ADVOCATES

David Pannick is a Barrister practising in London. He is a Fellow of All Souls College, Oxford, where he was elected to a Prize Fellowship in 1978. In 1992 he was appointed a QC.

He has appeared in many of the leading public law cases of the last decade. He represented *The Sunday Times* in the *Spycatcher* affair, acted for Tiny Rowland in the battle to win control of Harrods from the Fayeds, unsuccessfully attempted to persuade the European Court of Human Rights to give a transsexual woman the right to marry a man, spoke for the Commonwealth Games Federation when Zola Budd and Annette Cowley sought to compete in the 1986 Commonwealth Games, was briefed by Penguin Books when an attempt was made to prosecute Salman Rushdie's *Satanic Verses* for blasphemy, appeared for the female cook who won the first case of equal pay for work of equal value, and told the Court of Appeal that a solicitor should have a right of audience to read out an agreed statement in settlement of a libel action. He has appeared in court on behalf of the Attorney-General, Robert Maxwell, the Chief Rabbi, L. Ron Hubbard, and a waitress complaining that she had been dismissed from her job because her employers considered her bust was too large.

David Pannick's other books include *Judges* (also available in Oxford Paperbacks).

ADVOCATES

DAVID PANNICK

QC; Fellow of All Souls College,
Oxford

Oxford New York
OXFORD UNIVERSITY PRESS

Oxford University Press, Walton Street, Oxford OX2 6DP
Oxford New York Toronto
Delhi Bombay Calcutta Madras Karachi
Kuala Lumpur Singapore Hong Kong Tokyo
Nairobi Dar es Salaam Cape Town
Melbourne Auckland Madrid
and associated companies in
Berlin Ibadan

Oxford is a trade mark of Oxford University Press

First published 1992
First issued as an Oxford University Press paperback 1993

British Library Cataloguing in Publication Data
Data available

Library of Congress Cataloging in Publication Data
Pannick, David.
Advocates/David Pannick
p. cm.
1. Lawyers—Great Britain. 2. Practice of law—Great Britain.
I. Title.
KD460.P36 1992 349.41'023—dc20 [344.10023] 91–24461
ISBN 0–19–811948–8
ISBN 0–19–285289–2 (Pbk.)

3 5 7 9 10 8 6 4 2

Printed in Great Britain by
Biddles Ltd.
Guildford and King's Lynn

To DENISE, SAMUEL, JOEL, *and* SHULA

and to the memory of

MAURICE SLOAM

PREFACE

It may seem somewhat presumptuous for a barrister whose first client was hanged to write a book on advocates.[1] By way of mitigation I emphasize that this is not a book about *advocacy*. It does not purport to tell others how to perform. It has the more modest—and, I hope, more entertaining—purpose of exploring and defending the role of the advocate.

I am grateful to clients, opponents, judges, and leading counsel (in particular Anthony Lester QC and Michael Beloff QC) for providing some of the stimulation for what follows. If I have not always listened carefully enough to what they have been saying in the long hours of a court day, I have, at least, been using my time productively.

I also much appreciate the sympathetic and helpful editing from Judith Luna at Oxford University Press. Joshua Rozenberg (Legal Affairs Correspondent for BBC Television) has, as always, helpfully provided useful information. All Souls College, Oxford has been a provocative environment for thinking about the issues raised in this book.

I thank Patricia Wynn Davies (Legal Affairs Editor of the *Independent*) and Frances Gibb (Legal Correspondent of *The Times*) for assistance and encouragement.

[1] *Ong Ah Chuan v Public Prosecutor* [1981] AC 648 (Judicial Committee of the Privy Council). My client was hanged in Singapore in February 1981: *The Times* 6 Mar. 1981.

I have dedicated this book to the memory of Maurice Sloam (my father-in-law), a non-lawyer who could argue either side of any case. The book is also dedicated to my wife, Denise, and to my children, Samuel, Joel, and Shula. Each of them tells me, courteously but firmly, when I am taking a bad point.

DAVID PANNICK

2 Hare Court,
Temple,
London EC4

CONTENTS

CHAPTER 1

Introduction

THE task of the advocate is to be argumentative, inquisitive, indignant or apologetic—as the occasion demands—and always persuasive on behalf of the person who pays for his voice. He earns his living propounding views to which he does not necessarily subscribe, and which are sometimes anathema to him, on behalf of clients whose conduct may not interest him, will often offend him, and can occasionally cause him outrage. When making submissions to a judge, seeking to hold the attention of a jury, or cross-examining hostile witnesses, the advocate is required to entice, to flatter, to insult, all in order to advance the cause for which he is instructed, however unworthy of his efforts it, or his client, may be. As counsel accurately told the House of Lords in 1967, 'in criminal cases a large number of the clients are rogues and in many civil cases the clients are unreliable'.[1]

The professional function of the advocate is, essentially, one of supreme, even sublime, indifference to much of what matters in life. He must advance one point of view, irrespective of its inadequacies. He must belittle other interests, whatever their merits. Politely though the task is performed, many barristers spend much of their working day accusing respectable members of the community of being liars. It is not for counsel appearing in court to express equivocation, to recognize ambiguity or to doubt instructions. His client is right and his opponent is wrong. The wider consequences can be left to the judge or jury to consider.

'The orator', as Socrates emphasized in his criticism of advocacy, 'does not teach juries and other bodies about right and wrong—he merely persuades them.'[2] He seeks to accomplish this task by using whatever arguments are likely to be effective in the tribunal before which he is appearing. He does not confine himself to those points which he thinks are correct. He does not pause to assess whether his submissions have academic respectability. The fundamental role of the advocate, as Felix Frankfurter understood, 'is not to enlarge the intellectual horizon. His task is to seduce, to seize the mind for a predetermined end, not to explore paths to truth.'[3] Indeed, while the professor and the editor of the law review are left to focus on verities, the advocate may need positively to lead the judge in the opposite direction by skills akin to dissimulation. As Cicero explained, the advocate will base his efforts 'on points which *look like* the truth, even if they do not correspond with it exactly'.[4] To excuse wrongdoing and to promote injustice, as some advocacy demands, requires an ability to focus the attention of the judge on anything other than the central weaknesses of the client's case. Today, as in Cicero's time, the effective advocate remembers that 'men decide far more problems by hate, or love, or lust, or rage, or sorrow, or joy, or hope, or fear, or illusion, or some other inward emotion, than by reality, or authority, or any legal standard, or judicial precedent, or statute'.[5] The highest praise an advocate can receive is for it to be noted that he has the skill 'to dress up the wholly unarguable as if it had a scintilla of a basis of reason'.[6]

At the start of the Guinness fraud trial in 1990, a woman

was excused from jury service because she suffered from migraine. It was, she explained, 'things like this which start it off'.[7] For a variety of reasons, legal proceedings can cause severe headaches for advocates. Fellow lawyers have sympathy for the defence counsel who told the jury in his closing speech that he was doing his job 'to [the] best of my ability with what I have had to work with'.[8] The advocate may have difficulty capturing the mood of the court: Norman Birkett, a judge at the Nuremberg War Crimes Trial in 1945, recorded that one of the American prosecutors had begun his submissions by explaining that 'the voice you hear is the knocking of my knees. They haven't knocked so hard since I asked my wonderful little wife to marry me.'[9] Counsel may have problems coping unaided with the responsibilities imposed. In 1985, a judge reprimanded defence counsel in a criminal trial. The case, listed to last for two weeks, had taken 75 days to try. Counsel's closing speech, which had occupied 28 hours, was criticized by the judge for its lack of structure and its irrelevant content. 'You required prompting from the prosecution and the court', remarked the judge, 'and even from the foreman of the jury.'[10]

Outside pressures may make it difficult for the advocate to do his best for his client. But he should avoid announcing to the court that he will not take long to make his closing speech to the jury because 'I would like to move my car before 5 o'clock'.[11] In 1991, a solicitor issued a writ claiming damages for assault, unlawful arrest, and false imprisonment after his efforts of advocacy on behalf of a client in a Magistrates' Court had been interrupted by the solicitor being placed in a police cell for an hour. A police officer had arrested him (while the Magistrates were out of the courtroom) for declining immediately to hand over a document requested by the police. The solicitor had, understandably, been released from the police cell without charge.[12] When counsel is instructed, he must ensure that he does not involve himself in activities inconsistent with his professional status as advocate. In 1964, Chief Justice Wylie of the Borneo High Court held that it was improper conduct for a barrister also to act as a travelling salesman in ladies' underwear and dresses.[13]

The advocate's difficulties may be the result of judicial foibles. In 1973, a Californian judge was removed from office for vulgar and profane behaviour, including an incident in chambers in which he assaulted defence counsel with 'a battery-operated object resembling a penis and sometimes referred to as a "dildo"'. Later that day, in court, when defence counsel was cross-examining prosecution witnesses, the judge suggested that he speed up the process otherwise the judge would 'get the machine out'. It was, the Supreme Court of California concluded, inconsistent with the due administration of justice for the defence counsel to be told by the judge during the hearing, 'Hurry David. We've got a fifteen volt battery for you.'[14] However hard the advocate tries, the judge may not appreciate his efforts. The Supreme Court of Michigan has held that the judicial cursing of an advocate in court merited public censure when, at 'the conclusion of a lengthy exchange' during a preliminary hearing in the District Court, the judge had said to counsel:

> Now the question is, am I still dispassionate in the case? And I'm not sure that I am now . . . I'm not sure that I haven't come to a conclusion that whether your client is guilty or innocent, you're a despicable son-of-a-bitch.[15]

An advocate who has a really bad day may find (as occurred in Tennessee in 1981) that the court tells him, 'we shall have no more of this', and issues an injunction to restrain him from bringing any similar cases in the future.[16] By contrast, the advocate must not be on too close terms with the judge. In 1976, the Supreme Court of South Dakota censured a judge for allowing his wife to appear as an attorney in cases before him.[17]

But no matter how hopeless the cause, however unmeritorious the client, notwithstanding the antipathy of the judge, irrespective of the risks to his own reputation, and despite the other pressing concerns which may be preying on the mind of the lawyer, what counsel must do is to follow and defend the great tradition of advocacy: to make mountains out of molehills, to find a point of law where none had previously been known to exist, to ensure that his client does not lose the case without everything possible (and, on occasion, some things impossible) being said on his behalf. As Mr Justice Darling told counsel in 1912, 'there may be a great deal to be said for it. I do not think there is any proposition nowadays of which that may not be said . . .'.[18] It is rare indeed for counsel to concede, as once occurred, that 'it is difficult to contend that such a right [as claimed by his client] exists, when every principle of the constitution and all the authorities upon the subject are opposed to it, and the most diligent search has failed to discover a single atom of authority in its favour'.[19]

Apparently hopeless cases are—with skill, judgment, inspiration, and a great deal of luck—occasionally (though not often) won. In his willingness to have a go, Abraham H. Hummel is (in this respect, if not in others)[20] an example to us all. At the end of the nineteenth century in the United States, Hummel successfully defended three night-club dancers ('Philadelphia Egyptians called Zora, Fatima and Zelika') charged with indecent belly-dancing at a night club. As Richard H. Rovere explained, the court records did not state which of the two points taken by Hummel on behalf of his clients was decisive in winning the case. The first was that the dancing 'was part of an ancient ceremony which devout Moslems like Zora, Fatima and Zelika were bound by their faith to perform'. The second was that the prosecutor had described the dance as a 'lewd and lascivious contortion of the stomach', but the stomach, as Hummel pointed out, 'was nothing but a small sac in the abdominal region whose contortions, if any, could not be perceived except from inside the body'.[21]

Miracles cannot always be performed. We cannot all achieve the success of the Manhattan attorney Mo Levine who was said to be 'so good that he made money on the side by selling tape recordings of his final arguments'.[22] The advocate can expect to lose as many cases as he wins. He therefore requires a thick skin. He must accustom himself to being told that what he has confidently submitted, convincing himself (if no one else) of its accuracy and eloquence, is without foundation in law or fact or common sense. This can be hard, since advocates tend to be fiercely competitive, anxious (sometimes obsessed) to win. Only in theory, but certainly not in practice, is it true that, as Lord Eldon suggested in 1822, 'the result of the cause is to [the advocate] a matter of indifference'.[23]

Whatever his professional ethics may teach him, the advocate will be troubled by the fact that what he has submitted may influence the case, and perhaps the general law, in a direction contrary to what is fair or just. The prosecutor knows that, as Cicero taught, 'to make repeated accusations of the sort which involve defendants in the loss of their civil rights looks heartless, one might almost say inhuman'.[24] He is aware that nature, as Cicero explained, 'bestowed eloquence on human beings for their safety and preservation; and it is therefore the height of inhumanity to divert such a gift to the ruin and destruction of honest men'.[25]

Acting in the interests of a client does not always promote the interests of society in general. Because he is paid to use his skills for causes which are at best dubious and may be positively dangerous, the advocate daily faces difficult moral dilemmas. He must comply with a complex code of ethics which purports to reconcile his duties to his client with his duties to his society. So, for example, a prosecutor should not announce in his closing speech, as occurred in a recent trial in the USA, 'defence counsel gave his opinion, and I'm going to give you mine. The son-of-a-bitch [indicating] is guilty as hell.'[26]

In 1844, Mr Justice Crampton contended that the 'British Advocate' has 'duties as a man and as a christian [which] are paramount to all other considerations'. It does not require a degree in jurisprudence to predict the likely response of most clients if their advocate were to tell them that he proposed to adopt and apply the views of Mr Justice Crampton that 'if he be the Advocate of an individual, and *retained* and remunerated (often inadequately) for his valuable services, yet he has a prior and perpetual *retainer* on behalf of truth and justice'.[27]

But the barrister knows that there are limits to acceptable advocacy, problems concerning the extent to which he can and should act as a mouthpiece of his (perhaps unscrupulous) client. He appreciates that there is a fine line between, on the one hand, brilliant advocacy which focuses on the strengths of his case and tugs at the emotions of the audience and, on the other hand, sharp practice and sham theatricals which mislead the court. He will often be uncertain where his duties to his client end and his obligations to society, and the court, begin.

Travers Humphreys recalled George Elliott defending a man on a criminal charge at the turn of the last century. He had

> not challenged a single witness and his only cross-examination has been of the surveyor who proved the plan of the turkish bath (where the men had been arrested). He got the admission that the room where the men were is approached by a swing door, and you cannot see through a swing door. No one has ever suggested that they did see anything through the swing door, but that doesn't matter to George. He is now addressing the jury on the assumption that the issue in the case centres round that swing door.

When he began 'waving his hands and swaying his body to and fro, and some of the jury are beginning to do the same', it became obvious that the jury were going to acquit his client.[28] In such circumstances, there is substance in the suggestion made to Alan M. Dershowitz, a prominent US defence lawyer, by his son, a professional magician:

> 'You and I both do the same thing', he would chide me, 'sleight of hand—making things appear to be what they're not'.[29]

On occasion, the advocate may despair of what he is instructed to do on behalf of his client. He may find it necessary to remind himself that, as Lord Esher declared in a judgment in 1889, counsel is not 'bound to degrade himself for the purpose of winning his client's case'.[30] A lawyer has no professional obligation to punch his client's opponent outside court (as allegedly occurred in Madrid in 1989).[31] When a Canadian judge, summarizing the evidence for the jury in a criminal case, reached the part most damaging to the defendant, his counsel, 'anxious to distract the jurors from hearing what he preferred them not to hear, started to brush his teeth at the counsel table'.[32] In 1981, the Supreme Court of Florida ordered the suspension from practice for thirty days of an attorney who had appeared in court 'on a stretcher attired in bedclothes', despite the fact that he had been walking about in normal clothes the day before. Whether or not this had been done with the intention of pressurizing the court into granting an adjournment of the case, his conduct was, thought the court, likely to have that effect. It was inexcusable because 'he could have requested his wife, who had accompanied him, or an ambulance attendant, to advise the judge of his condition before he was carried into the courtroom on a stretcher'.[33]

Some lawyers go to heroic lengths in the interests of their clients. The advocate cannot be expected to inflict scratches on himself with a nail file in order to test whether an expert witness for the other party could, as he claimed in evidence, determine whether such injuries were caused by a struggle (the selfless conduct of a lawyer defending Claus von Bulow, tried and acquitted of assault with intent to murder his wife in 1985).[34] It is equally beyond the call of duty for a lawyer acting for a defendant in civil litigation to offer to be hit by the plaintiff in place of a settlement which would have involved his client paying $50,000. 'The client is very pleased,' explained the Texas defence lawyer involved. 'He likes to have a lawyer . . . who will go to the mat for him.'[35] The enactment of the Courts and Legal Services Act 1990 may enhance consumer choice in the field of legal services, as the Lord Chancellor intends. But there rightly remain some things that English lawyers will not do for their clients.

Trial by battle was not finally abolished as part of English legal procedure until 1819.[36] This reform was regretted by Mr Justice Harman when hearing a case in which one boxer sued another concerning their respective entitlements to be called the welterweight champion of Trinidad.[37] More often, courts recognize that for all its moral ambiguity, inherent contradictions, and plain absurdities, the essence of which will be considered in the following pages, advocacy is central not only to our legal system but also to our way of life. Advocacy has, in its manifestation of freedom of expression, its protection of liberty, and its vital contribution to the rule of law, an essential morality which justifies its practice, excuses its excesses, and makes intolerable any society which lacks its presence. The advocate makes a valuable contribution to the maintenance of a society in which we have the protection that, whatever the allegations which may be made against us, the State can only punish or impose other detriments on us under the legal process by judging our conduct by reference to general rules laid down in advance and after hearing any points that can be made on our behalf. The role of the advocate is to ensure that in a legal system in which disputes are decided by rational debate, the viewpoints of those most affected are explained so that the court can properly decide where legal right lies. The advocate exemplifies the valuable principle that there is always another point of view, a different perspective, a contrary argument, of which account should be taken before judgment is delivered.

Indeed, the principles of advocacy in our legal system have much to teach us about the more general values of reasoned debate which are fundamental to the success, indeed the survival, of a civilized society. Our culture is threatened by the decline of advocacy, that is the reluctance to present a case by means of persuasion, the refusal to listen to the arguments for the other side, the resistance to considering the competing merits dispassionately, and the replacement of these methods of rational and objective debate and analysis by aggression and intolerance at all levels, domestic, national, and international.

There are, of course, many impediments to justice in our legal system, including the cost (inadequately met through current legal aid provision), the delay, and the complexity of the law. The maintenance of an independent profession of advocates, speaking on behalf of all litigants, cannot solve these difficulties. But it is important to appreciate the substantial contribution to justice made by the advocate. The essential principles of advocacy—a duty to act for any client, irrespective of the merits of his cause; an obligation to speak out on his behalf without fear or favour; and a legal immunity from action for what is said in court—are central to equality under the law.

There is surprisingly little written by advocates about advocacy. Apart from opinions and pleadings while in practice, and judgments when on the Bench, the legal practitioner rarely writes anything other than legal autobiography. Most of that material consists of little more than gossip about promising juniors who have long been forgotten and careful explanations of the strategy adopted, in ephemeral litigation, to win what had seemed a hopeless case. For reasons which can only be based on the reluctance of academic lawyers to subject themselves to pain in the interests of their science, the art of advocacy has received little attention from legal theorists.

Now that the practice of advocacy in the courts of England and Wales is subject to radical reform by reason of the Courts and Legal Services Act 1990 giving greater rights of audience to solicitors, it is appropriate to pause to reflect on, and in some respects to celebrate, the principles and the policies of advocacy, the honourable profession of the advocate, and the valuable tradition of speaking for all manner of people.

It will, I hope, serve a useful purpose to consider the extent to which the advocate receives, and deserves, protection from clients, judges, and opponents who wish to impede the performance of his functions; the duties of the barrister to the court; the morality of advocacy; possible reforms to the law—such as allowing advocates to be sued for negligence and confining the quantity of advocacy—which would improve the quality of justice; and some cautionary tales about what can go wrong (as well as right) for the advocate.

If the English Bar does wither away, as the opponents of the Courts and Legal Services Act fear, it is as well to have a record of what we have lost. If, as is hoped and expected, the Bar continues to thrive and prosper, its future members require an explanation of the characteristics of the unique profession of advocate which they are to join. And those solicitors who proudly display their advocacy certificate will wish to have an introduction to the pleasures and pains of the art which they intend to practise. This book aspires to fulfil those needs.

CHAPTER 2

Clients

I

THE diligent advocate will want to identify for whom he acts. This may be more difficult than at first sight appears. In this respect the advocate may need to display, in the course of his duties, a degree of flexibility of which any profession would be proud. Sometimes, this is taken to heroic proportions. In 1989, there occurred an example in the finest traditions of the resourceful advocate. When the prosecutor failed to attend the Hendon Magistrates' Court, the defence solicitor, Mr Patrick Cusack, was concerned that his client's case (he was pleading guilty to a motoring offence) would be adjourned, to the client's detriment. So, with the permission of the Magistrates, he performed the role of prosecutor by outlining the facts and then acted as defence advocate by mitigating on behalf of the defendant. His client was fined £300 and ordered to perform 200 hours of community service. As he later explained, Mr Cusack did not ask for prosecution costs against himself.[1]

There are few precedents for the economy of labour adopted by Mr Cusack. Most of them are disreputable. Allegations of corrupt practices by pleaders—collusion with the other party and deliberately making a defective pleading in order to lose the case—led in 1292 to a Royal decree that the judges should provide for a defined number of lawyers and apprentices to follow the courts and to have an exclusive right of pleading before them.[2] In about 1668, an advocate was prosecuted for betraying his client's cause and taking fees from the other side in the case.[3] John Evelyn recorded in his 1686 diary that he had dined with three serjeants-at-law who boasted 'how long they had detained their clients in tedious processes, by their tricks, as if so many highway thieves should have met and discovered the several purses they had taken'.[4] In the eighteenth century, lawyers were suspected of bowing to the temptation of acting for both sides in a dispute, as represented on stage by such characters as 'Mr Serjeant Eitherside'.[5] Lord Eldon (Lord Chancellor at the beginning of the nineteenth century) recalled that Sir Fletcher Norton 'was reputed to take fees on both sides and had acquired the nickname of Sir Bullface Doublefee'. In one case, Norton had accepted instructions from, and been paid by, the plaintiff and the defendant in the same case. When it was suggested to him that he should return both briefs, and all the remuneration received, he declined. The parties, said Eldon, 'were forced to compromise, and he kept both fees'.[6] Equally discreditable was the practice adopted by some counsel in the seventeenth century of sacrificing the interests of one client for the sake of another. It was said of one leading counsel that 'in a small-fee'd cause, [he] would give it up to the Judge's mistake, and not contend to set him right, that he might gain credit to mislead him in some other cause in which he was well fee'd'. Lord Campbell accurately observed that such barristers 'ought to have changed places in court with the highwaymen they were retained to prosecute'.[7]

There are also examples of too many advocates acting

for one client. In an admittedly extreme example of overmanning on the advocate's bench of the court in 1820, 'two counsel appeared upon a petition, for the same parties, one instructed to consent, and the other instructed by a different solicitor to oppose it, except on certain terms'. The wise Master of the Rolls directed the petition to be stood over so that the instructions of the client could be checked.[8] Similarly, in 1849, Vice-Chancellor Knight Bruce sensibly remarked that 'as two sets of counsel appeared for Mr Lewis, with apparently different instructions, he must in that state of circumstances decline to hear the motion'.[9]

Early in the nineteenth century, a Mr Shelly found that his opponent had retained all the King's Counsel at the Bar. And when 'the orphan children of the late Lord Lonsdale's agent were the plaintiffs in a suit instituted against that nobleman to obtain payment of a debt, which was all the property they had in the world, the defendant retained all the counsel at Carlisle', where the case was to be tried. When Lord Lonsdale died, his successor repaid, with interest and costs, all the sums owing.[10] More recently, on suing all those concerned with the publication of the magazine *Private Eye*, Randolph Churchill instructed his solicitor 'to send a retainer to every leading QC at the libel bar'. The skills of advocacy of the solicitor managed to persuade the client that three leading counsel would suffice.[11]

Overmanning by advocates may lead to a conflict of legal opinion as to how the case should be conducted. In 1813, Gibbs J said that if leading counsel and junior counsel for the same party disagree during a trial as to what is a strong point to make to the court, a judge will not thereafter allow the unfortunate client to have a new trial on the ground that junior counsel would (if allowed by his leader) have argued a good point rejected by senior counsel. 'The junior counsel . . . must confine himself to the line taken by the leader.'[12] If the client cannot benefit from the wisdom of his junior counsel in this respect, he is also protected against folly from that direction. In a 1915 appeal in the British Columbia Court of Appeal, Macdonald CJA explained that at the trial 'the appellant was represented by senior and junior counsel. Senior counsel, very properly, I think, declined to make any admission concerning the applicability of the Workmen's Compensation Act. . . . His junior, however, insisted upon making that admission', resulting in judgment for the other party. The Court of Appeal concluded that it 'must accept the attitude of the leader as representing the true attitude of the client'.[13] In such cases, the client may wish to be reminded that in 1977 the Bar abandoned the rule that, if a QC was briefed, the client had to be represented by two counsel.[14]

The presence of a number of advocates may lead to disputes as to which of them should be heard first. When the Attorney-General of England and the Lord Advocate of Scotland appeared as counsel for the same party in the House of Lords in 1834, 'a question arose between them at the bar on the right of precedency'. It was argued by them, and decided by the Lord Chancellor in favour of the Attorney-General.[15] Lord Chancellor Bacon (at the beginning of the seventeenth century) resolved questions of precedence in the Court of Chancery on the principle that 'besides these great ones (the Attorney and Solicitor-General) I will hear any judge's son before a serjeant, and any serjeant's son before a reader, if there be not many of them'.[16]

Counsel who have only one client in the case may have difficulty remembering which side they are on. In 1602, a barrister recorded in his diary that 'Serjeant Harris was retained for the plaintiff and he argued for the defendant; so negligent that he knows not for whom he speaks'.[17] Lord Eldon recalled that soon after his call to the Bar (in 1776) he was briefed in a case in the King's Bench as junior to Dunning.[18] His leader 'began the argument, and appeared to me to be reasoning very powerfully against our client'. The young Eldon (then John Scott) whispered to Dunning 'that he must have misunderstood for whom he was employed', whereupon the versatile leading counsel 'proceeded to state that what he had addressed to the court was all that could be said against his client' and powerfully rebutted all the points he had previously made.[19]

Clients who brief counsel are entitled to expect a degree of loyalty. In 1887, the Supreme Court of California held that an attorney who acted for the plaintiff at an inconclusive trial could not thereafter act for the defendant at a subsequent trial of the same issue.[20] In 1907, an Indian advocate was found guilty of highly unprofessional conduct after writing to a client to state that he had received an offer to appear for the other side in a case against her and would accept it unless she offered him five times the usual fee.[21] In 1917, the Judicial Committee of the Privy Council pointed out 'the impropriety of a legal practitioner who has acted for one party in a dispute . . . acting for the other party in subsequent litigation between them relating to or arising out of that dispute. Such conduct is, to say the least of it, open to misconception, and is likely to raise suspicion in the mind of the original client and to embitter the subsequent litigation.'[22] An American lawyer was, in 1981, disbarred by the Supreme Court of California for negotiating a commission with burglars on items to be stolen by them from his client's home, the lawyer having helpfully agreed to provide a diagram of the house to be invaded.[23]

In such circumstances, the client may well wish that he had never briefed counsel at all. An American lawyer, Roy Grutman, proclaims that he gives all his new clients 'a simple stress test. First I ask them to tell me everything they can about themselves and their case; then, using that information, I hit them with a barrage of insults and sarcasm.' Not surprisingly, 'some break down, go home and never come back'.[24]

There are clients who are more equivocal, appearing unsure whether they have, in fact, instructed counsel. In 1844, it was argued that counsel who had appeared at an earlier hearing to consent to a petition being dismissed had no authority to do so. The Master of the Rolls, Lord Langdale, rejected the application to restore the petition. 'The business of the court cannot proceed', he explained, 'unless credit is given to the statements of counsel that they have authority for what they do.'[25] In a peculiar case in New South Wales at the beginning of this century, the Supreme Court of that State dismissed a complaint by a party that an advocate purporting to represent him at an earlier hearing had not appeared with his permission. As Mr Justice Owen sensibly observed, 'if a person hears counsel say [that he appears on his behalf] and allows that counsel to go on examining witnesses and arguing the case, that person cannot turn round and say there was no retainer'.[26]

There are clients who make it plain that they definitely do not want the assistance of counsel. 'No person charged with a criminal offence can have counsel forced upon him against his will', as the Court of Criminal Appeal held in favour of a defendant who had been denied the right to represent himself.[27] The Supreme Court of Canada has adopted a similar rule.[28] When the US Supreme Court reached the same conclusion in 1975, Justice Blackmun (with whom Chief Justice Burger and Justice Rehnquist agreed) dissented, lamenting that 'if there is any truth to the old proverb that "one who is his own lawyer has a fool for a client", the Court by its opinion today now bestows a *constitutional* right on one to make a fool of himself'.[29] Other American courts have had occasion to remind persistent counsel that they should not continue to act for clients who have dispensed with their services.[30] For counsel to contend that he 'cannot be discharged and that he has the right to continue in the case . . . is without merit', as the Supreme Court of Georgia held in 1980, reprimanding counsel who attempted to represent a former client who he knew no longer wished to take advantage of his services.[31]

Other counsel are eager to be released from the duty to act for their client. In 1979 the Supreme Court of New York, Appellate Division, pronounced that counsel for the defendant in a criminal action is entitled to withdraw when 'she has been threatened with bodily harm by [the] defendant' and 'the defendant has already assaulted Legal Aid counsel in a previous case'.[32]

There are clients who have no need of counsel. A member of my chambers once lost a case in the Court of Appeal to what the law report described as 'persons unknown' who 'appeared in person'.[33] Some litigants desperately need the services of counsel but are unable to obtain them. During a trial at the Central Criminal Court for piracy in 1844, 'one of the jurymen inquired of Lord Abinger [the trial judge] why, in such a serious case, the prisoners were undefended; at the same time offering to bear the expense, if any learned gentleman would undertake the case'. Lord Abinger concluded that this was not possible: counsel could not prepare the case in the middle of the trial and 'therefore it was much better for the prisoners themselves that they should be allowed to tell their own tale to the jury, and explain away, after their own fashion, the facts alleged against them'.[34] One of the defendants was convicted, and sentenced to one year's imprisonment; the other defendant was acquitted by the jury.[35]

Some counsel have not fully understood that they can only wear one hat in court. Humphreys J explained in 1941 that a barrister 'should not act as counsel and witness in the same case'.[36] But clients may find that counsel later appears in another guise: the House of Lords said in 1858 that there is no absolute rule that having been counsel in a case operated as a disqualification to prevent the same person, when raised to the Bench, from taking part in the judgment of that cause if there was no practical alternative to avoid delay and further expense.[37] However, as the High Court of the Sudan held in 1966, a judge who subsequently becomes a member of the practising bar is precluded from representing a party in an action in which he has previously been involved in his judicial capacity.[38] The Bar Council avoided such difficulties by stating that it 'does not approve, as a matter of principle, of former Judges in England and Wales returning to practise at the Bar in any capacity'[39] (though the current edition of the Bar's Code of Conduct does not mention the matter). The Courts and Legal Services Act 1990 states that no person holding a full-time appointment of judicial office (from a Lord of Appeal down to a Chairman of an Industrial Tribunal) may practise as a barrister or a solicitor or 'provide any advocacy or litigation services (in any jurisdiction)'.[40]

An unfortunate confusion of roles was only narrowly avoided when a Canadian judge considered whether counsel had acted in contempt at an earlier hearing. The judge explained his recollection of events, and declined to accede to counsel's suggestion that he should submit to cross-examination. He was reluctant to have to decide whether to believe his own evidence.[41] The problems which would be caused by such a judgment should have been appreciated by the advocate held in contempt for subpoening the judge as a witness in the case being tried by that judge.[42]

Counsel who is not representing any party may assist the court. In the reign of Edward I (1272–1307), the pleaders 'sit in court and one will sometimes intervene as "amicus curiae" [friend of the court]. The reporters mention their opinions with almost as much respect as the opinions of the judges. . . . Parliament, too, refers difficult points of law to them as well as to the judges.'[43] It is said (though the account is probably apocryphal) that in about 1560 the young Thomas Egerton, a Bar student, was watching a case in which 'a verdict was about to be pronounced which would have ruined a worthy old lady'. He pointed out a 'fatal objection which had escaped her counsel as well as [the] Lord Judge'.[44] Students watching the proceedings in the Royal Courts of Justice today are not advised to follow his example. On one occasion, the court's judgment, concerning the true meaning of the Statute of Frauds and Perjuries, was given a seal of approval when 'Sir G. Treby (ut amicus curiae) said he was present at the making of the said statute, and that was the intention of the Parliament'.[45] That is one way of circumventing the rule that the contents of Hansard are not to be used as an aid to the construction of an ambiguous statute. Nowadays, the amicus curiae is invariably counsel appointed by the Attorney-General to assist the court when one party to a dispute is not legally represented and the judge thinks that he may benefit from hearing counsel present any points that could be made on behalf of that unrepresented party. Counsel may have no choice but to assist the court in a way he had not previously contemplated. In 1758, Lord Mansfield 'desired Mr Hussey [the unfortunate advocate] to state the case for the sake of the students'.[46] In another case, 'Lord Mansfield desired the Bar to take a note of this, and waited till several gentlemen made a memorandum'.[47]

In 1814, John Campbell recorded that 'a mad man at Oxford . . . has taken it into his head that he is a barrister-at-law. He has accordingly contrived to procure an old wig and gown, in which he travels about the country and walks into court, following us regularly from town to town. He is perfectly harmless, and people rather encourage his fantasy.'[48] Any layman who thinks an amateur could do the job of the advocate better than the professionals should reflect hard on the standards required and the dangers involved. As early as 1253 'a man who appeared for another was amerced [fined] because he was not an advocate'.[49] More recently, the Family Court of Australia held in contempt a layman who falsely purported to be a lawyer. Mr Macklin had appeared before the court stating that he was a barrister representing Mrs Slender. When the judge, Watson SJ, investigated this claim, and confronted Mr Macklin with his findings that he had not in fact been called to the Bar, Mr Macklin 'claimed that there had been a mistake'. The judge found that Mr Macklin's relationship with Mrs Slender was sexual. Therefore, concluded the judge,

> Mr Macklin's offence is grave. He has impersonated a legal practitioner. . . . His relationship with Mrs Slender infringes any

objectivity he may possess as an advocate. Counsel before this court will constantly find it much safer to take their instructions in chambers of conference rooms rather than in the bed-chamber.

Because it seemed that Mr Macklin had 'a propensity for personation' which 'could be dangerous to the community and to himself', the judge imprisoned him for 90 days for contempt of court and ordered that he should be released after 14 days if he agreed to seek and continue psychiatric treatment.[50] The Lord Chancellor's White Paper on *Legal Services* suggested[51] that in England it was not a crime to impersonate a barrister. Now, the Courts and Legal Services Act 1990 makes it an offence where a person does 'any act in the purported exercise of a right of audience ... when he is not entitled to exercise that right' (and adds that this is also a contempt of court), or 'wilfully pretends' to be entitled to exercise any right of audience when he is not so entitled.[52]

II

If the advocate is able to ascertain for whom he is acting, and in respect of what, he must then concentrate on what he is going to say on behalf of his client. The effective performance of the function of the advocate is rarely assisted by the client. It does not help if, as in one recent criminal case, the defendant in a criminal trial falls asleep during the judge's summing-up, indicating to the jury that the defendant has been there many times before.[53] In most cases, 'the wise advocate resists the twitch of the gown and shuts his ears to the suggestion' made by his client, though the client 'may insist on thinking that he knows best'.[54] The inability of the client to focus on what is at issue may be a positive menace to the successful presentation of his case. In 1927, the Court of Criminal

Appeal, considering an appeal against conviction, was told by defence counsel that at the trial he 'was unable to read all the various scraps of paper handed to [him] by [the] appellant, and was thereby prevented from calling a witness'. The Court of Appeal, generously, heard the evidence of the witness and allowed the appeal.[55]

It may be necessary for the advocate to take strong steps to repulse the efforts of those who attempt to assist him in presenting the case. Sir Patrick Hastings often suffered from a client who saw 'a hundred points all equally important in his eyes, but in fact of no real importance whatever' and was often afflicted with a solicitor who had 'devoted tireless industry in the exploration of any matter in which his client is so deeply interested, with the result that his counsel is flooded with a mass of largely irrelevant material'. Hastings had witnessed 'enthusiastic juniors assisting their leaders with repeated interruptions' and 'equally enthusiastic solicitors rising to their feet in order to remind their counsel of some apparently forgotten point'. Even the most pacifistic of counsel may sympathize with the actions of Hastings when he 'was once constrained to curb the repeated and indeed perpetual offers of assistance by a particularly irrepressible [solicitor] client by hitting him upon the head with a volume of the Law Reports in order to persuade him to resume his seat'.[56] John Mortimer's Rumpole characterizes his favourite instructing solicitor as one who 'keeps quiet, does what he's told and hardly ever tells me about his bad back'.[57]

The advocate's client will often expect the performance of miracles on his behalf. He may resent the fact that one of his witnesses is 'discredited and ridiculed' by the questions put in cross-examination by opposing counsel and may well be aggravated to be told that 'it is always inconvenient to a party when his witness is shown in cross-examination to have been saying that she saw things which it was physically impossible for her to see'. He will not necessarily appreciate that 'there is no known prescription by which counsel can "neutralise" such a "revelation" or stop a jury from drawing reasonable inferences from it'. He may disagree that the interests of justice make it undesirable that 'such a magic should exist'.[58] Clients often have the mistaken view that the term 'fraud' is 'some kind of legal lubricant which made the words of his statement of claim read better'.[59]

However hard the advocate tries, there are some clients who simply cannot be protected. The 1989 trial in North Carolina of Jim Bakker, a television evangelist accused of fraud, was unusual not least in that the defendant was committed to a psychiatric hospital for observation after being found 'lying in the corner of his attorney's office with his head under a couch, hiding, expressing thoughts that someone was going to hurt him'.[60] The judge ruled that Mr Bakker was not mentally ill and ordered the resumption of the trial.[61] Mr Bakker was convicted and hurt even more by being sentenced to 45 years in prison (later reduced to 18 years).[62] Sometimes the best that counsel can do is to bluster on behalf of his client. As one of A. P. Herbert's *Misleading Cases* indicates, a certain amount can be achieved by theatrical effects and a well-developed reputation: when 'Sir Ethelred Rutt . . . rose to cross-examine, . . . three well-dressed women fainted and were thrown out'.[63] The advocate may, in desperate circumstances, be reduced to making a virtue out of the unattractive character of his client. He may tell the jury that she is 'one tough bitch', as did the lawyer for Leona Helmsley, the New York hotel proprietor and society queen convicted of tax fraud in 1989[64] and sentenced to four years' imprisonment.[65] Or, as Gerry Spence told the New York jury on behalf of Imelda Marcos, counsel may submit that although his client was a 'world-class shopper', she was also a 'world-class decent human being' whose only crime was 'loving her husband for 35 years'.[66] Whether or not because of such advocacy, Mrs Marcos was acquitted of charges of racketeering and fraud. She held a party for members of the jury, and entertained them with her rendition of 'God Bless America'.[67]

Some advocates have resorted to desperate measures for their clients. Marshall Hall sometimes 'wept before the jury and allowed the tears to stream down his cheeks as he spoke'.[68] In 1897, the Supreme Court of Tennessee heard an appeal against a judgment for the plaintiff in an action for seduction and breach of contract to marry. One of the grounds of appeal was that counsel for the plaintiff, 'in his closing argument, in the midst of a very eloquent and impassioned appeal to the jury, shed tears, and unduly excited the sympathies of the jury in favour of the plaintiff, and greatly prejudiced them against [the] defendant'. The Court commented in relation to the shedding of tears that 'it would appear to be one of the natural rights of counsel which no court or constitution could take away'. The court suggested that if counsel has tears available, 'it may be seriously questioned whether it is not his professional duty to shed them whenever proper occasion arises, and the trial judge would not feel constrained to interfere unless they were indulged in to such excess as to impede or delay the business of the court'. It was, the Court concluded, largely a matter for the advocate what weapons he used, from 'logic' down to 'noise and gesticulation'.[69] At the close of his submissions on behalf of a defendant in a Texas murder trial in 1911, counsel sang to the jury, in a tear-stained voice, 'Home, sweet home'. The verdict of not guilty was greeted with applause from the spectators.[70] When William F. Howe, senior partner in the infamous New York law firm of Howe and Hummel (lawyers to the criminal fraternity at the end of the nineteenth century), 'spoke of mothers and children, he generally cried. . . . He could cry at will. . . . He could and would cry over any case, no matter how commonplace. . . . It was a sickening spectacle, but it often carried a jury to extraordinary conclusions.'[71] On one occasion Howe 'made an entire summation, hours long, on his knees'.[72] Appeal courts (and professional ethics tribunals) are not always impressed with such behaviour. In 1957, because of highly prejudicial conduct by the prosecutor, the Supreme Court of Illinois allowed an appeal against a conviction for murder. The prosecutor had wept during his closing speech to the jury and told them: 'I am not ashamed of what I am doing now, believe me. I knew the dead man.'[73] By contrast, in 1982, the Supreme Court of Arizona did not think that the 'spontaneous' and 'genuine' tears of the prosecutor during the evidence of the victim's mother gave grounds for allowing an appeal against a murder conviction.[74]

Quintilianus, in his first-century AD study of advocacy, had recognized that 'actions as well as words may be employed to move the court to tears. Hence the custom of bringing accused persons into court wearing squalid and unkempt attire, and of introducing their children and parents, and it is with this in view that we see blood-stained swords, fragments of bone taken from the wound, and garments spotted with blood, displayed by the accusers, wounds stripped of their dressings and scourged bodies bared to view.'[75] William F. Howe learnt this lesson well. The wife and children of the defendant would be placed in the front row of the court to gaze devotedly at the man on trial. And 'if by chance a particular defendant did not have a pretty wife, fond children, or a snowy-haired mother, he was not for that reason deprived of the sympathy they might create on his behalf. Howe would supply them from the firm's large stable of professional spectators. Repulsive and apelike killers often turned up in court with lamblike children and wives of fragile beauty.'[76]

If such tricks do not accomplish the goal of distracting the judge or the jury from the overwhelming case against the client, the advocate may, as Quintilianus recognized, 'alleviate [judicial] boredom by the introduction of entertaining matter derived from any source that may be available'.[77] The unscrupulous advocate may resort to disreputable means to attract the attention of the jury away from his opponent. Marshall Hall, acting for a defendant in a civil trial, would make a grand entrance after the opening of the case, preceded by his clerk 'carrying his cushion and other odds and ends which he arranged'. Just as his opponent was recovering from this disruption and beginning to formulate his submissions, 'Marshall Hall picked up what appeared to be a scent-spray and squirted it three or four times up his nostrils'.[78] When prosecuting counsel was outlining for the jury facts embarrassing to the client of Horace Rumpole (John Mortimer's fictional barrister), Rumpole slowly and noisily tore a page out of his notebook. 'I was grateful to see that some of the members of the jury glanced in my direction. . . . I began to tear my piece of paper into very small strips. More members of the jury looked in my direction.'[79] On occasion, 'a Howe client . . . came into court with his head swathed in yards of white muslin, as if to suggest an ailment of the mind that required bandaging lest the brains fall out or attract infection'. It did not avail the prosecutor patiently to explain to the jury that when he had questioned the defendant prior to the trial his head was unbandaged and undamaged.[80]

On the rare occasions when water is made into wine, the advocate may receive ingratitude from his client. 'There are', as Mr Justice Lawton reflected, 'some clients who would not be satisfied by the performance of an embodiment of all the forensic virtues of Erskine, Scarlett, Russell, Birkett and Hastings . . .'[81] Lord Campbell recorded that soon after his call to the Bar in 1806 he was defending a prisoner in court, consulted him in the dock, triumphantly secured his acquittal of the charge and his discharge from detention, 'but my joy was soon disturbed; putting my hand into my pocket . . . I found that my purse was gone'. (Campbell added that the incident caused 'much merriment', the presiding judge, Lord Chief Baron Macdonald, commenting: 'What! does Mr Campbell think no one is entitled to take notes in court except himself?')[82]

Unsuccessful clients, frequently those with the most unmeritorious cases, gratifyingly and without the slightest justification are habitually able to persuade themselves that they have done much better than they had any right to expect. And, although it has been suggested by Lord Justice Salmon that a 'client can hardly be more dependent upon anyone than upon his counsel, nor can their relationship be closer',[83] the reality is that it is one of the merits of the working practices of the independent advocate that 'clients rarely get close enough to his shoulder to weep upon it, whether metaphorically or otherwise'.[84] The proper performance of the function of a lawyer, according to the Supreme Court of Tennessee, 'does not include a self-appointed role as a paraclete, comforter, helper, or hand holder, under the guise of legal services and at a lawyer's compensation rate'.[85] It is rare for a barrister to devote himself, like Marshall Hall, so wholeheartedly to the cause of his client that he becomes 'not merely counsel but also detective, showman, rhapsodist, actor, friend, and even father confessor'.[86] Indeed, to assist a client—for example, by delivering a document on his behalf on the way home from chambers—may lead to unjustified charges of contempt of court (of which the advocate was rightly acquitted, the court concluding that his conduct was 'not . . . in any way dishonourable or discreditable').[87]

The demands of the job may make the advocate ill. 'Anyone who has practised at the Bar knows the stresses and strains that counsel undergoes during the course of a case,' said Lord Upjohn. 'It is [in most cases] all in public; immediate decision[s] may have to be made as to whether to call or not to call a witness and even more quickly whether to ask or not to ask a question.'[88] Norman Birkett 'gave all he had to all his cases, often to the point of nervous exhaustion'.[89] In general, as Mr Justice Bayley commented in 1819, 'a long attendance at the bar naturally . . . wear[s] away [the] health' of the barrister.[90] Boswell recorded in his Journal for 1788 that Dunning was 'getting £8000 a year by his profession but being killed by it'.[91] By 1935, Wilfrid Greene was 'utterly exhausted by a practice of legendary proportions and, after arguing a case in the Judicial Committee [of the Privy Council] . . . he confessed that he was "really done"'. He was appointed a Judge of the Court of Appeal.[92]

The hazards may be more specific. In about 1760, the roof fell in on a court and Mr John Lawes was killed.[93] When Carson was appointed Counsel to the Attorney-General for Ireland at the age of 33 in 1887, his life was at risk. 'Threatening letters reached him frequently; he received postcards adorned with a skull and crossbones, and other emblems of mortality such as model coffins were sent to him. . . . His name as that of an ogre would even be used by peasant women to frighten their children when they were naughty.'[94] In 1899, Fernand Labori, the advocate for Alfred Dreyfus at his second court martial, was shot and seriously injured on the way to the courtroom.[95] Marcel Proust sent a sympathetic telegram noting that it was not only soldiers who shed blood for their cause.[96] Lord Hailsham recalled that when he was a young barrister earlier this century, a witness he had cross-examined 'appeared suddenly from behind a pillar as I left the court and said, "Young man, you made me out to be a liar. Take that and that and that!". And hit me three times with her umbrella.' On another occasion, he said, the friends of his client's rival 'chased me down the corridor of the Central Criminal Court'.[97] In the emotionally charged atmosphere of the 1988 trial in Israel of John Demjanjuk, accused—and convicted—of mass murder as 'Ivan the Terrible' in the Treblinka concentration camp, a 70-year-old Holocaust survivor who had lost his family at Treblinka threw acid in the face of an Israeli defence lawyer. (He was sentenced to five years' imprisonment, two of them suspended.)[98] After the conviction in 1990 of youths for raping a woman who had been jogging in Central Park, New York, supporters of the defendants shouted abuse at the female prosecutor: 'She's going to pay for it. Devilish bitch.'[99] In many parts of the world, governments carry out or permit the murder, assault, or other persecution of advocates for the performance of their professional duties.[100]

The advocate may require protection by the court from abuse by those against whom he appears (he is generally left to cope unaided with insults from his own client).

Courts do what they can to protect the advocate from the wrath of the other party and his supporters. In 1824, Sir William McMahon, Master of the Rolls in Ireland, explained that it was a contempt for a party to abuse or threaten the other party or his counsel while attending court or as a result of an occurrence there.[101] The Supreme Court of Mississippi upheld, in 1942, a finding of contempt of court against a witness for the defendant in a criminal trial who, after being cross-examined, left the witness stand and 'walked directly past the District Attorney . . . gritted his teeth at [him] and scowled at him in a hostile and threatening manner and said through his teeth, "I'll see you when you come down"'.[102] In Illinois in 1971, a defendant who was convicted of armed robbery punched the prosecuting counsel on the nose. Counsel's pain was, no doubt, only partly assuaged by the finding of contempt against the defendant.[103] In 1979, in the Court of Appeal, 'a litigant in person, after losing his appeal, hit opposing counsel on the head with a carafe of water and for this serious contempt he was imprisoned for three months'.[104] A defendant should not insult the prosecutor in court by calling him 'corrupt' even if, as the defendant claimed and the prosecutor denied, 'the Crown Attorney had intimidated him in a parking-lot, had laughed at him and thumbed his nose at him'. In that case, a fine of $250 for contempt of court was upheld in 1980 by the Supreme Court of Canada.[105] In 1977, the Supreme Court of Georgia overturned a criminal conviction: the trial judge should have allowed a postponement of the proceedings after the defence attorney was threatened and hit by the deputy sheriff for the manner in which he was conducting the case, instead of which the judge merely commented that 'he understood the deputy's feelings'.[106] In one recent case, a litigant in person who resented the submissions he had heard in court attempted to make a citizen's arrest of opposing counsel for what he described as 'high treason'.[107]

However, Mr Justice Scholl in Victoria, Australia, did not think that it was a contempt for a litigant in person to make written 'attacks . . . of a violent and indeed absurd character' against counsel for the opposing party. It was only a contempt, the judge said, if it was suggested that the court was party to any wrongdoing by counsel. This restrictive approach to contempt did not much matter on the facts: the defendant was imprisoned for one month for contempt by filing affidavits which accused various judges of 'strangling' and 'massacring' his litigation and conducting a 'vendetta' against him.[108]

If, like Edward Marshall Hall, the advocate is habitually 'ill with nervousness and anxiety before he [goes] into court',[109] the pressure is likely to tell after a few years. On at least two occasions (in 1935 and in 1973), advocates arguing cases before the US Supreme Court have fainted.[110] Even petty irritants may make it difficult for the advocate to immerse himself in a case and ignore the strains of normal life. On the first day of a murder trial in 1920, Sir Gordon Hewart (the Attorney-General) was not 'in a particularly good temper . . . since he was still smarting under a feeling of considerable annoyance due to one of the leading barristers' clerks having gained access to his room in the Bell Hotel on the previous night and made him an "apple pie" bed'.[111] In 1786, James Boswell was humiliated by his colleagues who left a feigned brief for him, leading him to believe he was acting for a client charged with throwing a dead cat in the face of a man who had called him a 'ragged-arse dog'.[112] Three years later, Boswell was robbed of his wig while on Circuit: 'I suspected a wanton trick, which some think witty'.[113]

Circumstances may conspire to make the task of the advocate impossible to perform. The advocate must be prepared for the unexpected, especially as 'it is always impossible to foretell in advance what impression a witness will make upon the Court'.[114] If the client has previously provided his advocate with an explanation of his conduct which is at least logical, his failure to stick to that account in court can be exasperating. Such a failure is one of the least surprising events which may occur during the trial. In the 1969 trial of the 'Chicago 7', when the hearings were in their sixth week the trial judge ordered one of the defendants, Bobby Seale, to be bound and gagged in the courtroom because of his attempts to disrupt proceedings. The next morning,

> the marshals carried Seale into the courtroom in a chair with a massive gag covering most of his face and with his arms and legs strapped to the chair. Mr Weinglass was cross-examining the witness Frappoly and interrupted his cross-examination to call the judge's attention to Seale, who was groaning, attempting to communicate through his gag, and apparently in considerable pain. The judge excused the jury and directed the marshals to determine whether Seale needed assistance. Several marshals approached Seale's chair. A scuffle ensued in which the chair tipped over, apparently into the first row of temporary press seats in the well of the courtroom. Pandemonium broke out, with counsel, defendants, reporters and spectators on their feet.[115]

By then, no doubt, Mr Weinglass had forgotten his next question in cross-examination.

To add to the frustrations of the job, laymen habitually misunderstand the work of the advocate, to the profound annoyance of counsel, assuming that he appears only in *criminal* courts when much (in some cases, all) of his work is in civil courts. They habitually fail to appreciate the finer points of legal etiquette ('why do you defend people who have committed terrible crimes?'),[116] though the occasional, perspicacious individual will understand the nature of the job. During the *Oz* obscenity trial in 1971, one of the witnesses was the comedian Marty Feldman. John Mortimer QC remembered him 'whispering to me, on his way to the witness-box, "Great to be working with you at last"'.[117]

The advocate, then, 'is faced with a difficult task'. Although he 'is entrusted with great licence and potent weapons', there is, according to Lord Pearce in 1967, a 'constant difficulty of inducing men and women to undertake the profession of the Bar, with its strain, hazard and rather austere self-discipline'.[118] If he can assuage the temper of the judge, negotiate the barriers created by witnesses, overcome the impediments placed in his way by his solicitor, and tolerate the antics of his client, what the advocate may find impossible to bear is the inexplicably high reputation (or the high fees) earned by his contemporaries. Wilkes wisely advised Boswell against going to the Bar 'because I should be excelled by plodding blockheads'.[119]

In the light of the extraordinary nature of the job, it is hardly surprising that the profession of advocacy attracts more than its fair share of eccentrics. John Popham (who later became Chief Justice from 1592 until 1607) was said to be a highwayman in the period before and after his call to the Bar.[120] In the eighteenth century, Serjeant Hill spent his wedding night 'going to his chambers in the Temple, and continuing there reading cases till next morning'.[121] But why do otherwise sensible men and women take up advocacy for a career? What is it about their personalities that encourages them to subject themselves to daily aggravation from clients, witnesses, opponents, instructing solicitors, judges, and juries?

III

There is, of course, the excitement of an unpredictable court battle. Like Trollope's Mr Chaffanbrass whose 'business is to perplex a witness and bamboozle a witness', the advocate wants

> a case in which he has all the world against him; Justice with her sword raised high to strike; Truth with open mouth and speaking eyes to tell the bloody tale; outraged humanity shrieking for punishment; a case from which Mercy herself, with averted eyes, has loathing turned and bade her sterner sister do her work; give him such a case as this, and then you will see Mr Chaffanbrass in his glory. Let him, by the use of his high art, rescue from the gallows and turn loose upon the world the wretch whose hands are reeking with the blood of father, mother, wife and brother and you may see Mr Chaffanbrass elated with conscious worth, rub his happy hands with infinite complacency. Then will his ambition be satisfied, and he will feel that in the verdict of the jury he has received the honour due to his genius. He will have succeeded in turning black into white, in washing the blackamoor, in dressing in the fair robe of innocence the foulest, filthiest wretch of his day; and as he returns to his home, he will be proudly conscious that he is no little man.[122]

If he is very talented and extremely fortunate, the advocate may, like Sir Patrick Hastings, reminisce that he 'cannot look back upon one moment when I was bored. I cannot remember one day which was not tinged with some element of adventure, either of hope or disappointment, of failure or achievement.'[123] Habitually, however, the less gifted or less fortunate advocate will have to be satisfied with more mundane topics which cannot by any stretch of the imagination be described as provoking any type of excitement, other than the usual uncertainty as to when, if ever, his opponent's submissions will come to an end; when, if at all, the judge will get the point; whether he will be paid for his labours, and, if so, whether the fee will cover his expenses.

He must deal with obstinate clients who tell epic sagas based on ancient grievances which they translate into hopeless causes of action and in respect of which they insist on having their weeks (a day would not be too bad) in court. At the opposite extreme, he must seek to identify and articulate the representations of a client who (for a variety of reasons, most of them damning) is reluctant to provide his lawyers with other than basic instructions (and occasionally not even that much) on the facts of the case. It is, as Lord Pearce understood, often the task of counsel representing 'the unreasonable' to exercise 'firm suasion' and thereby 'mitigate their unreason and find some via media by which their case can be presented intelligibly and reasonably'.[124] It is not necessarily easy acting, to adopt the description used by Lord Justice Lawton, as 'a legal sieve' without whose herculean efforts 'those who were stupid and ignorant might bring their neighbours to court when there was not the beginnings of a case'.[125]

Not all cases will provide intellectual stimulation to every advocate. Dicey (later to become an eminent constitutional lawyer) was, in 1876, appointed junior counsel to the Inland Revenue Commissioners. He confided to an Oxford professor that this work 'bored him to the point where he spent as much time as possible thinking of Blackstone' (though he held the post until 1890).[126] All varieties of grievance and conduct are within the realm of the advocate. When a distinguished French advocate visited the court of the Lord Chief Justice in 1864, the occasion was 'unhappily inauspicious, for two learned gentlemen were arguing on a nice point of special pleading as to the precise difference between a "replication" and a "new assignment" . . . there being really nothing substantial in dispute'.[127]

He 'may have to speak upon subjects concerning the deepest interests of social life, and the innermost feelings of the human soul'.[128] Or he may be required to submit (or, worse still, reply to his opponent's submission) that 'the courts were not the place to deal with someone's sense of grievance that another person has been rude in print about their bottom'[129] or that a holiday to Switzerland was ruined, and the travel company should pay compensation, because (amongst other matters) 'the yodler evening consisted of one man from the locality who came in his working clothes for a little while, and sang four or five songs very quickly'.[130] Even the enthusiastic Patrick Hastings was compelled to concede that he had no memories of the Central Criminal Court 'beyond a sense of undiluted melancholy; the whole atmosphere reeks of misery and squalor . . .'.[131]

The professional duty of the advocate to represent any client[132] may oblige the lawyer to accept some odd customers. Bartholomew Chassenée, a French lawyer of the sixteenth century (when legalism extended to the trial and punishment of animals), was said to have 'made his reputation at the bar as counsel for some rats, which had been put on trial before the ecclesiastical court of Autun on the charge of having feloniously eaten up and wantonly destroyed the barley-crop of that province'. Like any good advocate, he did the best he could for his clients, despite the difficulty of taking instructions and the absence of any obvious defence to the charge. On their behalf, he argued technical points 'as seriously as though it were a question of family feud between Capulet and Montague in Verona or Colonna and Orsini in Rome'.[133] In 1983 the US Court of Appeals suggested a less generous approach to human representation in cases concerning animals' rights. The court dismissed a challenge to the constitutionality of a municipal ordinance imposing a business licence tax. The appellants were the owners and promoters of 'Blackie the Talking Cat'. The court concluded that they had failed to make out their case that the tax was an infringement of First Amendment rights of free speech. Even if an animal could enjoy such rights, the court noted, 'we see no need for appellants to assert his right . . . Blackie can clearly speak for himself'.[134] However, animal rights campaigners will be reassured to learn that a dog was called as a witness in an Industrial Tribunal in 1987[135] and I have heard of another case in an Industrial Tribunal where a barrister sent her apologies for being unable to attend that morning as her dog was ill.

Advocacy may require a professional devotion to causes hopeless beyond redemption even by the most skilful of exponents of the craft. In 1616 a defendant pleaded infancy as a defence to an action. However, 'it was found by sufficient proof, by oath, and by examination of the church book, that he was of the age of 63 years, and so it appeared to the court that he was of full age, and this was but a shift'.[136] The law report does not record what his counsel found to say on his behalf in his closing speech. No doubt he rose to the occasion. But the judge is likely to have thought, as Viscount Dunedin stated for the House of Lords in a hopeless case three centuries later, that 'I have listened for some hours without discovering that even the ingenuity of counsel could bring forward any argument that was much worth consideration, and I think they were driven, as they were in duty bound driven, to the ultimate virtue of persistency'.[137] John Mortimer, recalling his experience in an obscenity case, suggested that 'no one has felt the full glory of a barrister's life who has not, in wig and gown, been called to the podium in the committee room of the House of Lords by an official in full evening dress and, on a wet Monday morning, lectured five elderly Law Lords in lounge suits on the virtues of masturbation'.[138] Judges understandably complain that 'many hours are spent each year . . . in listening to wholly unbalanced attempts to re-open, without justification, a case which a party has lost and which, by brooding over it, he can no longer see in an objective light'.[139] A litigious client of mine, who had lost an important case, was unwilling to accept that this might be the end of the road: can we sue the judges for negligence, he enquired.

Lord Justice Danckwerts was correct to note that there were 'many members of the Bar who have longed to be quit of a client and the undesirable effect on their practices which such a client brings'.[140] But 'while the client may get rid of his counsel whenever he pleases, and employ another', the Scottish Court of Session has perceptively observed, 'it is by no means easy for a counsel to get rid of his client'.[141]

IV

An admittedly extreme example of a hopeless case kept alive by the reluctance of a client to accept the inevitable was the *Spycatcher* saga. It is of interest to examine in some detail the progress of this extraordinary series of cases to see the extent to which a client may seek to defy the laws of reality and insist that his (or, in this case, her) lawyers do not give up. Even the most competent lawyers cannot keep alive for ever a cause which has been mortally wounded.

'A secret agent who throws his secrecy to the winds from desire of vengeance, and flaunts his achievements before the public eye, becomes', as Joseph Conrad observed of Mr Verloc in *The Secret Agent*, 'the mark for desperate and bloodthirsty indignations.'[142] By publishing his memoirs, *Spycatcher*, Peter Wright flaunted his dubious achievements in the security services and sought to gain his vengeance for the denial of the pension to which he thought himself entitled. The October 1988 judgment of the House of Lords—dismissing attempts to prevent further circulation of the book and its contents in this country—was the culmination of over two years' legal indignations on behalf of the British Government.

There are two frequent features of litigation in the cause of freedom of expression: first, that most of the books which are the subject of a ban involving legal action are of little intrinsic worth; second, that attempts to use the courts to censor the publication in question almost inevitably promote massive sales. *Spycatcher* was, as Mr Justice Kirby observed in his judgment in the New South Wales Court of Appeal in September 1987, 'one rather cantankerous old man's perspective of things notorious, or description of technology long out-dated, people long since dead and controversies tirelessly worked over by . . . numberless writers'.[143] Yet, stimulated by an unprecedented series of legal actions across the world—it was, as Chief Justice Davison noted in the New Zealand High Court, rapidly becoming 'the most litigated book of all time'[144]—*Spycatcher* sold well over a million copies. Legal action designed to prevent the publication of information resulted in 'a literary work of almost unparalleled tedium and banality'[145] heading the bestselling lists throughout the world.

In 1985 the British Government learnt of the publisher's plan to publish *Spycatcher* in Australia and obtained an injunction from the Australian courts pending a trial of the legal issues between the parties. In June 1986, after the *Guardian* and the *Observer* had published articles in England about that forthcoming trial, injunctions were obtained from the English courts against those newspapers.

By the summer of 1987, the Government's attempts to keep the book's contents secret had failed. The Cabinet Secretary, Sir Robert Armstrong, had an unhappy experience travelling to Australia to give evidence in the vain attempt to persuade Mr Justice Powell to impose a permanent injunction against publication in that country. The most interesting of Peter Wright's allegations were disclosed in England in the *Independent* newspaper in April 1987. In July 1987, *Spycatcher* was published in the USA. It was an immediate bestseller. The Prime Minister told Parliament that the Secretary of State for Trade and Industry had advised against an import ban 'because it is likely to be ineffective'.[146]

Three English newspapers, the *Sunday Times*, the *Guardian*, and the *Observer*, applied for the discharge of the English injunctions in the light of US publication. The former CIA agent Philip Agee has described how the CIA considered legal action in the USA to prevent publication of his 1975 book *Inside the Company*. William Colby, the CIA Director, had tried to persuade the Justice Department to seek an injunction, 'but Justice said they couldn't get it because the book was already published in England'.[147] Such a sensible approach, that one cannot realistically seek to rebottle secrets once they are out, did not commend itself to the British Government, or to some judges.

In ten extraordinary days of litigation in July 1987, the preliminary issues were considered by three English courts.[148] Sir Nicolas Browne-Wilkinson (the Vice-Chancellor) held that there was no longer any basis for an injunction against the newspapers. As he explained, 'in the contemporary world of electronics and jumbo jets, news anywhere is news everywhere'. He concluded that 'the law could . . . be justifiably accused of being an ass and brought into disrepute if it closed its eyes' to the reality that the book's contents were no longer secret, but easily obtainable by anyone who took the trouble to order a copy from the USA by post or telephone.[149]

The Court of Appeal disagreed. Without being asked to do so by either the newspapers or the Attorney-General, it fashioned its own half-way house, allowing publication of 'a summary in very general terms of the allegations made by Mr Wright'.[150] Then, the following week, in a strained atmosphere, the Law Lords concluded by a majority of 3–2 that there should be an injunction pending a full trial of the action against the newspapers. 'To attempt', as Lord Oliver observed in his dissenting speech, 'to create a sort of judicial cordon sanitaire against the infection from abroad of public comment and discussion is not only . . . certain to be ineffective but involves taking the first steps upon a very perilous path.'[151] Lord Bridge (former Chairman of the Security Commission) noted, in his dissenting speech, that 'freedom of speech is always the first casualty under a totalitarian regime'.[152] By contrast, Lord Ackner—one of the judges in the majority—was concerned that the law should not cease to be a 'rock' and become a 'jellyfish' by refusing to grant an injunction because of publication in the USA.[153] Without being asked to do so by the Attorney-General, the judges in the majority extended the injunction to forbid the reporting in England of proceedings held in open court in Australia. The front-page comment in the *Daily Mirror*, 'You Fools',[154] was more polite than the views expressed throughout the Temple on the wisdom of the majority decision.

In September 1987, the Attorney-General of Hong Kong obtained an injunction from the Hong Kong Court of Appeal to prevent the *South China Sunday Morning Post* from publishing further extracts from the book.[155] The Chinese-language version (published as *The Man who Catches Spies*), available in Peking,[156] was beyond the jurisdiction of the courts. The *Sun*—not previously known for the quality of its leaders on jurisprudential issues—observed that this was all 'Velly Silly'.

The full trial against the *Sunday Times*, the *Guardian*, and the *Observer* to prevent those newspapers from publishing any information in *Spycatcher*, and to prevent the *Sunday Times* from serializing extracts from the book, began before Mr Justice Scott on 23 November 1987. In his opening speech, Robert Alexander QC, counsel for the Attorney-General, conceded, with admirable understatement, that 'as is well known, the Government has not been wholly successful in its objective of preventing any publication'. By that time *Spycatcher* had been at the top of the bestseller lists in the USA and Canada for several weeks. The book had also been published in Australia and Ireland. Copies had been distributed throughout the world. A large number had been brought into the United Kingdom. Robert Alexander QC informed Mr Justice Scott that 'on Friday evenings when there is always a queue on the [A40], there would always be one or two enterprising people who would jump out. . . . They would hold up a copy of the book and say, "Want one?".' Copies were not so easy to retain. 'My learned friend and my junior', Mr Alexander told Mr Justice Scott (as the official transcript records), 'have found that their copies have gone missing from the Court. [Laughter].'

Lengthy extracts had been printed by newspapers throughout the world: by the *Independent* and by the *Sunday Times* in London, by the *South China Sunday Morning Post* in Hong Kong, by the *Dominion* in New Zealand, by the *Daily Nation* in Kenya, and by *Gulf News* in the United Arab Emirates. Danish Radio and Swedish Radio had broadcast extracts in English. Bookshops in Scotland were trying to avoid legal restrictions by giving away copies of the book with other works purchased, in one case a remaindered publication about Secretaries of State for Scotland, in another case with every copy bought of Prince Charles' *The Old Man of Lochnagar*. A record, 'Ballad of a Spycatcher', had been played several times on BBC Radio 1, repeating the major allegations. Peter Wright's literary agents in New York had sold the foreign-language rights to publish *Spycatcher* in various translations, from Catalan to Icelandic.

The satirical television programme *Spitting Image* included a sketch in which it was suggested to the Prime Minister, Mrs Thatcher, by one brave adviser that possibly the time had come to give up attempts to prevent people learning about the contents of *Spycatcher* since a musical by Andrew Lloyd-Webber based on the book had opened in the West End, and Torvill and Dean had created a new ice-dance routine around Wright's main allegations. A letter in the *Independent* asked whether the Attorney-General knew that the BBC was planning to broadcast the comedy film *Carry on Spying* and, if so, was he going to obtain an injunction?

Mr Justice Scott concluded that in the light of the publication of the book in the USA, the inclusion in the newspapers of further information and extracts from the book could not cause any more damage to national security. He found himself 'unable to escape the reflection that the absolute protection of the Security Services that Sir Robert [Armstrong] was contending for could not be achieved this side of the Iron Curtain'.[157] The Court of Appeal dismissed the Government's appeal early in 1988. Lord Justice Bingham observed that 'the court will not seek to emulate the 15th-century pope who issued a papal bull against Halley's comet' and that 'most of the great works of the French Enlightenment were, for good reason, published outside France. But the Bastille still fell.' He commented that 'Mr Wright's disservice to this country would . . . be compounded if revulsion from his conduct were to lead the law into paths not indicated by an objective application of settled and very important principles'.[158]

On 2 June 1988, the High Court of Australia (that country's supreme judicial body) rejected the Government's claims for a financial remedy against Peter Wright and Heinemann, his publishers.[159] Contrary to the impression which many observers may have had at the time, and may still have after reading the account by Malcolm Turnbull, the lawyer who acted for Peter Wright and Heinemann ('the real damage to the British case had occurred during my cross-examination of Armstrong'),[160] the Australian case was not legally won or lost on the performance of Sir Robert Armstrong in the witness-box. The Australian courts refused to assist the British Government not because Sir Robert's evidence was disbelieved or found wanting, but because of a point of law, that the Australian legal system would not enforce what amounted to the public law of another State. Nor did any of the three Australian courts which heard the case accept the conspiracy theory of various events advanced on behalf of Peter Wright by Malcolm Turnbull. Nevertheless, Turnbull's ritual humiliation of the pom sent down under to bat for the Crown unsettled the British Government, provoked its public ridicule, and undoubtedly made it easier for the Australian judiciary to decide the case in favour of Peter Wright on a legal technicality.

Peter Wright was, in consequence, a millionaire. If the aim of the litigation had been to prevent him from profiting from his wrong, or to deter others, it had failed miserably.

The Government's case had also been dismissed by the New Zealand courts.[161] The Government had recognized at an early stage in the saga that American and Canadian law—which provide constitutional protection for freedom of speech—offered no prospect of a remedy. By this time (summer 1988) 1.5 million hardback copies of *Spycatcher* had been sold worldwide. Yet the Attorney-General was still asking the English courts to prevent English newspapers and bookshops from informing readers what people all over the world knew about *our* Security Services.

It was in this context that on 14 June 1988 the House of Lords began to hear the final appeal in the English proceedings. Alan Rusbridger, in his sketch in the *Guardian*, described how 'the Spycatcher Society held one of its periodic meetings in London yesterday. . . . Those present were given an interesting talk on the history of the Wright affair by one of the world's leading scholars on the subject, Mr Robert Alexander QC.'[162]

In their October 1988 judgment, the Law Lords put an end to the absurd injunctions and confirmed what had been obvious since July 1987: that as a result of worldwide publication, all secrecy in the contents of *Spycatcher* had been destroyed and no further harm could be done by publication in this country.[163] The legal actions continued. In July 1990, the European Commission of Human Rights unanimously held that the House of Lords, by their decision in July 1987 to continue the injunction after publication in the USA, had breached the guarantee of freedom of expression in the European Convention on Human Rights. Once the contents of the book were no longer secret, there was, concluded the Commission, no justification for preventing the British people from reading what was being read throughout the world, especially as the book concerned the alleged activities of the British Security Service.

In John le Carré's novel, *The Russia House,* MI5's in-house lawyer acknowledges that his 'old law tutor would have turned in his grave—not, I am afraid, for the first time. But it's always wonderful what a lawyer can achieve when nobody knows the law.'[164] The House of Lords imposed some harsh reality in this area of the law. However insistent the client, and however talented or industrious a litigant's lawyers may be, a hopeless cause is eventually doomed to failure.

CHAPTER 3

Judges and Opponents

I

THE maintenance of a proper working relationship with his client is one, but by no means the only, occupational hazard for the advocate to overcome. He will often find it more trying to resolve the difficulties posed by the judge and by his opponent in court.

The advocate must seek to persuade judges (who have heard it all before) and juries (who think they have) to listen carefully, or at all, to arguments when the adjudicator would rather be somewhere (anywhere) else or, at least, would prefer there to be silence in court. In 1881, Lord Justice Brett complimented a barrister for doing 'that which I think all counsel ought to do, [that is he] insisted on being heard'.[1]

To gain, and retain, attention is not always easy. 'The judge may, for even judges are human, be perhaps unreceptive to counsel's case',[2] as Lord Upjohn realistically recognized in 1967. The advocate is accustomed to facing the wrath of judges who have got out of bed the wrong side, who do not understand that counsel only received the brief that morning, or who apply the principle of Lord

Chancellor Lyndhurst that it is their duty 'to make it disagreeable to counsel to talk nonsense'.[3] At the Lincoln Assizes in 1606, Mr Justice Walmsley is said so to have intimidated the lawyers acting for Sir Richard Ogle that neither of them 'durst speak a word'.[4]

A variety of techniques may have to be employed by the eager advocate, according to the needs of the moment and the characteristics of the judge. In 1851, Lord Chief Justice Campbell recalled that Lord Cottenham had once given evidence 'to say how far he was influenced by a nod from counsel'.[5] On occasion, it may be necessary to show considerable enterprise. In a 1932 judgment concerning an action by a husband against a man who had enticed away his wife, Lord Justice Scrutton said that 'it was a squalid and not a very interesting case which had somehow been elevated by the newspapers into a case which afforded good copy, apparently because some ingenious counsel had considered that there was some likeness between this case and the Trojan War'.[6] In extreme circumstances, the advocate may have to resort to desperate measures. In one case, counsel 'cited extracts from an after dinner speech made by Mr Patrick Jenkin, the then Secretary of State for the Environment'. The judge, Mr Justice Macpherson, commented that he 'had not personally heard such citation made before in court'.[7]

In struggling to do his best for his client, the advocate must overcome impediments placed in his way by the judge, his opponent, the jury, and the witnesses. The advocate must tread a very fine line between standing up for the rights of his client and committing a contempt of court. The vital role of the advocate in ensuring that justice is done makes it essential that courts should treat sympathetically those lawyers who overstep the mark unwittingly, or in the heat of the moment.

II

The advocate's difficulties are often caused by the material with which he has to work. The efforts of a diligent instructing solicitor and the good fortune of an attentive judge cannot necessarily overcome the handicap imposed by the absence of a winning point. Even Cicero would have had problems persuading a court that there was substance in the grounds of appeal in a California case reported in 1988.[8] A defence lawyer, Mr Clark Head, was to appeal in the case of a client convicted of breaking and entering because, he contended, the prosecuting attorney 'farted about 100 times' during Mr Head's closing speech to the jury.

That case—unlikely as it is to be reported in the Law Reports or to be cited in the standard works on criminal jurisprudence—gives an insight into the unpredictable daily life of the advocate. More charitably minded readers may wish to reflect on the pressures imposed on counsel and to have sympathy with the California attorney and his co-workers throughout the legal world. The duty of the advocate is 'fearlessly to raise every issue, advance every argument, and ask every question, however distasteful, which he thinks will help his client's case'.[9] However unpromising the material supplied to him by his client, his solicitors, and fate, whatever the provocation from his opponent, and however strong the disapproval of the judge, it is the role of the advocate fearlessly to seek to persuade the tribunal that the law and justice (or at least one of them) are on his side.

As is invariably the case, whatever the point to be argued, the resourceful counsel will be able to find some law to support him. No doubt Mr Head was prepared to remind the appeal court that it is well established in

American courts that prosecuting counsel 'may prosecute with earnestness and vigour—indeed, he should do so. But, while he may strike hard blows, he is not at liberty to strike foul ones.'[10] In particular, it has been held, the advocate should not insult his opponent, for example if he 'loudly expelled air from his lungs' during his opponent's submissions to the court (as in an Illinois case in 1976)[11] or by commenting during a trial (as occurred in California in 1974) that he was 'sorry if I offended the high-priced lawyer' for the opposing party.[12] The English equivalent of prosecuting counsel offending his opponent is more refined than that to which Mr Clark Head took exception in California. In one of A. P. Herbert's *Misleading Cases*, 'both the famous advocates constantly thumped on the desk, raised their eyebrows, and blew their noses'.[13]

On occasion in the courts of the United States, an advocate has been known to use 'profane and insulting language towards opposing counsel in open court after being warned by the judge not to do so'.[14] American lawyers do not always maintain high standards of courtesy in these, and analogous, respects. Defence counsel have been held in contempt or otherwise disgraced themselves by referring to the prosecutor as 'you stiff' and 'Mr Voicestrong' (his name was Armstrong);[15] by describing the prosecutor as 'so lacking in mental capacity as not being able to find his way to the toilet, too big for his britches, a skunk [etc]';[16] by telling the jury, 'I am not going to ask for a show of hands on how many of you would like to go on a search party with [defence counsel] for truth and think you will be successful';[17] and by 'asking the jury if they would play miniature golf with the prosecutor' and 'if they would buy a used car from the prosecutor' and describing her trial tactics as 'cheat, cheat, cheat'.[18]

In 1935, the US Supreme Court fined an advocate $250, and suspended him from practice before that court for six months, for including offensive remarks in the written brief filed with the court.[19] In 1978, an attorney was disbarred by the Supreme Court of Indiana for his failure to comply with gentlemanly standards. When your opponent declines to agree to the cancellation of a hearing, it was, suggested the Court, inappropriate for an advocate to retort: 'You snake son-of-a-bitch, that leaves but one thing for me to do, to go down and load up both barrels of my gun, and I'll getcha.'[20]

Jan Morris, in Manhattan in 1979, observed how 'an aged court-appointed lawyer, down at the state courts, histrionically convinces the judge, with a florid wealth of legal jargon and gesture, that an adjournment is necessary, but spotting a row of hostile witnesses as he passes through the courtroom on his way out, loudly offers them a comment: *Too bad, assholes*'.[21] In 1982, the Supreme Court of Ohio reprimanded a lawyer for misconduct, which had included his response to a written request by his opponent: he 'rubber-stamped an obscenity on the face of the letter' (and wrote two more obscenities) before returning it.[22] It is seldom in any jurisdiction that a lawyer encounters an opponent comparable to the US lawyer, Roy Cohn. He had learnt many of his tricks of bribery, smear, and obfuscation as chief counsel to Senator Joseph McCarthy during the witch-hunt years. It was said that he was 'a man so altogether loathsome that his opponents would settle cases just to avoid dealing with him'.[23]

In 1971, the European Commission of Human Rights rejected a complaint by a German counsel reprimanded by the Law Society for insulting his opponent in a written brief (the statement of claim presented by the other side was, he said, 'a stammering filled with helplessness and despair') and for rudeness to a public prosecutor during a trial (he had commented that the submissions made by the prosecutor might be excusable since he 'was perhaps not of sound mind' and that the prosecutor 'reminded him of the ill-famed Nazi judge Freisler'). The duty of the advocate 'not to use aggressive or insulting language in no way hinders him from . . . submitting his client's case', the Commission concluded.[24]

In England advocates usually remain on civil terms with their opponents. So impersonally do most counsel treat the causes of their clients in the United Kingdom that it is rare for an advocate even to go so far as to contend, as did Cyril Radcliffe KC in a 1937 case, that 'my friends' (opposing counsel are always described in terms of amity no matter how bitter the relationship with them) 'have argued the case with a disregard of the facts and of the law which is applicable'.[25]

There have been examples of unhappy relations between opposing counsel at the English and Scottish bar. It is, regrettably, only to be expected, as Lord Clyde of the Scottish Court of Session noted in 1921, that 'the rhetorical javelins which opposing counsel employ sometimes overshoot the mark'.[26] There are bound to be exceptions to the rule that advocates display the best of behaviour in court and out. In the early seventeenth century 'ill feeling and disputes breaking out in exchanges of verbal abuse, and even physical violence, were certainly not uncommon'.[27] In 1887, a solicitor was found to be in contempt for calling his opponent (outside court) 'a d—d perjured scoundrel' (as the Law Reports somewhat sanctimoniously record). This was, according to Lord Esher MR, 'an insult to the administration of justice'.[28] In 1908, 'the Court of Mr Justice A. T. Lawrence was disturbed by an outbreak of fisticuffs between two K.C.s . . . the former of whom had made disparaging remarks about the latter's ancestry'.[29] A barrister recalled in 1911 a case where 'the leader on one side interrupted his opponent by declaring that his nerves would not allow him to remain in court, unless his learned friend moderated "his strident voice"' and the opposing counsel 'retorted that he would endeavour to do so if his learned friend would "turn away his ugly face"'.[30] In 1956 the Court of Appeal criticized the behaviour of counsel during a trial: 'there began, almost from the commencement of the case, a wrangling or quarrelling or bickering between counsel, and it lasted throughout the case'. The court expressed the hope that 'it will be a long time before this kind of thing happens again'.[31]

In contemporary England, any suggestion of ungentlemanly conduct at the Bar receives considerable attention and concern. During a libel trial in 1968, it was inaccurately reported by a newspaper that the judge, Mr Justice Cantley, had 'walked out of his court when QCs bickered' about the content of the evidence which had been given by a previous witness.[32] When the court next convened to continue the trial, Mr Justice Cantley made a statement that what had occurred in court 'seems to have given rise to a certain amount of misunderstanding . . . which I personally found rather distressing when I read about it'. He explained that he had 'adjourned the court for a short while so that [counsel] could look up a disputed passage in the evidence in the transcript'. He assured counsel that he 'was not rebuking either of you' and had not 'suggested that, in any way, you had misconducted yourselves'. Mr Ackner QC added that 'my learned friend and I do not bicker'. Mr Justice Cantley noted that 'bickering is something which I go to considerable trouble to avoid'.[33] So prized are the reputations of counsel for high standards of conduct towards each other that in 1988 two Northern

Ireland QCs were each awarded £50,000 libel damages for a newspaper article which falsely suggested that they had squabbled in a shop about which of them should have the opportunity to buy the last available chocolate eclair.[34]

If the words used by an advocate about his opponent were especially insulting, pronounced the Judicial Committee of the Privy Council in 1945, they could amount to a contempt of court: for example if 'an advocate threatened or attempted violence on his opponent, or conceivably if he used language so outrageous and provocative as to be likely to lead to a brawl in court'. However, judges are normally careful to ensure that the contempt of court power is not used 'to suppress methods of advocacy which are merely offensive' or 'the sort of tactless and intemperate statement that is not infrequently made in the heat of argument'. It would be different if the advocate 'persists in a line of conduct or use of language in spite of the ruling of the presiding judge . . . [for] then the offence is the disregard of the ruling and setting the court at defiance'.[35]

The advocate's temper may have been provoked by the judge, rather than his opponent. Judicial trampling on the rights of a client or various manifestations of other forms of judicial idiocy can try the patience of the advocate. A Californian judge was censured in 1983 for a variety of types of injudicious conduct, including his response when the District Attorney announced that a preliminary ruling was going to be the subject of an appeal: the judge 'poked [the District Attorney] in the chest with his finger and told [him], "Buddy boy, you're not going to get away with this"'.[36] (The District Attorney could consider himself fortunate: in 1975 the Supreme Court of California had upheld the recommendation of the Commission on Judicial Qualifications that a Municipal Court

Judge should be removed from office for a number of offences which had caused concern, including an order to the bailiff to bring before her in Court the policeman who had reprimanded her for a traffic offence on her way to work: she told the bailiff, 'Give me a gun; I am going to shoot his balls off and give him a .38 vasectomy').[37] In 1988, a US District Court judge threatened a female lawyer that if she persisted in using her maiden name or the title 'Ms' in court, 'you're going to sleep in the county jail tonight. You can't tell me how to run my courtroom.' He apologized a week later.[38]

Californian advocates would appear to require especial qualities of patience and self-control. In 1925, a California Court reversed the decision of a trial judge that an advocate was in contempt for disobeying the judge's order to conduct his cross-examination sitting down. 'The orderly conduct of a trial', pronounced the court, 'permits, if not requires, counsel in presenting his case . . . to stand'.[39] In 1979, the California Court of Appeal rejected the argument of counsel for the Superior Court of San Diego County that an advocate 'was disrespectful to the [San Diego] trial court in referring to the court as "sir", when he said "No, sir"', instead of responding, as he ought to have done, 'No, Your Honour'. The Court of Appeal dismissed the allegation that this was a contempt.[40] When courts take themselves too seriously and make rulings which impinge unreasonably on the ability of the advocate to do his job, it is not surprising if lawyers have trouble controlling their emotions.

It may be difficult for the advocate to resist the temptation to respond in kind to excessive judicial interventions, particularly if the judge threatens counsel that 'if you say another word I will have the Marshal stick a gag in your mouth';[41] or warns the advocate that if, during a preliminary hearing, he kept raising points that did not appeal to the bench, the judge would 'take care' of the lawyer during the trial.[42] In 1988, a judge of the US District Court was reprimanded for allowing her child to run around her courtroom; calling litigants 'pure trash'; and threatening to shoot a lawyer (presumably in descending order of seriousness).[43] A Californian judge was removed from office in 1988 for a number of lapses from proper judicial standards, one of which was to tell an offensive joke to two female attornies appearing before him at a preliminary hearing in his chambers.[44] In 1268, 'Robert de Coleville, pleader of the bench, assaulted a Justice', and was fortunate that his offence was pardoned.[45] We do not know what the judge had said to him by way of provocation.

There are, regrettably, an infinite variety of ways in which the judge may impede the effective performance of the functions of the conscientious advocate. There is a temptation for the fussy judge to seek to regulate every aspect of the advocate's court life. The judge may, for example, seek to impose dress codes on the advocate anxious to concentrate on arguing the case. In 1969, a New York judge prohibited a young female attorney from taking any further part in a case before him until she wore 'suitable, conventional and appropriate' clothes. She was wearing a dress the hemline of which was approximately five inches above the knee. The Supreme Court of New York, Appellate Division, quashed the judge's order, noting that there was no suggestion that her appearance 'in any way created distraction or in any manner disrupted the ordinary proceedings of the court' or was 'so immodest or revealing as to shock one's sense of propriety'. Justice Del Vecchio, dissenting, thought that the dress 'revealed substantially more of the human frame than is customarily displayed in a courtroom'.[46]

In an extraordinary case, that could only have occurred in California, an advocate was forbidden by a judge to appear in his courtroom wearing a turban when there appeared to be no religious or other legitimate reason to do so. The attorney refused to explain why he wore the turban. Associate Justice Butler, for the Court of Appeal of California, gave a grandiloquent opinion that 'to require a lawyer to disclose religious beliefs as a condition to appear before a judge returns us to those troubled times our ancestors fled in their search for freedom from religious oppression'. The appeal court therefore ordered the lower court 'to permit the turbanned [advocate] to appear and practice law before it without having to reveal why he wears a turban, unless the court can establish through proper procedure [that] the turban interferes with or disrupts justice'.[47] By contrast, the Court of Appeals of New York held, in 1975, that a judge could prohibit an attorney who was also a Roman Catholic priest from wearing clerical garb in court when acting as defence counsel in a criminal trial. Chief Justice Breitel explained that a 'juror might view differently statements made by a member of the clergy than those made by others'.[48]

Appeal courts usually find that the trial judge has a broad discretion to regulate the dress of lawyers in his courtroom. In 1976, the Supreme Court of Florida held by a majority of 4–3 that it had no jurisdiction to consider an attorney's petition in respect of a finding of criminal contempt for his refusal to wear a necktie in court. One court had sentenced him to three days in jail for this offence, and another court had fined him $500. Justice England, dissenting, pointed out that the advocate's 'personal appearance and attire, which included a suit, clean and pressed shirt, and a hanging gold medallion, were otherwise neat, attractive and proper'. He wisely rejected 'any inference that respect for the judicial system is dependent upon male attorneys wearing neckties'.[49] In 1964, an optimistic ground of appeal against a conviction for perjury was that, on the first day of the trial, the judge had requested the female attorney for the defendant to appear hatless in court on subsequent days of the trial. The attorney declined and appeared with her hat on each day of the proceedings. Her client's conviction was, held the District Court of Appeal of California, in no respect due to the judicial request about the hat. In any event, it was well within the judge's discretion to make such a request if he thought the hat to be distracting to the jury.[50] It is a curious feature of human nature that judges who have sufficient to occupy their minds in the facts and the law relevant to the case they are trying often have a peculiar preoccupation with the dress of those who appear in their courtroom.[51] In the middle of his cross-examination of a witness, John Mortimer's Rumpole is passed a message from Mr Justice Prestcold: 'your bands are falling down and showing your collar-stud'. As Rumpole curses to himself, 'what was this, a murder trial or a bloody fashion parade?'[52]

If the judge is prepared to concentrate on the case, and put out of his mind the couture of the advocate, he may, by his constant interruptions, make it impossible for the advocate properly to present the case on behalf of his client.[53] Or the judge may, exceptionally, make wholly unjustified allegations that, by doing his job and cross-examining prosecution witnesses, the defence advocate is wasting court time. At the end of a criminal trial in 1975, Mr Justice Melford Stevenson criticized defence counsel for conducting a 'mud-slinging defence' which had involved 'wild accusations of fraud, forgery and general dishonesty' which were 'flung' at police officers 'recklessly and without any factual basis'. He complained that the defence counsel had acted as 'mere loudspeakers' by making the 'insulting suggestion' of police misconduct. The Court of Criminal Appeal held that the judge had no power to interfere with the payment of legal aid fees to the defence counsel involved (as he had purported to do) and the Professional Conduct Committee of the Bar rejected the judge's complaints about the conduct of the lawyers as wholly unjustified: the counsel were performing their professional duty to present their client's case without fear or favour.[54]

But however irrelevant to the issues the comments expressed by the judge, however extreme the provocation coming from the direction of the Bench, however incompetent or prejudicial to a fair trial the performance of the judge, there are limits to what an advocate—whatever his seniority—can say or do, even on instructions. Sometimes, in the course of the contest, proper standards of behaviour 'are not only forgotten but completely disregarded and dragged in the mire'.[55] The cautious barrister who wishes to avoid being prevented from earning his living at the Bar may welcome some general guidance in this sensitive area, derived from an analysis of other such cases in various jurisdictions.

Some general principles can confidently be stated. It is unwise for an advocate to pick a fight with the judge. The authorities tend to frown on advocates who make threats of personal violence to the judge who has not been persuaded by the advocate's submissions. An advocate should not call a judge a 'contemptible cur' and threaten to 'settle with him outside'[56] or to 'get even with you'.[57] In 1871, the US Supreme Court upheld an order striking counsel's name from a lower court's roll of attornies for having 'threatened the judge with personal chastisement' at the end of a court day during which he had convinced himself that the judge had insulted him. 'A greater indignity could hardly be offered to a judge,' the court concluded. 'A judge who should pass over in silence an offence of such gravity would soon find himself a subject of pity rather than of respect.'[58] In a New Mexico court, an advocate who had been held to be in contempt for ignoring judicial rulings 'took off his tie and took off his coat and approached toward the Bench in a fighting attitude', according to the recollection of the unfortunate judge. The advocate later urged that this was 'a symbolic demonstration that he was from that point on a prisoner and not a lawyer'. The Supreme Court of New Mexico declined to decide which version was correct.[59] An advocate should not threaten the judge that if he repeats his ruling outside the court, 'I will take on you [*sic*] certainly'. (Abdoolcader J in the Malaysian High Court allowed an appeal against the sentence of two days' imprisonment for contempt, as the advocate had not been given an adequate chance to answer the charge before the judge had convicted and sentenced him, but he referred the matter to the Bar Committee for an inquiry into the conduct of the advocate).[60]

The lawyer should ensure that he is present at the beginning of the hearing. The absence of the advocate from court when his case is called may amount to contempt,[61] especially (as the Ontario Court of Appeal held in 1978) if it is a deliberate failure to attend or shows 'an indifference to his obligation to the court and to the client. . . . Whether an inadvertent lapse constitutes a contempt of court depends on the particular facts of the case . . .'[62] In 1978, the Scottish High Court of Justiciary harshly upheld a fine of £25 imposed on a solicitor advocate for not being present in court when the case in which he was acting was called on for hearing: he had misjudged the length of time which the previous case was likely to take.[63] In 1987, the National Court of Papua New Guinea fined a prosecuting counsel for contempt for arriving late at court.[64]

During the hearing, the advocate must resist the temptation to insult the judge for failing to appreciate the strength of his case.[65] An advocate who, upset that his opponent's objections have been consistently upheld, inquires of the judge, 'Surely the court knows the merest elementary rules of law?' is likely to be held to be in contempt of court.[66] Similar consequences (and possibly suspension from practice) will follow for the rash advocate who reprimands the judge in court by suggesting that 'you ought to be ashamed of yourself' and 'you should cite yourself for misconduct';[67] or comments, 'this court obviously doesn't want to apply the law';[68] or replies to a question from the judge by saying that he has not come to court 'to listen to a whole lot of stuff from you; I am not in the mood for it';[69] or responds to judicial admonishment with the words, 'I'm getting out of this court, if you can call it a court';[70] or describes a judge in court as 'a horse's ass';[71] or claims that the judge's ruling 'smacks of Stalinism and Hitlerism and Mussoliniism';[72] or says in court that the judge's ruling is 'about the most outrageous statement I have ever heard from a bench', that he feels 'disgraced to be here', and that 'if this is what your career is going to end on, if this is what your pride is going to be built on, I can only say to your Honour, "Good luck to you"'[73] (the appeal court there rejected the defence that this was 'merely heated legal argument' by the advocate on behalf of his client).[74]

Criticisms of the performance of the judge should be

expressed politely during the hearing of the case. It is unwise for the advocate to make an 'offensive and insulting' suggestion that the magistrate was failing to keep a proper record of the proceedings. In 1943, the Transvaal Provincial Division of the Supreme Court of South Africa dismissed an appeal by an advocate who had been fined £5 by a magistrate for contempt for interrupting his opponent's cross-examination of a witness to assert that 'the record contains a number of inaccuracies'.[75] In 1985, the Supreme Court of Malaysia upheld a fine imposed by a magistrate on a barrister who had complained that the court was 'unnecessarily tormenting the witness'. He had become 'emotional and made several allegations of bias against the magistrate'. He then refused to leave the court. This was, concluded the Supreme Court, a serious contempt. 'Whilst we accept that counsel can plead for his client without fear and favour, he certainly has no right to abuse the court and interrupt the proceedings.'[76]

If the case is not going too well, owing to lack of judicial sympathy for the cause for which the advocate is contending, the lawyer must resist the temptation to imitate the example of Serjeant Sullivan, walk out of court and (successfully) seek from the appeal court an order for a retrial.[77] It may not be a contempt for a barrister to leave the court if he believes his client is not receiving a fair trial,[78] but it will not necessarily assist his client if he does so. 'If it be open for counsel . . . to break off a losing battle when the court appears to be very much against him, and then to ask [the Court of Appeal] for a rehearing, it would create an opportunity for many applications to this court by undeserving litigants.' So, said the Court of Appeal, it is only in 'very exceptional circumstances' that the Court of Appeal would assist 'litigants who have voluntarily left the field before the battle is concluded'.[79]

After the hearing, and before judgment is given, the ambitious advocate should not write a letter to the judge, as did a barrister in 1836 (in a case heard by a Master), making threats and seeking to induce him to form a particular view on the merits of the case. The Lord Chancellor committed the barrister to prison, noting that there were 'expressions in the letter which no gentleman could permit to be used towards himself'. He was released from prison after three weeks.[80]

Because 'it is not every act of discourtesy to the court by counsel that amounts to contempt, nor is conduct which involves a breach by counsel of his duty to his client necessarily in this category', the failure of a barrister to attend court to hear the judgment in the case he has argued is not invariably a contempt of court.[81] But if the advocate is going to attend the judgment, he should try to restrain expression of his opinion on the quality of the judicial decision.

It is rare for the judge to give the advocate the opportunity of letting off steam after judgment has been pronounced. Lord Mansfield (Chief Justice of the King's Bench 1756–88) did so on one occasion. After the court of four judges had given their decision, Lord Mansfield asked Serjeant Hill, who had appeared for the unsuccessful party, to 'tell us your real opinion and whether you don't think we are right'. Hill replied that 'he always thought it his duty to do what the court desired and . . . he . . . did not think that there were four men in the world who could have given such an illsounded judgment as you four, my Lords judges, have pronounced'.[82] More often, the advocate is expected to, and the wise advocate does, keep his views to himself.

The disappointed advocate should not interrupt the judgment with such words as 'that is a most unjust remark', conduct which led to a solicitor advocate being committed to prison for six days for contempt in 1888.[83] On hearing the judgment, the unsuccessful advocate must (unless he welcomes a fine) resist the temptation to comment in court that the judge has 'set the seal upon dishonesty'.[84] When the judge announces his decision, it is unwise for the losing advocate to seek to withdraw the claim, remove a court document, and throw it into the fire, as did an Aberdeen advocate unhappy at a sheriff's refusal in 1867 to grant an interdict (injunction) prohibiting the sale of certain bathing machines. The advocate was 'thereupon seized and lodged in prison, where he remained till the following day, when he was released'. Optimistically, he brought a claim seeking £5000 damages for his imprisonment. Lord Chancellor Cairns, dismissing the claim, described the advocate's conduct as 'a gross and unjustifiable contempt of court'.[85]

In 1989, the Visitors to the Inns of Court (Vinelott, Rose, and Swinton Thomas JJ) decided that Mr Rudy Narayan (whose own work on advocacy had warned that the life of a defence barrister is one of 'loneliness and ostracism')[86] had exceeded the licence accorded to an advocate and so should be suspended from practice at the Bar for eighteen months for accepting two different briefs in different criminal trials to be heard in different courts on the same day. The sentence ran concurrently with a sentence of six months' suspension for intemperate comments made by Mr Narayan. He had complained in court that the two judges who were to hear the criminal cases, and who had been less than impressed with the arrangements proposed by Mr Narayan, were guilty of 'racial bias' and 'racism'. Mr Narayan had, before a disciplinary tribunal, accused one of those judges of 'being mad and berserk' and 'compared him with Adolf Hitler'. Mr

Narayan accepted before the Visitors that these charges were wholly unfounded.[87]

A less assertive response is to be recommended to the advocate who feels the urge to express his critical opinions of the wisdom or competence of the judge before whom he is appearing. Counsel may, for example, escape a finding of contempt for saying, 'I don't believe this', when the judge gives a ruling adverse to her submission on the admissibility of evidence.[88] It is also a wise policy to keep your voice down on these occasions. The US Court of Appeals held in 1961 that it was not a contempt for counsel to comment in court of a judicial ruling, 'that is crazy', when this observation 'was addressed to his co-counsel . . . and was not intended to be heard by either the court or the jury'.[89] Indeed, as a general principle, the advocate should not shout at the judge (unless he is deaf). Even if the advocate is told he is inaudible, he should not (as did one Sierra Leone counsel who was held in contempt) continue his submissions 'by shouting at the top of [his] voice most contemptuously and rudely, which caused general laughter in court'.[90]

The barrister who allows the stresses and strains of a lengthy trial to become too much of a burden, and whose response tests the patience of the judge, may receive no sympathy from an appeal court. In dismissing an appeal against conviction in 1981, Lord Chief Justice Lane rejected the ground of appeal based on the fact that the trial judge had 'exhibited and expressed irritation'. It was, in the judgment of the Lord Chief Justice, counsel who had been to blame. 'Counsel must of course not shrink from representing his client's interest with fearlessness and determination', said Lord Lane. But 'that does not mean that he is permitted to interrupt the judge, to be offensive to the judge, or to cast aside the common standards of politeness which have always been the aim and pride of the Bar of this country'. The judge had, Lord Lane observed, 'on a number of occasions felt impelled to rebuke [counsel] for interrupting him, for failing to submit to rulings from the Bench; for rudeness, and on one occasion for an outrageous piece of blasphemy'.[91] The advocate should not use the appellate process to express his indignation at the decision of the lower court. In 1885, the Supreme Court of Canada objected to the appeal documents filed by a party as 'framed in such a scandalous manner, in fact in such a virulent and malignant spirit of invective of the judgments of the learned judges whose decision is appealed from, as to disgrace not only the counsel by whom it was prepared, but this court also if it should be permitted to remain upon its files or among its records'.[92]

The advocate who finds it difficult to move his attention to his next case, and to forget the previous one, should be aware that judges can show extreme sensitivity to criticism and have punished barristers who have acted on a continuing grievance once the case has finished. A lawyer should not write the judge a letter 'reflecting on his judicial conduct, containing matter disrespectful and insulting to the court, and injurious to the administration of justice'. In such a case in 1822, the Court of Session in Scotland found that this was 'a high offence against the dignity of this Court' and reprimanded the lawyer for his contempt.[93] Nor should he write to the judge pointing out that his decision 'is directly contrary to every principle of law . . . and everybody knows it'. In such circumstances, an appeal against a fine for contempt is unlikely to succeed, as the Supreme Court of Kansas held in 1877, on the ground that the letter 'simply tells the judge, in a plain, matter-of-fact way, that he has committed an error of law in his decision'.[94]

It is dangerous to moan about the treatment you have received from the court as an advocate. In 1944, the Court of Appeals of Georgia upheld a finding of contempt against an attorney who told a judge in open court,

> I think your Honor has such antagonism toward me personally that I just can't, your Honor, seem to try a case before you without you jumping on me unnecessarily . . . I don't think it is called for, for you to jump at me, and holler at me like you do from the bench . . .[95]

A Nova Scotia lawyer who wrote to the Chief Justice complaining (as many advocates, before and since, have believed in all courts of the world) that 'I can't help thinking that I am not fairly dealt with by the Court or Judges, and that the well-beaten track is often departed from for some bye-way to defeat me', was, in 1866, found guilty by the Judicial Committee of the Privy Council of a contempt which was, according to Lord Westbury, 'of a most reprehensible kind'.[96] Advocates from that province seem to have had peculiar difficulty in understanding this principle. In 1921 another Nova Scotia lawyer wrote to the Chief Justice telling him that his decision in a case in which the lawyer had appeared as an advocate 'virtually . . . annuls all [relevant] provisions of the Arbitration Act'. The recipient of the letter, Chief Justice Harris, explained, on fining the barrister $100 for contempt of court, that his 'first inclination was to consign it—as I have had other communications from Mr Miller—to the waste-basket and take no notice of it'. But then 'a re-reading of it convinced me that it was intended to be, and was, a gross insult to the whole court'. He pointed out that in almost every case a barrister is on the losing side; it would, he thought, be 'intolerable' if the unsuccessful barrister should habitually 'write an insulting and abusive letter to the Court'.[97]

A similar case arose in Malaysia in 1986. An advocate acted for a plaintiff who succeeded in the High Court but lost on appeal. As Mohamed Azmi SCJ explained on behalf of the Supreme Court of Malaysia (upholding the contempt conviction), the advocate was 'needless to say . . . extremely unhappy and disappointed with the outcome'. He unwisely 'embarked on the extraordinary mission of writing various letters to the court and to the solicitors of the appellants and copied to others, criticizing the court's judgment in allowing the appeal'. Those letters were 'highly derisive' of the court, alleging that the decision was 'unjust and biased' and threatening that unless the judgment were to be reviewed, 'there is no justice in the court'. In particular he suggested (and this will strike all advocates as astonishing even to contemplate of any members of the judiciary in any jurisdiction) that the court had 'employed a complete non-sequitur to arrive at its decision' and that the court's judgment was reached 'without cogent rationalization'. The Malaysian Supreme Court imposed a fine of $5000. He had exceeded 'the limits of reasonable courtesy and good faith'.[98] It is dangerous for an advocate who has not enjoyed success in court to publish in a newspaper an article insulting the judge. In 1906 the Privy Council upheld a decision of the High Court in Allahabad, India, to suspend a barrister from practice for four years for contempt in such circumstances.[99]

III

The advocate must also avoid insulting members of the jury. In his closing address to the jury in 1864, a barrister for the defendant said that he 'thank[ed] God that there is more than one juryman to determine whether the prisoner stole the property with which he is charged, for if there were only one, and that one the foreman, from what has transpired today there is no doubt what the result would be'. After his client was convicted, the barrister was fined £20 for contempt of court.[100] In 1933 the US Court of Appeals upheld a contempt ruling against an attorney who, at the end of a trial, met a juror on the steps of the court building and abused him for the small amount of damages awarded to his client ('that was a damn rotten verdict').[101] It is also incumbent on the advocate to avoid going to the other extreme in his relations with the jury. In 1979, the US District Court declined to hear counsel further after he had been responsible for a number of breaches of professional standards, including 'unprofessional solicitude for the jurors' welfare. For example, on one Friday afternoon, after the jury had been dismissed and as they were leaving the courtroom, [counsel] smiled, waved and told the jury to "have a nice weekend". This remark constituted an unprofessional, patronizing comment intended to "gain special consideration" by the jury.'[102]

In 1989, a juror was fined £125 for contempt for walking out of a trial in London because he was 'fed up hanging around' during legal argument.[103] We are unlikely to receive more articulate comment from jurors on the quality of the advocacy they have heard because of the blanket restrictions imposed by section 8 of the Contempt of Court Act 1981. This provision, pushed through Parliament by a group of legal peers against the advice of Lord Hailsham (then Lord Chancellor)[104] and Lord Mackay (then Lord Advocate and now Lord Chancellor),[105] ensures that it is the policy of the criminal law in a supposedly open society that anyone who conducts academic research into whether the jury understood the charges, the evidence, the lawyers, or the judge in the proceedings in which they have participated, should be punished, no matter how reputable the researcher, and irrespective of the degree of anonymity guaranteed to the juror and the defendant.

It may be wise for the advocate to be careful what he asks the witness in cross-examination. An Australian psychiatrist has explained that a 'psychologically unsophisticated barrister may goad a patient into a highly dangerous and homicidal frame of mind'.[106] The court may insist, for reasons other than concern for the welfare of a lawyer, that the advocate is polite to witnesses. This can be especially difficult when they succeed, deliberately or not, in frustrating his best endeavours to perform his task competently or at all. In 1989, a fraud trial was halted when the defendant, who was about to be cross-examined, indicated to the judge that she had superglued her lips together in protest at the proceedings.[107] If the witness does not so impede the conduct of the case, he or she may, by answers to cross-examination, indicate contempt for the questions being put by counsel. In 1989, Mr Justice Owen advised a jury trying the case of a Baroness accused of murdering her ex-husband not to attach significance to the fact that she had used the word 'bollocks' in answer to a question put by counsel in the course of his cross-examination.[108] She was acquitted by the jury.[109]

Whatever the provocation offered to counsel by the witness, there are strict limits to the permissible response from the advocate. Verbal abuse of the witness can be damaging to the career of the attorney. The conduct of defence counsel in a criminal case in calling upon 'every one in the courtroom to bear witness to what this witness says' was, said the Supreme Judicial Court of Massachusetts in 1944, 'highly improper'.[110] In 1933, the Supreme

Court of Washington upheld a finding of contempt against the attorney for the defendant in a criminal trial after he had asked the State's witness, in cross-examination, 'You are a scab, aren't you, Mr Walters?' The court, unpersuaded by the argument that this was a common expression for a person who breaks a strike, noted that 'much depends upon the manner, expression and attitude of the party adjudged in contempt. . . . A finding of contempt is not necessarily based alone upon the language used.'[111] There are limits to what is acceptable in cross-examination. In South Africa in 1914, the Appellate Division of the Supreme Court upheld a fine of £3 for contempt imposed by the magistrate on an attorney acting for the defence in a criminal trial. He had been repeatedly warned not to shout at witnesses. But he continued to do so, 'banged the table with his hand making a loud report, and shouted, "Did you say so?"'. The magistrate thought that the advocate's style of cross-examination had 'terrorised the witness. . . . He had shouted spasmodically for seven hours.'[112]

Nor is a physically aggressive response to be recommended to the advocate who loses patience with the witness. When counsel for a plaintiff during a personal injuries trial asked a defendant giving evidence to come down off the witness-stand to help in a reconstruction of the incident which led to the plaintiff's injury and 'kicked [him] in the back in front of the jury box with sufficient force to drive him from where he was into the jury box', he was in contempt of court. The court was unimpressed by the attorney's defence that 'he was simply discharging his obligation to represent his client zealously'.[113] Similar consequences may follow when physical violence is threatened, as when an attorney for the defendant in a criminal trial 'while cross-examining [a] witness for the

State did with clenched fist drawn back step toward the witness in a menacing manner as if to strike the witness'. The court was unpersuaded by his plea that 'he acted as any man would act upon being called a liar', although the judge in the appeal court, while upholding the finding of contempt, confessed that he 'might have been tempted under similar circumstances and might have done exactly what the appellant did'.[114]

Litigants in person, lacking the benefit of representation by counsel, sometimes fail fully to understand the rules of the game. In particular, such litigants have had difficulty appreciating that they, and not the court, are on trial and that the court must not be insulted.[115] In 1983, a defendant in a criminal trial in Guernsey interrupted the proceedings against him by attempting to make a citizen's arrest of the magistrate hearing the case.[116] A defendant in criminal proceedings in the Huntingdon Magistrates' Court 'attempted, until restrained, to climb over the dock in order to arrest the justices'.[117] In 1989, I heard a litigant in person who had lost his case in the High Court suggest to the judge that he should not have to pay the costs because it was the judge's fault for making the wrong decision. The judge was understandably unimpressed with this argument. A litigant in person, complaining that he had been wrongly convicted because his advocate had failed to show that he had acted in self-defence in biting off a man's ear lobe, told the Court of Appeal, 'it sounds difficult to understand in cold blood but I can demonstrate it . . .'. Lord Denning, in his judgment, recorded that 'we did not accept the offer'.[118] Some litigants in person satisfy the highest standards of advocacy. In dismissing an appeal by an ex-employee in relation to compensation for his unfair dismissal, the Master of the Rolls, Lord Donaldson, provided a useful character reference by expressing his 'admiration for the employee's quality as an advocate and for the way in which he has conducted this appeal. His intelligence and ability to apply himself have been amply demonstrated and I can only say that it is surprising that no employer has been found who wishes to harness these qualities to his service.'[119]

There are a number of old cases in which contempt powers have been exercised against those litigants who expressed their feelings about judges before taking legal advice. It is, for example, a contempt for a defendant on being served with a court order to curse the Lord Chief Justice with the words, 'G—d d—n the Lord Reeves and the Court' and to state 'that he neither cared for him or them';[120] similarly if a defendant reacts to the person serving him with a writ by endeavouring to 'beat him and . . . make him eat it';[121] or if the defendant tells those seeking to serve a court order on him that they should take it 'back again to those from whom it came, and bid them wipe their backsides with it';[122] or when the defendant, on being served with the order of the court, said that 'he did not care a fart for the rule of court';[123] or if, 'when the plaintiff told him he came to serve him with an Order from the Master of the Rolls, the defendant said, "the Master of the Rolls kiss my Arse"'.[124]

IV

In past centuries advocates needed to be even more careful in their criticism of established authority than is now required. In 1607, it was held by all the judges and Barons of the Court of Exchequer that 'if a counsellor at law, in his argument, shall scandal the King or his government, temporal or ecclesiastical, this is a misdemeanour and contempt to the court; for this he is to be indicted, fined and imprisoned . . .'.[125] In 1613, a barrister was prosecuted for contempt of court for giving an Opinion to his client expressing the view that the prerogative powers of the Crown were narrow in a particular respect. The barrister, James Whitelocke, made an abject apology and was pardoned.[126] According to Lord Chancellor Hyde in 1663, a lawyer could not speak sedition in defence of his client.[127] In 1677, a barrister was fined for saying that a particular Baron of the Exchequer was a 'Judge de gratia'.[128]

In most legal systems of the world, courts have now accepted that it is the right and duty of the advocate to say, on behalf of his client, everything he considers relevant to the issues in the case. There are, therefore, few circumstances in which the court may legitimately punish or censure the courteous exercise of freedom of expression by advocates. It is vital for courts to ensure that the imposition of a sanction against the advocate for the performance of his function does not inhibit the presentation of the case for the litigant, in the instant case or generally. Punishment for gross discourtesy to the Bench may (as in some of the cases mentioned above) be justifiable. But the court must be very careful to avoid penalizing the advocate for comments which the court finds offensive but which are a legitimate part of the case being presented on behalf of the client.

In 1989, a barrister was suspended from practice for five months for telling the jury at a trial at Southwark Crown Court in 1986 that some judges were prejudiced and unfair and that the presiding judge might have particular views favouring the prosecution.[129] In 1984, the High Court of Australia rightly adopted a more liberal position in relation to such a statement. It allowed an advocate's appeal against a conviction for contempt for telling the jury, in his speech for the defence at a criminal trial, that the judge had favoured the prosecution case. The High Court correctly stated that a judge 'should be slow to hold that remarks made during the course of counsel's address to the jury amount to a wilful insult to the judge, when the remarks may be seen to be relevant to the case which counsel is presenting to the jury on behalf of his client'. Although the counsel's conduct was 'extremely discourteous, perhaps offensive, and deserving of rebuke', it was not punishable as a contempt of court.[130]

It is a matter of considerable concern that, in some jurisdictions, it has been dangerous, even on instructions from a client, for counsel to impugn the integrity of a court. In 1899, the New Zealand Supreme Court adopted a very strict approach to such matters. It held, astonishingly, that the existence of prejudice or bias on the part of a judge, or of grounds (other than direct pecuniary interest) on which a probability or possibility of such prejudice or bias might be suggested, would not disqualify a judge from adjudicating in a case. Consequently, any such allegation 'cannot be averred or proved or discussed in any proceeding'. An affidavit filed in support of such an application was therefore ordered to be removed from the file.[131] In disciplinary proceedings, the guilty solicitor (who conducted his own defence) was suspended from practice for three months. The court concluded that 'he had availed himself of the opportunity to inflict a series of studied insults' on the judge. An appeal to the Judicial Committee of the Privy Council was dismissed. Lord Macnaghten said that the solicitor had 'allowed himself to be carried away possibly by zeal for his client, possibly by his own feelings, when in the very difficult position of counsel on his own behalf, and so made charges and insinuations which he ought not to have made'.[132]

In 1952, the Appellate Division of the Supreme Court of South Africa accepted that it was the right of counsel, on behalf of his client, to ask a judge to recuse himself from continuing to hear a case because of bias. But it dismissed an appeal by an advocate whom a magistrate had fined £10 for contempt for making such a submission. In the circumstances, the court held, the objection had been a pretext for insulting the magistrate. The Appellate Division had difficulty understanding what had made the advocate behave in this way. 'Perhaps', suggested Schreiner JA, 'his vanity had been hurt because his objections, despite his strenuous arguments, had been so regularly overruled, and he might have been aiming at restoring his self-esteem and possibly his position in the eyes of the public by a daring attack on the magistrate.'[133] For an advocate to object, without any reasonable basis, to a particular judge sitting on the Court hearing an appeal in which he acted was, according to the Canadian Supreme Court in 1957, a contempt of court. 'There is no doubt that a counsel owes a duty to his client,' the court acknowledged, 'but he also has an obligation to conduct himself properly before any court . . .'. He was fined $2000.[134] In 1968, the New Zealand Court of Appeal sentenced a solicitor to three months' imprisonment for contempt of court in that the affidavits sworn by him on behalf of a client 'impute the most improper motives' to various judges who had heard the relevant cases in which the client was involved. In mitigation, the solicitor touchingly explained that he was 'usually concerned with conveyancing and if I made a few mistakes I am sorry'.[135]

In 1963 the Privy Council held that it was a contempt of court for counsel acting for a trade union to inform an Industrial Court in Ceylon that because his clients believed that 'an impartial inquiry could not be had' before the court, his clients were withdrawing from the proceedings. This was, concluded the Privy Council, 'an act calculated to bring the Industrial Court into disrepute. . . . [It] clearly suggested that the court was prejudiced against the union and could not be trusted to give impartial consideration to the inquiry. . . . It was not and could not be contended that because the appellant was acting on instructions he was entitled to any special privilege.' There was, the Privy Council held, no justification for making such an attack on the integrity of the court.[136]

These authorities express or imply a wholly unacceptable limitation of the right and duty of the advocate politely, but fully, to present his client's case. It is fundamentally wrong that the advocate should face criminal or disciplinary sanctions for making points of this nature which embarrass the court (unless the points are made in bad faith or in an abusive manner). A more realistic attitude to such matters is indicated by recent authority. In 1989, a Committee of the House of Lords heard a charge of contempt of court against Lonrho plc, some of its directors (including Mr Tiny Rowland), and the *Observer* newspaper. The charge arose from the newspaper's publication of extracts from the Report of Government Inspectors who were highly critical of the Fayed brothers' takeover of House of Fraser, the owners of Harrods. The Law Lords were unimpressed by the submission of counsel for the defendants that 'the circumstance that the father of one of their Lordships had been Mr Rowland's dentist many years ago made him an unsuitable member of the Committee'. Although Lord Keith, for the Committee, thought there was no substance in this and other grounds for objecting to the composition of the Committee, 'their Lordships were reluctant to leave Lonrho with a sense of grievance, however misguided' and so a fresh Committee heard the charges (and acquitted the defendants).[137] No one suggested that it was a contempt for counsel courteously, but firmly, to submit that the tribunal should be reconstituted because his clients doubted that their case would receive a fair hearing.

It is to be hoped that all courts will now accept that for counsel to express his client's lack of confidence in the tribunal before whom he is appearing is not, absent bad faith or an abusive manner, a contempt of court. Indeed, contempt of court problems have sometimes been caused by the advocate failing to express himself with sufficient clarity in this respect. In 1975, the High Court in Trinidad and Tobago imprisoned a barrister for seven days for contempt. The judge said that he was guilty of 'a vicious attack on the integrity of the court'. The Privy Council allowed an appeal, concluding that 'the judge mistakenly persuaded himself that the appellant had made such an attack on him'. Had the judge explained to the barrister the precise nature of the alleged contempt, the barrister would, the Privy Council confidently believed, 'have explained that the unjudicial conduct of which he complained had nothing to do with the judge's integrity but his failure to give the appellant's clients a chance of being heard before deciding against them'.[138] At a further hearing, the Privy Council found that there had been a breach of the constitutional rights of the barrister.[139] He recovered damages in the courts of Trinidad and Tobago.[140] As Lord Justice Sankey suggested in 1929, 'the Bar is just as important as the Bench in the administration of justice, and misunderstandings between the Bar and the Bench are regrettable, for they prevent the attainment of that which all of us desire—namely, that justice should not only be done, but should appear to have been done'.[141]

As the examples already given indicate, there are, regrettably, many indications in case-law of the unjustified eagerness of some judges to resort to sanctions against barristers who exercise freedom of expression out of court after the case has ended. It would be preferable in such circumstances for the courts to ignore the comments of the disappointed advocate, unless, of course, his grievance has some substance to it, in which case it should be acted upon, and not punished. Judges ought to be very slow to penalize the advocate for expressing his views out of court after the case has ended. By becoming a barrister, an individual does not sacrifice his right to freedom of expression. Other than in very extreme circumstances, the public comments of the advocate are unlikely to impede the administration of justice. The disadvantages of restricting free speech (in particular, the risk of preventing the publication of something of value by someone in a position to make an informed contribution on a matter of public importance, and the danger of increasing the readership of rubbish by giving added publicity to it by contempt proceedings) caution judicial restraint in this context. That is so even where the exercise of free speech by the advocate is unwise or even reprehensible. An American lawyer, whose female client lost a well publicized action in 1989 for maintenance from the film-star man with whom she had lived, was fortunate to avoid disciplinary action after he insulted the female judge for her decision. He announced that his client would be appealing on the absurd ground that the judge was 'so madly in love with this defendant . . . that we never could have gotten a fair shake'.[142] It is unusual for counsel to take the precaution, as did F. Lee Bailey before his unsuccessful defence of Patty Hearst at her trial in 1976 (on a charge of bank robbery with her kidnappers, the Symbionese Liberation Army), of agreeing that part of his fee was the entitlement to write a book about the case.[143] Such a precedent is not to be followed: the advocate has duties to his client and the court which might conflict with his duties to his publisher.

The US Supreme Court has, on occasion, taken a justifiably liberal approach to freedom of expression for advocates, providing useful principles to be applied by other courts. In 1964, the Court overturned the conviction by the State court of a District Attorney for criminal defamation after he had held a press conference at which he accused certain State court judges of laziness and inefficiency. The Supreme Court concluded that the 'vacation-minded judges' (as the District Attorney had termed them) did not need the protection of the law to defend their reputations.[144] In 1985, the Supreme Court allowed an appeal by a lawyer who had been suspended for six months from the practice of law in the federal courts for refusing to retract or apologize for a letter he had sent to a District Court Judge complaining about low fees for legal aid work and the complex procedures for recovering sums owed to him. He was, he said in the letter, 'extremely disgusted' and he asked for his name to be removed from the list of attornies prepared to undertake such work: 'I have simply had it'. The Court held that 'a lawyer's criticism of the administration' of the relevant legislation was not a reason for disciplining him; and 'even assuming that the letter exhibited an unlawyerlike rudeness, a single incident of rudeness or lack of professional courtesy—in this context—does not support a finding of contemptuous or contumacious conduct'.[145]

Regrettably, this approach is not adopted in every jurisdiction. Any aspiring or practising advocate should appreciate that (to varying degrees depending on the country in which he works and the judge before whom he appears) there are severe restrictions on what he may legitimately say and do in and out of court and substantial risks of punishment (which may be severe) for those who overstep the boundaries of what is considered acceptable legal behaviour. Since judges have been known to impose and apply unreasonable regulations which serve no purpose but to protect their own vanity, self-esteem, or reputation, some of the limitations applied to advocates have been wholly unjustified and have served to frustrate the administration of justice.

Many of the extraordinary cases to which reference is made above did not merit the sanctions imposed. The courts were impeding the proper function of the advocate by deterring forceful advocacy that represented the legal interests of the client and informed the court of information and argument which it needed to hear (embarrassing or inconvenient though it may have been to the judges), or which was an exercise of the legitimate right of the advocate to freedom of expression once the case had ended. It will rarely, if ever, be appropriate to restrain or penalize submissions made in court courteously and in good faith, unless in defiance of an express judicial direction. Even when the advocate displays less than a judicious approach to his job, it will often serve the cause of justice better for judges to ignore challenges to the dignity or wisdom or impartiality of the court. It will rarely, if ever, be appropriate to use the sanctions of contempt or to bring disciplinary proceedings against an advocate who, in good faith, expresses outside the court, once the case has finished, critical comments about the judge. This is not to say that such statements by the advocate are necessarily wise. Rather it is to doubt the legitimacy of imposing sanctions to restrain and punish such statements. Judges ought to recognize that freedom of expression is to be protected, even for those who use it to make complaints (justifiable or not) against the judiciary.

In using the law of contempt or disciplinary procedures against those who have insulted the judge, or the opposing advocate, a sense of proportion is required. Advocates may have said what they did not intend or would much prefer (with the benefit of hindsight) to have kept to themselves. Judges usually recognize that 'the adversary process . . . must make allowance for counsel . . . coming out with remarks in the heat of battle . . . that would not normally be expected from those same persons'.[146] It is inevitable that, on occasion, 'in the zeal of advocacy . . . [and] in the full tide of impassioned eloquence, the most honourable and most conscientious advocate may easily overstep the boundaries of discretion and justice'.[147] No punishment should be imposed other than in the most extreme cases where a penalty really is necessary to protect the proper functioning of the administration of justice. The advocate, on behalf of his client, has a vital interest in practising free speech in court and out. The objective of ensuring that the client has his case determined on its legal merits, and the right of the advocate to his freedom of expression outside court, create a very strong presumption against any interference with the freedom of speech of the advocate.

V

Judges, as human beings, are not immune from vanity. It is, then, 'always a good principle of advocacy' for counsel to base his submissions on the previous decisions of the judge trying the case,[148] since, as Lord Donaldson MR has acknowledged, 'nothing appeals to judges quite as much as something which they have thought of themselves'.[149] Little has changed since Quintilianus advised all aspiring advocates in the first century AD that 'we shall win the good-will of the judge not merely by praising him, which must be done with tact and is an artifice common to both parties, but by linking his praise to the furtherance of our own case. For instance, in pleading for a man of good birth we shall appeal to his own high rank, in speaking for the lowly we shall lay stress on his sense of justice, on his pity in pleading the cause of misfortune, and on his severity when we champion the victims of wrong, and so on'.[150]

In the light of all the difficulties which he faces, it is unsurprising that in the interests of his present and future clients and in the hope of making tolerable his often unattractive working conditions, the advocate may feel the need to display a degree of sycophancy to the foibles of those who sit in judgment which is scarcely credible in intelligent human beings. When Sir Patrick Hastings, appearing for George Robey, was asked by Mr Justice Darling who his client was, he replied, making a friend of that injudicious judge, 'My Lord, the Darling of the music-halls'.[151] There are few, if any, judges who would expect (or, indeed, tolerate) such treatment nowadays. Still, there remain at the Bar leading counsel who tell judges who show the slightest sign of understanding the point being made, 'Your Lordship puts the point so much better than I could possibly hope to achieve', and laugh uproariously at any attempt at judicial wit in the endeavour (usually unsuccessful) to ingratiate themselves (their client is not always in the forefront of their mind) with the occupant of the Bench. In 1988, a most eminent leading counsel, anxious to do his best for his client in an important case in the House of Lords, imitated the inexplicable judicial mispronunciation of a standard English word rather than use the standard pronunciation and thereby risk offending his Lordship.

By contrast, to protect the genuine interests of his client the advocate may need to show firmness and resolve before the unsympathetic and intimidating figure of the judge who is unimpressed by the advocate's efforts to advance a litigant's cause. In 1784, Thomas Erskine, defending his client against a charge of seditious libel, insisted that Mr Justice Buller record in full the verdict of the jury, which the judge was unwilling to do. Mr Justice Buller told Erskine to 'sit down, or I shall be obliged to interpose in some other way'. Erskine, undaunted, bravely replied, 'Your lordship may interpose in what manner you think fit', but continued to protect his client.[152] When, in the 1860s or 1870s, Mr Justice Blackburn told the barrister Samuel Carter to stop wasting the time of the court, he is reputed to have replied, 'Your Lordship means—Your Lordship's dinner'.[153] The American nineteenth-century lawyer Joseph Choate, on being told by the Judge, 'If you say that again I shall commit you for contempt', is said to have answered, 'I have said it once. It is therefore unnecessary to say it again.'[154] F. E. Smith (later a Lord Chancellor) is credited, no doubt apocryphally, with responding to an irritable judge who had complained that having listened to the arguments he was no wiser: 'Possibly not, my Lord, but far better informed'.[155] Serjeant Sullivan is said to have interrupted a judge who informed him of the way his mind was operating 'by sweetly suggesting that the operation of what his Lordship was pleased to call his mind would become relevant if his Lordship would first listen to the facts of the case'.[156] Earlier this century, Sir Andrew (then Mr) Clark, told by an irritable judge that he was 'getting a little tired of your jewels of Chancery learning', is reputed to have replied, 'if Your Lordship will bear with me a few moments longer I am about to cast my last pearl'.[157]

None of these examples is to be recommended to the junior barrister as appropriate for him to follow. It is only if one has reached the dizzy heights of Attorney-General that it is advisable to interrupt the judgment of the Master of the Rolls in the Court of Appeal to inform him that if he went on to decide a second point there would be an application for leave to appeal but if the judges were content to find against his client on the first point alone then leave to appeal would not be requested.[158] No beginner would survive telling a judge, as Serjeant Hill told Mr Justice Willes during argument, 'pray don't think of poh, pohing me—I won't submit to it'.[159] One of Theo Mathew's most instructive *Forensic Fables* concerns 'the beginner who thought he would do it himself'. He adopts the practice of a 'big pot' counsel (who had been his opponent in a previous case) and puts words into the mouth of his client giving evidence. The judge 'rebuked the beginner for his gross misconduct and discussed the question whether he would commit him for contempt or merely report him to the General Council of the Bar'. The moral of the story—'Wait till you're a big pot'—is a sound one.[160] Some aspects of the practice of advocacy displayed by the giants of the Bar as ways of dealing with difficult judges, or clients, or opponents, or witnesses, and for which they are highly remunerated and much lauded, cannot be recommended to the aspiring junior counsel who wishes to pursue a successful career as an advocate.

CHAPTER 4

Duties and Powers

I

THOSE who have earned their living from advocacy have adopted a range of different perspectives, social, political, and moral. Some see themselves as fighting alongside their client. According to one practitioner, Mr Rudy Narayan, there are 'potential leading Barristers for the Defence' who adopt the approach that they are 'the Frontline Fighters and will receive Frontline attention from hostile sections—but, if your Powder is Dry and your Hands Steady—then: "Pass the Ammunition, Brother, I am going over that Hill"'.[1] Some understand their role as assisting society to deal appropriately with their client. 'The first job of a revolutionary lawyer', it has been suggested, 'is not to argue that his client is innocent, but rather to determine if his client is guilty and, if so, to seek the sanction which will best rehabilitate him.'[2] Most advocates adopt a more conventional approach, somewhere between these two extremes.

There is a general consensus amongst the vast majority of advocates that they have two primary duties: a duty to represent the client and a duty to the court. 'He wishes to promote his client's interests, and it is his duty to do so by all legitimate means. But he also', as Sir John Donaldson MR noted in 1985, 'has an interest in the proper administration of justice, to which his profession is dedicated, and he owes a duty to the court to assist in ensuring that this is achieved.'[3] The duty owed by the advocate to his client is far from absolute. The scope of the advocate's duty to the court is very significant in any assessment of the morality of his function. The potential and actual conflicts which these duties create, and the competing demands which they make on the heart and mind of the advocate, add to the terrors of the profession. It is perhaps fortunate that there is 'no basis for a contention that [advocates] owe any independent duty to their lay client's opponent'.[4]

II

The advocate owes a very substantial duty to the person who puts his life, liberty, finances, reputation, or general happiness into his hands. The client 'must rely on him at times for fortune and character and life'.[5] His obligation is to represent his client, any client, no matter how unmeritorious the case, 'no matter how great a rascal the man may be . . . no matter how undeserving or unpopular his cause'.[6] The advocate must 'make every honest endeavour to succeed . . . [and to] put such matters . . . as in his discretion he thinks will be most to the advantage of his client'.[7] He has a professional duty 'to promote and protect fearlessly and by all proper and lawful means his lay client's best interests and do so without regard to his own interests or to any consequences to himself or to any other person (including his professional client or fellow members of the legal profession)'.[8]

It is the duty of the advocate (sometimes a difficult one

to discharge in the face of an unsympathetic tribunal) to ensure that the court listens to such submissions as the advocate thinks it appropriate to make on behalf of his client. During the trial of Thomas Williams for blasphemy in 1797 the judge, Lord Kenyon (the Chief Justice), uttered the exasperated words echoed by judges down the ages, 'I cannot sit in this place and hear this kind of discussion'. Counsel for Williams, Mr Kyd, correctly reminded the judge that

> I stand here on the privilege of an advocate in an English court of justice: this man has applied to me to defend him; I have undertaken his defence; and I have often heard your lordship declare that every man had a right to be defended; I know no other mode by which I can seriously defend him against this charge, than that which I am now pursuing; if your lordship wish to prevent me from pursuing it, you may as well tell me to abandon my duty to my client at once.

Lord Kenyon replied, 'Go on, sir'.[9] Courts should, as the US Supreme Court emphasized in 1952, 'unhesitatingly protect counsel in fearless, vigorous and effective performance of every duty pertaining to the office of the advocate on behalf of any person whatsoever' (though this does not, added Mr Justice Jackson on behalf of the Court, 'equate contempt with courage or insults with independence').[10]

This duty imposes substantial responsibilities. The advocate knows that if, in his conduct of the case, he 'makes a decision or takes a course which later appears to have been mistaken or unwise, that generally speaking has never been regarded as a proper ground for an appeal', save where there has been injustice caused by what the Court of Appeal has described as 'flagrantly incompetent advocacy'.[11] Similarly, the US Supreme Court will set aside a conviction only where the defendant can show that the advocacy of his counsel fell below an objective standard of reasonableness so as to deny him a fair trial by prejudicing his defence.[12] But subject to such exceptional circumstances, the general principle is, as Mr Justice Eyre observed in 1713, 'the mistake of the judge or jury is a good cause of granting a new trial; but I never yet heard that the mistake of counsel was so'.[13]

When counselling the client, a lawyer can and should express his opinions fully and frankly about all aspects of the case, legal and ethical. The client will insist on having clear and definite advice as to what is going to happen in court (and, in many cases, what is going to be reported in the newspapers whose journalists are present at the hearing). He may not be satisfied if his lawyer accurately informs him, echoing Jeremy Bentham (and allowing, of course, for inflation), that 'on many cases . . . as well-grounded a guess might be had of an astrologer for five shillings as of a counsel for twice or thrice as many guineas'.[14] He may wish to know more than that, as the Advocate repeatedly tells K in Kafka's *The Trial*, 'progress had always been made, but the nature of the progress could never be divulged'.[15]

Once the case reaches court, the advocate is required to keep his personal opinions of the merits of the case (legal or otherwise) to himself and not make them the subject of his submissions.[16] The advocate's duty to his client authorizes and obliges the advocate to say all that the client would say for himself (were he able to do so). This is often pitifully little once the relevant and the helpful have been stripped from the inconsequential or damaging aspects of the client's account of the history of the matter. The advocate is entitled to take all possible points, bad as well as good. He has no right 'to set himself up as a judge of his client's case' and should not 'foresake [his] client on any mere suspicion of [his] own or any view [he] might take as to the client's chances of ultimate success'.[17] As Baron Bramwell explained in 1871, a 'man's rights are to be determined by the Court, not by his [solicitor] or counsel. . . . A client is entitled to say to his counsel, I want your advocacy, not your judgment; I prefer that of the Court.'[18]

In 1963, the Court of Appeal allowed the appeal of a solicitor who had acted as an advocate for a defendant before a Magistrates' Court and had been ordered personally to pay fifteen guineas towards the costs of the prosecution because he had taken a bad point. Lord Denning explained the width of the licence allowed to the advocate. It was 'his duty to take any point which he believed to be fairly arguable on behalf of his client. An advocate is not to usurp the province of the judge.' The advocate 'only becomes guilty of misconduct if he is dishonest. That is, if he knowingly takes a bad point and thereby deceives the court.' Lord Justice Harman agreed, adding that 'if it be misconduct to take a bad point, a new peril is added to those of the legal profession'. He concluded that 'unless a bad point be taken knowing it to be bad and concealing from the court, for instance, an authority which shows it clearly to be a bad point, then it would be a very dangerous doctrine indeed to say that the advocate ought to be mulcted in the costs because he took a point which failed'.[19] It is central to the function of the advocate that 'even if a legal proposition is untenable, counsel may properly urge it in good faith; he may do so even though he may not expect to be successful, provided of course that he does not resort to deceit or to wilful obstruction of the orderly processes'.[20]

Of course, the fact that an advocate may properly take

hopeless points does not mean, as any judge will make very clear, that it is wise or in the interests of the client to do so. And there are limits to the duty of the advocate to his client in this respect. In 1872, Mr Justice Keating said that it was 'the duty of counsel to say so when he finds a point not to be arguable'. Mr Justice Brett agreed: 'when the counsel has satisfied himself that he has no argument to offer in support of his case, it is his duty at once to say so, and to withdraw altogether'.[21]

Chief Judge Coffin, for the US Court of Appeals, adopted a similar approach in a 1973 judgment. He thought that 'the mere finding that a position advanced was frivolous must not be cause for discipline of the attorney because of the danger that such action might inhibit the bar from the most vigorous advocacy of clients' positions and restrict meaningful access to the court'. Such considerations meant, he said, that courts should 'indulge every presumption in favour of the attorney who presents or defends a position which is found to lack support. We must ensure that there is breathing room for the fullest possible exercise of the advocacy function.' However, he explained, 'there must be limits'. The Court therefore held that filing petitions for review in immigration cases, none of which raised any substantial issue but which caused automatic stays in deportation, justified disciplinary action against a lawyer.[22] The High Court of Australia has adopted an analogous principle: 'counsel have a responsibility to the Court not to use public time in the pursuit of submissions which are really unarguable'.[23]

III

In carrying out his duties the advocate enjoys broad powers and a blissful immunity from legal consequences for what he says. He has, as C. P. Harvey observed, a standing invitation 'to be clever at someone else's expense'.[24]

In order to 'encourage due freedom of speech in the lawful defence of their clients',[25] advocates have a wide range of immunities. Counsel 'is at liberty to make strong, even calumnious observations against the party, the witnesses and the attorney in the cause'.[26] No action will lie against him for defamatory words spoken with reference to and in the course of a court hearing, even if they were spoken not with the object of furthering the cause of his client, but rather from personal ill-will and without justification. This is because, according to Brett MR in 1883,

> a counsel has a special need to have his mind clear from all anxiety. A counsel's position is one of the utmost difficulty. He is not to speak of that which he knows; he is not called upon to consider whether the facts with which he is dealing are true or false. What he has to do, is to argue as best he can, without degrading himself, in order to maintain the proposition which will carry with it either the protection or the remedy which he desires for his client. If amidst the difficulties of his position he were to be called upon during the heat of his argument to consider whether what he says is true or false, whether what he says is relevant or irrelevant, he would have his mind so embarrassed that he could not do the duty which he is called upon to perform.[27]

To ensure that counsel are not 'harassed with suits', no action for defamation may be brought for statements in court even if 'malice and misconduct' could be shown.[28] Hence the courts have dismissed actions for slander brought against an advocate for saying, during the course of trial, that the other party had 'defrauded'[29] his client or 'plundered [him] to a frightful extent'.[30] For similar reasons, in 1818 an action against a barrister for defamation failed in respect of comments made by him, during the course of a trial, that the solicitor for the other party was 'fraudulent and wicked' and that 'some actions are founded in folly, some in knavery, some in both, some in the folly of the [solicitor], some in the knavery of the [solicitor], some in the folly and knavery of the parties themselves'. Mr Justice Abbott thought that 'it would be impossible that justice could be well administered if counsel were to be questioned for the too great strength of their expressions'.[31] It was, no doubt, this legal immunity which provoked three cases in Ireland in the nineteenth century where victims of advocates' eloquence sought to provoke duels with, or sent rude letters to, the advocate who they considered had insulted them by his speech for their opponent in court. In each case the barrister responded by commencing criminal proceedings. And in each case the judges wisely ordered that no further step should be taken in the criminal proceedings without the permission of the court.[32] American courts have recognized similar immunities for the advocate from liability for statements made in court.[33]

Advocates do not need, or deserve, immunity from suit where malice can be shown. No doubt (because of a risk that advocates would otherwise be deterred from performing their professional duty) the court should be very slow to allow such actions to proceed unless there is a strong prima facie case of such malice. But, if the evidence exists, it is difficult to see why the victim should be left without a remedy.

Although the advocate owes important duties to his client, even the wishes and instructions of the client form only a partial restraint on the liberty of counsel. When an ungrateful client claimed damages against counsel in respect of alleged misconduct in an action in 1876, the Court of Session pronounced that the nature of the advocate's office makes it clear that in the performance of his duty he must be entirely independent, and act according to his own discretion and judgment in the conduct of the cause for his client. His legal right is to conduct the cause without any regard to the wishes of the client, so long as his mandate is unrecalled, and what he does bona fide according to his own judgment will bind his client, and will not expose him to any action for what he has done, even if the client's interests are thereby prejudiced. These legal powers of counsel are seldom, if ever, exercised to the full extent, because counsel are restrained by consideration of propriety and expediency from doing so. But in such a case as this it is necessary to have in view what is the full extent of their legal powers.[34]

When a dissatisfied client alleged that a barrister had compromised a claim without authority, Chief Baron Pollock explained that 'the conduct and control of the cause are necessarily left to counsel'. He is only bound by his client's instructions as to the conduct of the action if they expressly so agree. Otherwise 'counsel is not subject to an action for calling or not calling a particular witness, or for putting or omitting to put a particular question, or for honestly taking a view of the case which may turn out to be quite erroneous'.[35] This was, it must be said, a rather unusual claim against a barrister: the defendant was the Lord Chancellor, Lord Chelmsford (formerly Sir Frederick Thesiger, Attorney-General), who was being sued for what he was alleged to have done during the conduct of the plaintiff's case while he had been at the Bar. In addition to the allegation that he had compromised the plaintiff's claim without her authority, he was accused of having entered into the compromise 'by collusion with the learned judge who tried the cause'.[36] It does seem as if the defendant barrister had made a serious mistake in his handling of the case.[37]

The continuing applicability of these old authorities is doubtful. More recently, it has been accepted that counsel's failure to comply with the instructions of the client may entitle the client to some remedy, albeit not a remedy against the advocate. In 1985, the Court of Appeal of New Zealand set aside a conviction for rape and ordered a new trial because counsel for the defendant had, contrary to instructions from the client, ignored an alibi defence and argued that the complainant had consented to sexual intercourse. The Court held that 'following any advice he thought it proper to give to his client, [counsel's] duty was either to act on the instructions he then received or to withdraw from the case. . . . Counsel may not take it upon himself to disregard his instructions and to then conduct the case as he himself thinks best.'[38] Similarly, in 1987, the Court of Appeal in London allowed an appeal against a conviction for criminal damage where, on a re-trial, defence counsel decided not to call alibi evidence (which had been called at the first trial) and did not discuss this tactic with the defendant.[39] However, more recently the Court of Appeal has said that no principle was stated in that case and that 'generally speaking this court will always proceed upon the basis that what counsel does is done with the authority of the client who has instructed counsel to conduct his case'. The court would intervene only if it had any lurking doubt that the litigant might have suffered an injustice as a result of flagrantly incompetent advocacy.[40]

There is a report of a County Court case in 1885 in which damages were awarded against a solicitor advocate for his negligence in the presentation of a case in that Court. The aggrieved litigant established that he had lost his action because of the solicitor's 'want of familiarity with the facts'.[41] There appears to be no case in which a barrister has ever been successfully sued for negligent advocacy. 'This cannot be because there have been no dissatisfied clients', as was pointed out by counsel representing a barrister who was sued.[42] It is because the courts have created an immunity from suit in negligence for the barrister whose eloquence is alleged to have fallen short of an acceptable standard. The rationale for this immunity used to be that barristers did not enter into a contract with their clients and could not recover fees. But it is now recognized that this 'facile explanation' should be rejected as 'legal folklore',[43] and that the absence of contractual liability has no connection with the rule conferring immunity from actions for negligence[44] since 'liability for negligence might exist in the absence of a contract for reward'.[45] The House of Lords held in 1967 that it is the demands of public policy (in particular, the advocate's overriding duty to the court and the importance of avoiding relitigation of matters previously decided) that require the advocate to be immune from an action for negligence brought by a client in respect of his conduct and management of the case in court.[46] This reasoning has been approved by the majority of the High Court of Australia.[47] By contrast, the Canadian courts have declined to recognize such an immunity.[48] The wisdom of granting such an immunity is extremely doubtful.[49]

There are limits to the barrister's immunity from suit for negligence. In 1967, Lord Morris announced that 'there is no sound legal principle which can support or justify the broad and sweeping statements that have in the past been made that barristers are in all circumstances immune from liability'.[50] Lord Pearson thought that 'no doubt, if a barrister were guilty of collusion or otherwise dishonest conduct, the client would have a remedy'.[51] In

1978, the House of Lords decided (by a majority of 3–2)[52] that the immunity extends to some, but not all, pre-trial work. When the barrister is advising out of court, the public policy factors which justify immunity from action for negligence have less force.[53] So, held the majority, there was no immunity for the allegedly negligent advice of counsel to the plaintiff in a civil action concerning whom to sue as defendants before the expiry of the limitation period. The majority of the Lords of Appeal[54] applied the test earlier stated in the New Zealand Court of Appeal: 'the protection exists only where the particular work is so intimately connected with the conduct of the cause in court that it can fairly be said to be a preliminary decision affecting the way that cause is to be conducted when it comes to a hearing. The protection should not be given any wider application than is absolutely necessary in the interests of the administration of justice . . .'[55] However, when an advocate advises a defendant in a criminal trial whether to plead guilty or not guilty, the immunity does apply, as this is intimately connected with the conduct of the case in court, in the terms suggested by the New Zealand Court of Appeal.[56] Similarly, the immunity applies when the alleged negligence of counsel was in advising the plaintiff to settle the case at the end of the oral evidence and failing to ensure that the terms of the settlement as recorded by the court were consistent with the terms agreed between the parties.[57] The immunity protects the advocate against claims by the other party to the case in which he acted, as well as claims by his disappointed client.[58]

This immunity was not confined to barristers: it also applied to solicitor advocates in courts in which they have a right of audience.[59] This is now confirmed by the Courts and Legal Services Act 1990.[60] Parliament has reached a similar conclusion as to the requirements of public policy in this context by providing that the implied term that the supplier of a service will use reasonable care and skill does not apply to the services of an advocate in court or before any tribunal, inquiry, or arbitrator, or in carrying out any preliminary work directly affecting the conduct of the hearing.[61] The Court of Appeal has also held that, irrespective of the immunity of advocates from liability for negligence, it is an abuse of the process of the court for a plaintiff to bring an action which necessarily involves an attack on a decision of another competent court (civil or criminal). So for a plaintiff to complain that, because of the negligence of his advocate, he was wrongly convicted, or failed in his civil litigation, is an abuse of the process of the court, and any such claim will be struck out.[62]

In addition to the broad immunities from liability enjoyed by the advocate, it should be noted that courts have held that the duty fearlessly to represent the client does not in law impose a liability on the advocate to repay his fee if he fails to turn up for the big day in court. In 1792 an aggrieved plaintiff sued a barrister who, he alleged, had been briefed and paid to attend court as one of his counsel at a trial. The plaintiff (not unreasonably, if the facts were as he alleged) wanted his money back. Lord Kenyon (no doubt to applause from the barristers in court and to general derision from laymen) 'mentioned the general opinion of the profession, that the fees of barristers and physicians were as a present by the client, and not a payment or hire for their labour'. On hearing this, the parties settled the case. But not before counsel, Mr Garrow, had announced that he 'held a brief for [the defendant barrister who denied that he was] guilty of the negligence imputed to him, for that it never was intended that he should attend the cause, but the fee was given him as a compliment for the trouble he had taken in the former stage of it'.[63] A similar decision—that no cause of action lay on behalf of a client who claimed to be disappointed that his barrister had failed to attend court on the relevant day, causing the loss of the case—was reached by the Irish Court of Exchequer in 1860.[64] Any barrister who insisted on retaining his fee even though he had failed to perform his obligation to turn up in court would, nowadays, receive an unsympathetic hearing from the disciplinary tribunal of the Bar before being suspended from practice for a considerable period of time.

The client did, at least, have the consolation that his incapacity to sue in respect of fees was reciprocal. Under the old cases, 'it ha[d] been a settled principle of English law that the arrangement between barrister and client . . . for the barrister to conduct litigious business for the client is not a contractual or otherwise legally binding arrangement'.[65] For this reason, 'the inability of a barrister to sue for his fees [was] deep rooted in the law'.[66] It was well established that 'an advocate and his client are in point of law mutually incapable of entering into contracts of hiring with respect to advocacy in litigation. . . . No legal contract existing between the parties, neither can sue the other for breach of its supposed terms. . . . Whether the advocate sues the client . . . for non-payment of the promised fee, or the client sues the advocate for the non-performance of the promised advocacy, the same principle applies, and neither can succeed'.[67] In this respect, counsel's 'fees are payable as a matter of honour',[68] such that a 'counsellor cannot demand [them] without doing wrong to his reputation'.[69] The court would not, said Lord Chancellor Hardwicke in 1742, 'suffer a gentleman of the Bar to maintain an action for fees, which is quiddam honorarium'.[70] So the barrister who does perform his side of the bargain has no right to sue the solicitor, or the client, for fees earned. In 1870, Sir G. M. Giffard LJ 'hope[d] never to see the day when a counsel coming into court to enforce his claim for fees as such against the client will be successful'.[71] In 1896, Lindley LJ suggested that 'it is of the utmost importance that the Court should not assist barristers to recover their fees. If they do so, the whole relation between a barrister and his professional client will be altered. . . . The inevitable result will be to do away with that which is the greatest protection of counsel against an action for negligence by his client.'[72] (It was not the inevitable result, as explained above.)[73]

A promise by a client to pay money to an advocate, whether made before, during, or after the litigation, had no binding effect. In 1863, Chief Justice Erle stated this rule in a case in which a barrister was promised by his client that if he won the case, she would pay him £20,000: he did win, but she refused to keep her side of the bargain. Chief Justice Erle suggested that the rule was a necessary one, because 'if the law allowed the advocate to make a contract of hiring and service, it may be that his mind would be lowered, and that his performance would be guided by the words of his contract rather than by principles of duty'.[74] In 1884, the Judicial Committee of the Privy Council agreed that this was the rule, but—sensibly—were 'not prepared to accept all the reasons which were assigned for that decision' by Chief Justice Erle.[75] One defendant, unsuccessful in proceedings, argued that he should not have to pay the costs incurred by the successful plaintiff in employing counsel since the plaintiff was not legally obliged to pay his counsel. The court was unpersuaded by this logical argument. Mr Justice Best thought that there was 'nothing which has so great a tendency to secure the due administration of justice as having the courts of the country frequented by gentlemen so eminently qualified by their education and principles of honour as at this time appear to discharge the duties which they are called upon to fulfil'.[76]

Counsel can, however, take steps to ensure that he is paid: except where the work is done on legal aid,[77] 'the solicitor can, if so required by counsel, be compelled either not to retain him or to pay his fee with the brief. That is the remedy of counsel, and he has it in his own hands.'[78] He also has the remedy (which the Bar Council will exercise on his behalf)[79] of reporting to the Law Society an offending solicitor who refuses to pay fees owing, and that is 'likely to cost the solicitor far more than the fees he retains'.[80]

In 1965, Mr Justice Lawton adopted a more sceptical attitude to the rule that barristers could not sue for their fees. He said that it was not for him 'to speculate whether, in this day and age, the young barrister struggling with family responsibilities shares the regrets' expressed by judges at the prospect of being able to sue for unpaid fees.[81] Some judges in New Zealand had suggested that barristers there may sue a client for their fees,[82] though this issue has been left open by the New Zealand Court of Appeal.[83] It is quite absurd that English law should for so long have retained the fiction that the proper professional fee of the barrister for the services provided by him was an honorarium. It is impossible to understand how ignoring the commercial reality of an agreement by a client to pay for the services of a barrister can have been thought necessary to the maintenance of proper professional standards by barristers. The legal position has been altered by the Courts and Legal Services Act 1990 which has abolished all rules of law which prevented a barrister from entering into a contract for the provision of his services. But this does not affect the power of the General Council of the Bar to make rules prohibiting or restricting such practices.[84]

IV

Some advocates have claimed that the obligation to a client must be paramount over all other considerations. Henry (later Lord) Brougham announced to the House of Lords in his defence of Queen Caroline in 1820 against the charge of adultery, that the advocate

> in the discharge of his duty knows but one person in all the world, and that person is his client. . . . Separating the duty of a patriot from that of an advocate, he must go on reckless of consequences, though it should be his unhappy fate to involve his country in confusion.[85]

Brougham repeated this fundamental principle in 1864.[86]

Such a conception of the role of the advocate would not now be widely shared. He has important responsibilities to the court as well as to his client. Chief Justice Burger of the US Supreme Court has rightly criticized 'cynics who view the lawyer much as the "hired gun" of the Old West'.[87] The advocate is more than a mouthpiece. As Mr Justice Blackburn explained, 'few counsel . . . would accept a brief on [such] terms'.[88] He 'owes allegiance to a higher cause'.[89]

The nature of the advocate's duty to the court has been variously described by judges over the decades. He is, thought Lord Justice Singleton, 'a helper in the administration of justice' whose task it is to assist in reaching 'a proper result in the dispute between the parties'.[90] He has, according to Lord Pearce, a duty to use the weapons of advocacy 'in the pursuit of justice and to elucidate the truth in the public interest with an approach which is as biased in favour of his client's contentions as public considerations allow'.[91] For Lord Langdale, the 'zeal and arguments of every counsel, knowing what is due to himself and his honourable profession, are qualified not only by considerations affecting his own character as a man of honour, experience and learning, but also by considerations affecting the general interests of justice'.[92] Chief Justice Cardozo believed that the advocate has been 'received into that ancient fellowship for something more than private gain. He becomes an officer of the court and, like the court itself, an instrument or agency to advance the ends of justice.'[93] Because (according to Lord Upjohn) 'the courts rely on the integrity and fairness of counsel in the presentation of the case',[94] there is, for Sir John Donaldson, a 'requirement of absolute probity' imposed on advocates in the public interest.[95] For all these reasons, Lord Morris concluded that 'to a certain extent every advocate is an amicus curiae [friend of the court]'.[96]

Despite the antiquated language and medieval concepts of honour involved in some of these statements, counsel need to be reminded that it is not simply their task to speak on behalf of their client. They do have additional, and sometimes conflicting, responsibilities. So broad are the legal privileges of the advocate and so vital his role in the administration of justice, that there must be limits to what he is entitled to say or do on behalf of his client. But where, and how, are the boundaries to be drawn?

The basic duties of the advocate to the court are well established. 'In giving his opinion beforehand', Lord Denning explained, 'he must only advise proceedings if there is a reasonable case to be made—putting away from himself, like the plague, any thought of the extra fees which would come to him if the case was fought—and remembering the hardship on the other side if harassed unfairly'.[97] During the hearing, he must 'assist the Court in the administration of justice and must not deceive or knowingly or recklessly mislead the court',[98] that is 'either on the facts or on the law'[99] (although 'consistently with the rule that the prosecution must prove its case, he may passively stand by and watch the court being misled by reason of its failure to ascertain facts that are within the barrister's knowledge').[100] He should refrain from tendering evidence 'that he knows to be false as a matter of fact' or presenting 'arguments or points that are obviously specious, or frivolous. Counsel is not expected to stultify himself in an attempt to advance his client's interests.'[101] He 'must not allow a charge of fraud to be made unless there is evidence to support it'.[102] In a criminal case, 'it is the duty of counsel not to note an irregularity and keep it as a ground of appeal . . . but to take the point then and there'.[103] He should guard against being made the channel for questions or statements which are only intended to insult or annoy either the witness or some other person.[104] He 'must not lend himself to casting aspersions on the other party or witnesses for which there is no sufficient basis in the information in his possession'[105] (though 'questions of considerable nicety may arise as to what constitutes sufficient foundation or relevance to justify the particular aspersion which his client wants him to make').[106]

He 'must not withhold authorities or documents which may tell against his clients but which the law or the standards of his profession require him to produce'.[107] This may require advocates 'to face the embarrassment of bringing to the attention of the court authorities of which their opponents have been ignorant and which they know will lose the case for the client who has paid their fees'.[108]

Lord Birkenhead, for the Appellate Committee of the House of Lords, explained in 1921 that to withhold from the court 'any authority which might throw light upon the matters under debate was . . . to convert this House into a debating assembly upon legal matters, and to obtain a decision founded upon imperfect knowledge. The extreme impropriety of such a course could not be made too plain.'[109]

Before the case reaches court, and before the advocate has an opportunity to display his oratorical skills, there are restraints on the manner in which a case may be conducted.[110] In 1660, counsel who signed a pleading containing scandalous matter was fined £5.[111] A 'frivolous and vain' pleading in 1603 led Lord Chancellor Egerton to ban a particular counsel from drafting any further such documents.[112] A finding of contempt of court was made in 1749 against a solicitor who inserted 'scandalous matter' in a written pleading 'and put counsel's name to [it] without having any authority for so doing'.[113] In 1951, a solicitor was held to be in contempt for endorsing on a writ a statement which was, to his knowledge, 'wholly fictitious and was designed to conceal from the court the true nature of the plaintiff's claim' (it was, in truth, a claim for money alleged to be won on bets—a cause of action not maintainable in law—but the solicitor had disguised the claim as one for money due under an account between the parties).[114] The Court of Criminal Appeal stated in 1966 that counsel should not 'put pen to paper to draft grounds [of appeal] without being certain in their own minds that they were arguable grounds'.[115] For this reason, a barrister who accepted a retainer was obliged to give the client his opinion on a legal matter, but was not obliged to sign pleadings asserting a claim.[116] Counsel who encouraged a man to bring false actions through malice and for the purposes of oppression was found guilty of a criminal offence in 1686.[117] Counsel must not advise his client to commence baseless prosecutions against an innocent solicitor with the purpose of intimidating him into ceasing to act for a third person in other proceedings against the barrister's client.[118]

Advocates must behave themselves while the hearing is continuing. Counsel for the defendant in a criminal trial should not substitute another person for his client at the table in court with intent to provoke a misidentification.[119] It was a contempt for an advocate to indulge 'in the regrettable practice of needling the Court in the hope that something might be said or done which would ensure a new trial, if one became necessary' (that is, if the advocate's client was convicted of the offence charged).[120] Similarly in contempt of court was an advocate appearing for a defendant in a criminal trial, who 'attempted by misconducting himself to bring about a situation in which the learned chairman of quarter sessions would be constrained to order him out of court and thus to compel the chairman to discharge the jury and order a retrial of the case'.[121] In Queensland, Australia, Chief Justice Lilley suspended from practice a barrister who, defending a man on a capital charge, adopted the 'trick' of telling the jury that because of a comment from the judge he would decline to cross-examine the prosecution witness, but that if he had asked such questions very material evidence might have emerged. 'It was a statement to the jury that . . . the whole matter was not before them, and they were not in a position to determine the case'.[122]

Of course, an advocate should not conspire with his client to deceive the court, as Mr Justice Kay found to have occurred in 1888 when counsel (who was imprisoned for contempt) 'knew that affidavits were going to be used containing matter amounting to chicanery'.[123] It would be very improper for the advocate to present on behalf of his client evidence which he knows to be perjured. Such an advocate may, as the Supreme Court of California stated in 1969, 'be subject to criminal prosecution . . . as well as severe disciplinary action'.[124] More difficult is the case of the client charged with a criminal offence who insists on giving evidence which he tells his lawyer (before or after testifying) is perjured.[125]

Hard cases have arisen as to what constitutes deceiving the court. In 1961, the Court of Appeal was correct to allow the plaintiff's appeal on the ground that at the trial of an action for damages for alleged assault and false imprisonment, the defendant's counsel had not made known to the court that the defendant—a police officer—had been reduced to the ranks from Chief Inspector for deception of a court. The case turned on the credibility of the parties. The plaintiff's counsel and the Judge referred to the defendant as 'Chief Inspector', not knowing of the change in his status. Lord Justice Holroyd Pearce appreciated that 'it is very hard at times for the advocate to see his path clearly between failure in his duty to the court and failure in his duty to his client. . . . But in my judgment the duty to the court was here unwarrantably subordinated to the duty to the client.' Lord Justice Willmer explained that the course adopted 'resulted in the judge and the jury, as well as the plaintiff and his advisers, being deceived into thinking that the defendant was, and remained, a high-ranking officer of unblemished reputation'.[126]

The Court of Appeal found more difficult a case in 1951 where a trial witness for the plaintiff had been brought from prison in plain clothes and this fact had not been disclosed to the judge or to the defendants. The defendants appealed against the trial judgment of damages for the plaintiff and asked for leave to produce, at a new trial, fresh evidence concerning the credit of the witness. The Court dismissed the appeal. Lord Justice Somervell said, surprisingly, there had not been any 'trick'. Lord Justice Singleton expressed 'regret that a false picture of the witness . . . was before the judge', but did not dissent from the dismissal of the appeal. Lord Justice Denning said that nothing improper had here occurred. So long as he did not deceive the court, it was for counsel to 'put such matters in evidence or omit such others as in his discretion he thinks will be most to the advantage of his client'.[127] The principle is uncontroversial, but its application to the facts somewhat disturbing. If the advocate's duty not to mislead the court is more than a platitude, it must prohibit conduct which, as in that case, will inevitably throw a seriously misleading light on the evidence which is presented.

There are some cases which go further and imply a general duty on an advocate to assist the court by providing it with relevant information, even if harmful to the interests of the advocate's client. In 1919, Mr Justice Coleridge suggested, in relation to a divorce petition and the fact that the petitioner himself had been guilty of adultery, that 'both counsel and solicitors ought to disclose all the true facts to the court. It is their duty not to conceal anything, as the court implicitly relies upon them.'[128] In a factually similar case in Canada in 1949, the judge said that if counsel 'have good reason to suspect that they are being deceived, they . . . are under an obligation to bring their attitude of mind in that respect to the attention of the court'.[129] In the Supreme Court of Victoria in 1909, Chief Justice Madden observed, more generally, that where there were matters corrupting the administration of justice in court, counsel 'was under an obligation to state that which he knew, whatsoever he knew, and howsoever he knew it, which appeared to have caused the actual elements of corruption to have come into the conduct of the case and to be likely to come into the process of the court'. The alternative, he warned, was for the Bar to become 'merely learned tricksters' who would constitute 'a never-failing source of trouble to the community'.[130]

Impassioned advocacy may be counterproductive. As the Supreme Court of California explained in 1969, such 'intemperate and unprofessional conduct by counsel . . . runs a grave and unjustifiable risk of sacrificing an otherwise sound case for recovery, and as such is a disservice to a litigant'.[131] In 1862, an English court ordered a new trial of an action for assault in which the plaintiff had been awarded damages of five guineas by the jury: the sum was excessive, said the court, and was the result of the plaintiff's counsel improperly submitting that unless she was awarded at least that sum, she would not recover her costs.[132] If an appeal court 'can see that the jury in assessing damages have . . . been misled by the speeches of the counsel, those are undoubtedly sufficient grounds for interfering with the verdict'.[133] In 1901, the Court of Appeal allowed an appeal against libel damages awarded to a plaintiff because her counsel, Marshall Hall, had made a speech at the trial unjustifiably containing 'a monstrous charge' which 'had a very serious effect in inflaming the damages' awarded by the jury.[134] This judgment had a very serious effect on Marshall Hall: 'it destroyed his confidence and, taken with other related circumstances, well-nigh ruined his practice', partly because he tried to conceal his humiliation 'under a mask of recklessness'.[135] The Supreme Court of New South

Wales allowed an appeal against a jury award of damages in a defamation action because of what the court described as 'prejudice engendered by speeches of and statements by counsel for the plaintiff'.[136] Appeals to the emotions may be counterproductive in other ways. An American advocate acting for the plaintiff in a personal injuries case described for the benefit of the jury the appalling injuries suffered by his unfortunate client. The 'attorney thought he had the jury in his hands, until one juror in the front row leaned over the railing and vomited. The result was a mistrial.'[137]

In a personal injuries case, it is, said the Supreme Court of California in 1964, 'improper to appeal to the jury to fix damages as if they or a loved one were the injured party'.[138] In 1953, the Ontario Court of Appeal allowed an appeal, ordering a new trial on the assessment of damages in a personal injuries action. At the trial, counsel for the victim had said to the jury in relation to the amount of damages they should award, 'if any of your wives manifested the symptoms that have been manifested to you today—do you think money would compensate?' This was, held Hogg JA, 'an appeal to the jury to fix the amount of damages upon an appraisement governed by emotion and not by reason based upon the evidence'. Such a plea was, he concluded, 'beyond the ordinary and legitimate use of rhetoric'.[139] It is equally improper for counsel for the defendant in a personal injuries case to tell the jury that the question for them was whether to ensure, by their verdict for the plaintiff, that the elderly defendant should be sent to a home for indigents.[140]

In 1916, it was held that counsel acting for a plaintiff in a personal injuries action before a jury should not have asked the defendant in cross-examination if he was insured. Mr Justice Rowlatt said that 'counsel are not entitled to do such a thing in order to prejudice the minds of the jury'.[141] That principle was later held not to apply to a trial before a judge without a jury,[142] and, in any event, it would have limited application now in personal injuries cases when compulsory third-party motor insurance is required. Still, as a matter of principle, an advocate 'should not be permitted to bring the fact of insurance to the attention of the jury where that fact has no proper relationship to the issues in the case'.[143]

There is some authority for the proposition that lawyers 'do not do their duty to their clients by insisting upon the strict letter of their rights. That is the sort of thing which, if permitted, brings the administration of justice into odium.'[144] So it might be inappropriate for a lawyer to take advantage of a slip or an error by his opponent.[145] But there must be limits to this doctrine: in order to defeat an otherwise valid claim, lawyers frequently, and properly, take technical points (such as reliance on limitation periods) which have no relation to the merits of a dispute.

V

Some advocates have distinct obligations to the court which override their duty to their client. Prosecuting counsel 'are to regard themselves as ministers of justice, and not to struggle for a conviction'.[146] The function of the prosecutor 'is not to tack as many skins of victims as possible to the wall'[147] but 'to present the case fairly and completely'.[148] So, if information comes to the knowledge of the prosecuting counsel which may assist the defence, he is under an obligation to see that it is disclosed.[149]

The origin of the duty of Crown Counsel appears to be the conduct of Thomas Erskine when acting for the prosecution at the trial in 1797 of Thomas Williams for blasphemy by publishing Thomas Paine's *The Age of Reason*. After Williams had been convicted, Erskine declined to seek punishment of him. Erskine later wrote that he had been influenced by the fact that when walking near Lincoln's Inn Fields one day he 'felt something pulling me by the coat, when on turning round I saw a woman at my feet, bathed in tears and emaciated with disease and sorrow, who continued almost to drag me into a miserable hovel in the passage, where I found she was attending upon two or three unhappy children . . .'. This was the defendant's wife and family. Erskine was 'most deeply affected with what I had seen', and so advised the prosecutor, the Society for Carrying into Effect His Majesty's Proclamation against Vice and Immorality, that Christian charity required no punishment of the defendant. The prosecutor declined to instruct Erskine so to submit to the judge. But Erskine considered that 'I had still a duty of my own to perform, considering myself not as counsel for the Society, but for the Crown'. Erskine suggested to the court that a lenient sentence was appropriate: 'recollecting [that] this prosecution was brought to vindicate the honour and character of the Christian religion, I thought I owed it to the prisoner not to forget the charity which it so very peculiarly inculcates'. Mr Justice Ashhurst, explaining that the court would 'not pass so severe a sentence as it perhaps would, only upon account of Mr Erskine's suggestion', ordered that Mr Williams be imprisoned for one year. Williams enquired whether 'it will not be too great an indulgence that I may have a bed' in prison. Lord Kenyon replied that he could not so order.[150]

The obligation to act fairly does not mean that the prosecuting counsel is compelled to avoid advocacy. In 1925 Judge Hand, for the US Circuit Court of Appeals, rejected an attempt 'to confine a prosecuting attorney to an impartial statement of the evidence. He is an advocate, and it is entirely proper for him as earnestly as he can to persuade the jury of the truth of his side . . .'[151]

But although the District Attorney may 'present the government's side of the case in forcible and direct language', this does not entitle him to use 'arguments . . . calculated to inflame the minds of the jurors and prejudice them against the accused'.[152] For a prosecuting counsel, in a trial of a defendant for alleged sexual intercourse with a girl aged 14, to appeal to the jury to 'protect young girls from men like the prisoner' would now be considered more than 'a matter of taste', the approach of the Court of Criminal Appeal in 1916.[153] Five years later, that court understandably allowed an appeal by a Russian-born Jew against his conviction for stealing the property of a seaman. One of the grounds upon which the Lord Chief Justice quashed the conviction was that prosecuting counsel had used 'highly improper' language when submitting that 'these brutes' were 'robbing our British subjects' and 'now they have got Palestine or Mesopotamia they are not satisfied'.[154]

There are some decisions of courts in the United States which allow the prosecuting attorney a far greater degree of latitude to introduce emotional arguments than should be acceptable. In 1944, the Supreme Court of Illinois declined to overturn the criminal conviction of a defendant for indecent acts committed with a child although prosecuting counsel, in his closing speech to the jury, had said that 'the only way these kind of people are going to be put out of circulation, these morons that hang around . . . is by juries'. The court stated that 'the State's Attorney in his argument has a right to dwell on the evil results of a crime and to urge a fearless administration of the criminal law and to comment on the conduct of the accused'.[155] Similarly, in 1927 the Supreme Court of Pennsylvania held that the prosecuting attorney was entitled to say in his opening address to the jury in a murder trial that if the facts were as he had stated them to be, 'the electric chair is too good' for the defendant.[156]

It is of particular importance that prosecuting counsel should not 'express . . . by inflammatory or vindictive language his own personal opinion that the accused is guilty'.[157] Attorney-General Coke set an appalling example in the 1603 trial of Sir Walter Raleigh for high treason, telling the unfortunate defendant, 'I will prove you the notoriest traitor that ever came to the bar . . . thou art a monster'. During his submissions, it was suggested to Coke that he might moderate his abuse of the defendant. He asserted that this would 'encourage traitors' and 'sat down in a chafe, and would speak no more, until the Commissioners urged and entreated him. After much ado, he went on . . .'[158] In 1913, the Supreme Court of North Dakota allowed an appeal against conviction for rape where the prosecuting attorney had said to the jury, 'I do not come here to try a case unless the defendant is guilty'.[159] As the US Court of Appeals has stated, 'to permit counsel to express his personal belief in the testimony . . . would . . . create the false issue of the reliability and credibility of counsel. This is peculiarly unfortunate if one of them has the advantage of official backing.'[160] The US Supreme Court, allowing an appeal by a defendant convicted of a criminal offence, rightly held that prosecuting counsel breached the duty of fairness at the trial when he made 'improper suggestions, insinuations and, especially, assertions of personal knowledge'.[161]

Some US courts have shown a regrettable reluctance to control the introduction into the trial of the personal views of prosecuting counsel. In 1955, the US Court of Appeals held that 'it is not misconduct on [the District Attorney's] part to express [to the jury] his individual belief in the guilt of the accused if such belief is based solely on the evidence introduced'. The prosecuting attorney had there told the jury that 'if I don't believe he is guilty, no one is going to make me stand here and prosecute him'.[162] Similar decisions (some fairly ancient and of doubtful validity today) can be found in the jurisprudence of Arkansas ('He is guilty. I know it, and you know it, and the defendant knows it'), California, Michigan, and New Jersey.[163]

Courts have considered what to do where each side has given the jury its own personal view of the guilt or innocence of the defendant. If defence counsel, in his closing speech to the jury, suggests that 'there's not a person in this courtroom including those sitting at [counsel's] table who think that [the defendant was guilty of the crime charged]', and the prosecutor replies to the jury, 'Well, I was sitting there and I think he was', both counsel are at fault for introducing their personal opinions and there is—according to a bare majority of the US Supreme Court—no unfairness sufficient to justify reversing the conviction.[164] Similarly, when a prosecuting attorney told the jury he believed the defendant was guilty, but did so only in answer to 'the charge of appellant's attorney in his speech that he [the prosecuting attorney] was seeking an unjust conviction by his ambition to win', the US Circuit Court of Appeals declined to accept that this was a ground for reversing the conviction of the defendant.[165]

This must be erroneous. That defence counsel is also at fault is no excuse whatsoever for misbehaviour by the prosecution to the detriment of the unfortunate defendant: the impediment to a fair trial caused by the prosecutor introducing his personal opinions is the same whether or not he was provoked. If defence counsel impermissibly asserts the personal views of the advocates, the prosecuting counsel should explain to the jury that such opinions are irrelevant to the issue and that he will therefore keep his opinions to himself and will concentrate on presenting to the jury the case for the prosecution. It is essential for courts to control and punish the introduction by prosecuting counsel of their personal opinions of the guilt or innocence of defendants in criminal trials. There is an unacceptable risk that the jury will decide the case by reference to the opinion of the authoritative prosecuting counsel rather than on the evidence presented in court; defence counsel will be tempted, by way of rebuttal, to express their own view of their client's innocence; and any lawyer who, showing greater sensitivity and a finer appreciation of the true role of the advocate, does not wish to express a view may wrongly be thought by the jury to be a prosecutor who does not believe the defendant to be guilty or a defence attorney acting for a client whose innocence he doubts.[166]

In Charles Dickens's *A Tale of Two Cities*, the Attorney-General tells the jury that

> they never could lay their heads upon their pillows; that they never could endure the notion of their children laying their heads upon their pillows; in short, that there never more could be, for them or theirs, any laying of heads upon pillows at all, unless the prisoner's head was taken off. That head Mr Attorney-General concluded by demanding of them, in the name of everything he could think of with a round turn in it, and on the faith of his solemn asseveration that he already considered the prisoner as good as dead and gone.[167]

The guarantee of a fair trial requires that Crown counsel should not adopt as a precedent that style of prosecuting, nor its modern equivalent in totalitarian States. In Arthur Koestler's *Darkness at Noon*, the Public Prosecutor's speech to the court ends with the words, 'I demand that all these mad dogs be shot'.[168] Less dangerous to the pursuit of justice, but also to be avoided as a model, is the American District Attorney (as characterized by Tom Wolfe) who 'never went near a courtroom. He didn't have time. There were only so many hours in the day for him to stay in touch with Channels 1, 2, 4, 5, 7 and 11 and the New York *Daily News*, the *Post*, the *City Light* and the *Times*.'[169]

In civil cases, counsel who appear for the Crown similarly act as ministers of justice with a duty to ensure fairness to the other party. The Treasury devil (there is one in common law matters, and one on the Chancery side) represents the Crown in court. He is an independent counsel whose expertise is sought by all government departments on their most difficult and sensitive legal problems. It would be a mistake to 'underestimate the advantages of an independent mind in the inner closets of government'.[170] The burden of such work now makes it impossible for the Treasury devil to follow the example of Sir Valentine Holmes (appointed to the post in 1935): he performed the task 'without any abatement of his private practice' as a libel specialist.[171] The ever-increasing quantities of litigation by and against the Crown has led to the creation of a panel of Crown counsel, all of whom (with the exception of the Treasury devil) also accept instructions for private clients as well as for the Crown. So objectively do Crown counsel perform this work that it is most unusual for it to be said of a former Treasury counsel, as it was of Lord Parker as Lord Chief Justice, that 'the years he had spent as "Treasury devil" [1945–50, succeeding Sir Valentine Holmes] had caused him to have a greater tendency to support the actions of the Executive than had been the case with some of his predecessors'.[172]

VI

It will therefore be appreciated that advocates have substantial duties to the court which may override the duty to their client. The duty to the court must, as Lord Denning explained, be performed notwithstanding 'the wishes of the client, no matter how pressing and no matter how high the fee'.[173] A barrister is obliged to decline to act further for a client who refuses to allow him to comply with his professional obligations, for example the duty to make a disclosure to the court.[174] He must not do anything which would 'permit his absolute independence and freedom from external pressures to be compromised'.[175]

As Lord Pearce recognized in a 1967 judgment, it can be 'very unpleasant' and 'hard' for the advocate 'to explain to a client why he is indulging in what seems treachery to his client because of an abstract duty to justice and professional honour'.[176] As Lord Reid understated it, by complying with his professional duties the advocate 'may well incur the displeasure or worse of his client'.[177] Because of this responsibility for the proper administration of justice as well as for promoting the interests of his client, the job of the advocate involves 'divided loyalties' with 'the potential for conflict' being 'very considerable'.[178] The application in borderline cases of the rules governing the advocate's duty to the court 'may call for a degree of sophistry not readily appreciated by the lay client, particularly one who is [a] defendant in a criminal trial'.[179]

The advocate's duty to the court binds him 'to guard against abuse of the powers and privileges entrusted to him, by a constant recourse to his own sense of right'.[180] Lord Reid thought that 'it can be said with confidence in this country that where there is any doubt the vast majority of counsel put their public duty before the apparent interests of their clients'.[181] But it must be acknowledged, as Chief Justice Erle warned, that 'in the class of advocates, as in every other numerous class, there will be bad men, taking the wages of evil, and therewith also for the most part the early blight that waits upon the servants of evil'.[182] It is necessary to guard against what Sir William Blackstone condemned as 'the unseemly licentiousness of prostitute and illiberal men, a few of whom may sometimes insinuate themselves even into the most honourable profession',[183] especially as the unscrupulous advocate who refuses to abide by proper standards may well impede—whether by misunderstandings or worse—the administration of justice.

The court has considerable powers to punish errant barristers for contempt of court.[184] The central means by which the Bar itself controls the conduct of advocates and 'jealously guards' its 'reputation for the maintenance of high professional standards'[185] is the application of disciplinary sanctions for infractions of its code of conduct. 'The legal profession', Judge Coffin observed, 'has developed over a considerable period of time a complex code of behaviour.'[186] The ethical rules of the profession make membership of the Bar what Mr Justice Cardozo termed 'a privilege burdened with conditions'.[187] The rules of professional behaviour are contained in the *Code of Conduct* published by the Bar Council. Many of these rules 'rest essentially on nothing more and nothing less than a generally accepted standard of common decency and common fairness'.[188] Geoffrey Hazard has accurately analysed the rules of professional conduct as being capable of distillation into three main groups: those dealing with confidentiality, with conflicts of interest, and with prohibited forms of assistance to clients. That these rules may raise types of dilemmas experienced by non-lawyers in their working or social lives does not make the resolution of the problems any easier.[189]

From at least the seventeenth century, the power to suspend from practice a barrister who does not comply with professional standards was exercised by the Inns of Court. Complaints against barristers are now considered by the Bar Council. There is an appeal to the Judges as Visitors to the Inns.[190] The rules of professional conduct 'do not require the imprimatur of the judges as a condition of their validity', as the Visitors to Lincoln's Inn (Whitford, Ewbank, and Bingham JJ) held in 1981. 'If any rule acceptable to the Bar were held by the judges (in whatever capacity) to be contrary to public policy or to be liable to undermine the proper administration of justice, that rule would of course be ineffective, but subject to that the responsibility for formulating rules of professional conduct rests with the Bar through its appropriate procedure.'[191] The Visitors there rejected a challenge to the validity of the rule of the profession that a barrister may only act on the instructions of a solicitor, despite the fact that there is no rule of law so requiring.[192] However, professional rules cannot properly be used to compel barristers to pay a subscription to the Bar Council, since the essential purpose of the rules of professional conduct is to ensure that the right of audience is confined to fit and proper persons, and an individual may be an admirable person to practise at the Bar irrespective of whether he has paid such a subscription.[193]

The Professional Conduct Committee of the General Council of the Bar fulfils the role of prosecutor, considering complaints of breaches of professional standards, and bringing appropriate cases and charges before the disciplinary tribunal. Its decisions are subject to judicial review, as the Divisional Court held in dismissing a complaint by one barrister that another member of his former chambers should have been charged with professional misconduct for alleged irregularities in the administration of chambers business.[194]

Professional discipline regulates the conduct of all counsel, no matter how eminent. The manner in which the Attorney-General, Sir John Hobson, conducted a case in the Divisional Court in 1963 led to his being reported to the Benchers of his Inn by a fellow Bencher for alleged unprofessional conduct.[195] Although the Attorney was acquitted of the charge after an oral hearing, it was, according to counsel (Harold Lever) who acted for the complainant, 'plain that during the hearing the Attorney's standing with the Benchers had not increased'.[196] If a barrister is found to have fallen short of professional standards, the punishment can be harsh, amounting in extreme cases to permanent disbarment, or suspension from practice. If a disbarred barrister applies to be re-admitted to the ranks, he should be careful not to say that he 'accepts' rather than 'agrees with' the original decision to disbar him. The court may otherwise, as occurred in the New South Wales Supreme Court in 1961, dismiss his application on the basis that 'the only conclusion to be drawn is that he has exhibited and still exhibits a degree of casuistry, a lack of humility and an intellectual arrogance which are incompatible with a sincere understanding of and a genuine belief in the code of honour of the Bar'.[197] The Supreme Judicial Court of Massachusetts took a more realistic approach to this issue in 1975: reinstatement to the Bar of a person (Alger Hiss) struck off for a criminal offence did not depend on his admitting that he had been correctly convicted when he sincerely believed that he was the victim of a miscarriage of justice.[198]

In an 1821 case, a litigant in person was fined for his contempt of court in making blasphemous statements during legal proceedings. He lamented that 'no barrister will undertake and uphold an honest defence in a cause like mine'. Mr Justice Bayley confidently stated that 'when a case is conducted by counsel . . . they have that regard for their own character which generally prevents them from doing anything which may break in upon the rules of decency and decorum'.[199] That advocates have occasionally disappointed such expectations—in breach of, or sometimes in compliance with, professional standards—leads to a consideration of the morality of advocacy.

CHAPTER 5

Morality

I

BY becoming a member of the bar', Judge Downey of the Florida District Court of Appeal explained, 'a lawyer does not terminate his membership in the human race.'[1] But the practice of advocacy can create severe strains on the human instincts of the lawyer and can pose profound moral dilemmas. However unjust or unfair the result for which the client wishes to contend, it is the task of the advocate to argue to that end, as best he is able within the limits of his professional responsibility to the court.[2] The advocate's difficulty is to comply with the 1882 dictum of Sir James Hannen, President of the Probate, Divorce and Admiralty Division of the High Court, that 'there is an honourable way of defending the worst of cases',[3] and, in extreme circumstances, to reconcile with his conscience the fact that he is being paid to promote human misery.

Some of those for whom counsel acts will unquestioningly accept the propriety of the arrangement. 'A barrister is an old taxi plying for hire', Rumpole explains to a client.

> 'So it's my sacred duty, Mr Morry Machin, to take on anyone in trouble. However repellent I may happen to find them.'

'Thank you, Mr Rumpole.' Morry was genuinely grateful.
'Think nothing of it.'[4]

More often, members of the public doubt the morality of advocacy. They are at least suspicious, and often downright abusive, of those who are paid to argue vehemently for that to which they are, at best, personally indifferent.

Swift's description of advocates as a 'society of men . . . bred up from their youth in the art of proving by words multiplied for the purpose, that white is black, and black is white, according as they are paid',[5] is well understood and appreciated by laymen. Hazlitt's 'fee'd, time-serving, shuffling advocate'[6] is rarely the subject of public approval in any culture in any century. Few works of literature have lawyers as their heroes.[7] Indeed, on occasion, resentment of the legal profession has become so pronounced as to provoke major disorder in society. The professional conduct of lawyers was one focus of the anger of those who participated in Wat Tyler's rebellion of 1380 and the Gordon riots of 1780.

It is, perhaps, understandable that lawyers are not universally loved. Most of those who come into contact with the advocate do so in times of trouble or distress. Because lawyers necessarily lose half of the cases which are decided by courts there are likely to be many dissatisfied clients. It should, however, be noted that the public does not have a consistent hatred of lawyers. As Charles W. Wolfram has observed, 'many persons who speak ill of lawyers would be delighted if a son or daughter were admitted to law school'.[8]

The case against advocacy cannot, however, be dismissed as the grumblings of those who fail to win their cases. There is a principled objection to the practice of advocacy and it is well expressed by Jeremy Bentham:

A man has committed a theft; another man who, without a licence, knowing what he has done, has assisted him in making his escape, is punished as an accomplice. But the law (that is the judges . . .) have contrived to grant to their connexions acting in the character of advocates, a licence for this purpose. What the non-advocate is hanged for, the advocate is paid for, and admired.[9]

By so assisting the wrongdoer to escape, the advocate, said Bentham, 'lets out to the malefactor and wrongdoer his best endeavours'.[10] John Stuart Mill similarly complained that the lawyer 'hires himself out to do injustice or frustrate justice with his tongue'. Mill objected to hearing the 'advocate boasting of the artifices by which he had trepanned a deluded jury into a verdict in direct opposition to the strongest evidence'. He suggested that 'more regard for truth and justice might be expected than now' and that advocates were quite wrong to imagine that 'on such easy terms as those of putting on a wig and gown, a man obtains, and on the most important of all occasions, an exemption from both' of those qualities.[11] Lord Macaulay asked whether it was right 'that a man should, with a wig on his head and a band round his neck, do for a guinea what, without those appendages, he would think it wicked and infamous to do for an empire.'[12] Trollope's Lord Chiltern 'never believe[s] anything that a lawyer says when he has a wig on his head and a fee in his hand. I prepare myself beforehand to regard it all as mere words, supplied at so much the thousand.'[13] The central objection to advocacy implied by all these critics is that expressed by Socrates: that oratory is employed in the service of evil and so impedes the punishment of wrongdoing.[14]

It is on the function of defence counsel that critics of advocacy focus (though Socrates added that 'no honest man would prosecute an innocent party').[15] As explained by Mr Justice White of the US Supreme Court, counsel for the defence does not have any 'obligation to ascertain or present the truth. . . . He need not furnish any witnesses to the police, or reveal any confidences of his client, or furnish any other information to help the prosecution's case. If he can confuse a witness, even a truthful one, or make him appear at a disadvantage, unsure or indecisive, that will be his normal course.' In this respect, 'we countenance or require conduct which in many instances has little, if any, relation to the search for truth'.[16] Travers Humphreys (called to the Bar in 1889) recalled attending a conference in which leading counsel, Willie Willis, told his client, whom he was defending on some serious criminal charge, that he would do his best for him if the client gave him an undertaking: 'Promise me, my friend, that if I get you off this time you will never do it again.'[17]

As a young advocate, Lord Denning 'wasn't concerned so much with the rightness of the cause, I was concerned only, as a member of the Bar, to win it if I could'.[18] But there are many lawyers who have shared the popular view of the ethics of advocacy or, at least, had doubts about its propriety. In his early years at the Bar, Matthew Hale (later Chief Justice from 1671 to 1676), adopted the principle that 'if he saw a cause was unjust, he . . . would not meddle further in it but to give his advice that it was so; if the parties after that would go on, they were to seek another counsellor; for he would assist none in acts of injustice'.[19] In 1685, the infamous Judge Jeffreys (when Lord Chief Justice) criticized an eminent counsel in court with the words, 'Mr Wallop, I observe you are in all these dirty causes'. The judge suggested that counsel 'should have more wit and honesty than to support and hold up these factious knaves by the chin'.[20] Lord Chancellor Eldon recalled that as a young barrister he had remarked to a leading counsel that he had observed that 'in all causes in which you were concerned, good, bad, indifferent, whatever their nature was, you equally exerted yourself to the utmost to gain verdicts'. Eldon reflected that 'it may be questioned whether . . . this can be supported'.[21] On occasion, counsel have considered it appropriate to substitute a different morality for that which is normally observed in court. Lord Chancellor King, immediately prior to his retirement in 1733, 'often dozed over his causes when upon the bench'. This did not prejudice the litigants because counsel, Sir Philip Yorke and Mr Talbot, 'were both men of such good principles and strict integrity, and had always so good an understanding with one another, that, although they were frequently and almost always concerned for opposite parties in the same cause, yet the merits of the cause were no sooner fully stated to the court, but they were sensible on which side the right lay; and, accordingly, the one or the other of these two great men took occasion to state the matter briefly to his Lordship, and instruct the Register in what manner to minute the heads of the decree'.[22]

A critical assessment of advocacy is becoming increasingly fashionable and prevalent amongst conservatives (who are concerned that, by reason of the efforts of lawyers, villains might not be receiving their just deserts) and amongst liberals and socialists (who do not understand why barristers who share their political views should speak in court for persons, and so promote causes, they find repellent). Lord Hutchinson QC regretted that throughout his career at the Bar 'I have met people from time to time who have addressed me on the basis,

"I was very surprised to see you mixed up in a case like that". That is the attitude of so many laymen to the advocate.'[23] Defendants often have little sympathy for the ethics of the bar. One of the Guildford Four, wrongly convicted and imprisoned for the 1974 IRA bombing which murdered five people, 'got the impression that any of our barristers [at the trial] could easily have . . . taken over the running of the prosecution. They were no different.'[24] Many young barristers are dubious about the ethics of their profession.

II

The defence of advocacy as a respectable profession for an honest and liberal individual is based on identifying its central principles. First, that the advocate is not expressing his own opinions, but is speaking on behalf of his client. Second, that the advocate is prepared to perform this task for any client, irrespective of the views or conduct of that client. Third, that the performance of this function is necessary to assist the court properly to determine the legal rights and duties of relevant persons.

The advocate does not endorse the views or beliefs of his client. He is, as Lord Macmillan explained, there to 'present to the court all that can be said on behalf of his client's case, all that his client would have said for himself if he had possessed the requisite skill and knowledge. . . . His duty is to see that those whose business it is to judge do not do so without first hearing from him all that can possibly be urged on his side.'[25] When an editorial in *The Times* commented on the difficulty of obtaining convictions in obscenity cases when the defence had the advantage of being represented by John Mortimer QC with his 'passionate devotion to defence of the freedom of pornography', Mortimer responded with an eloquent statement of the duty of the advocate. 'Any barrister's duty is to be "passionately devoted" to the defence of his client. It would be a sad day if a defendant charged with an alleged crime could not be defended without his counsel being accused of devotion to murder or robbing banks.'[26]

While the case is in court, the opinions of the advocate are not of central relevance. The advocate is paid to argue the point, not to decide it. He should not assert a personal opinion of the facts or the law to the court unless invited to do so by that court.[27] If so invited, he should politely remind the court that he is there only to perform his function as an advocate. He is therefore obliged to conceal from the court his own opinions (favourable or unfavourable) of the merits of the case, the veracity of the witnesses, the wisdom of the judge, and (subject to his duties to the court)[28] subsume them all to the furtherance of the goal—victory for the cause, petty or wrongheaded, dangerous or wicked though it may be.

The ethical rule is as stated by Lord Campbell in his direction to the jury in the trial of William Palmer, accused (and convicted) of murder by poisoning. The judge told the jury to attend carefully to everything that had been said by Serjeant Shee, counsel for the defendant, 'with the exception of his own personal opinion. . . . You are to try the prisoner upon the evidence before you . . . and by that alone, and not by any opinion of his advocate. I feel also bound to say that it would have been better if his advocate had abstained from some of the observations which he made in his address to you, in which he laid great stress upon his own conviction of the prisoner's innocence of the crime imputed to him.' But for the application of this principle, then 'if the advocate withholds an opinion, the jury may suppose that he is conscious of his client's guilt, whereas it is the duty of the advocate to press his argument upon the jury, not his opinion'.[29] Lord Herschell (Lord Chancellor in 1886 and from 1892 to 1895) explained (in 1889) that but for the principle that the advocate must not express his own views, the unscrupulous counsel 'would express a belief which he did not entertain, whilst a scrupulous one, from the very desire to avoid exaggeration in the indication of his views, would probably do his client less than justice'. More fundamentally, as Herschell added, 'the mischief calculated to flow from the appearance of an advocate of position and character in support of a case which proves to be without merit can only be obviated if it be distinctly understood that he is an advocate only, and that it is his client's case, and not his personal views or opinions to which he is giving expression'.[30]

For these reasons, Serjeant Buzfuz should not have opened the breach of promise of marriage case of *Bardell v. Pickwick* by representing to the jury, on behalf of the plaintiff, that

> never, in the whole course of his professional experience—never, from the very first moment of his applying himself to the study and practice of the law—had he approached a case with feelings of such deep emotion, or with such a heavy sense of the responsibility imposed upon him—a responsibility, he would say, which he could never have supported, were he not buoyed up and sustained by a conviction so strong, that it amounted to positive certainty that the cause of truth and justice, or, in other words, the cause of his much-injured and most oppressed client, must prevail with the high-minded and intelligent dozen of men whom he now saw in that box before him.[31]

Nor should counsel have added, at the end of his submissions to the US Supreme Court in an important constitutional case, that he wanted to 'say just one final and somewhat personal word. I have tried very hard to argue this case calmly and dispassionately. . . . But I do not want your Honors to think that my feelings are not involved, and that my emotions are not deeply stirred. Indeed may it please your Honors, I believe I am standing here today to plead the cause of the America I have loved . . .'[32]

That the advocate is speaking on behalf of the client, and not endorsing the views or opinions of the person he represents, is linked to the second principle of advocacy: that counsel accepts the responsibility of performing this task for any client prepared to pay for his services, irrespective of whether the lawyer personally accepts the truth or validity of those submissions, or sympathizes with the conduct and predicament of the client. To the extent that the advocate picks and chooses between potential clients on the basis of whether their conduct and opinions are acceptable to him, he is, implicitly, associating himself with his clients and their causes and giving a personal endorsement to the submissions he makes on their behalf.

The House of Lords recognized in 1969 that a central principle of advocacy is that 'no counsel is entitled to refuse to act in a sphere in which he practices, and on being tendered a proper fee, for any person however unpopular or even offensive he or his opinions may be'.[33] This 'cab-rank rule' requires a barrister to accept any brief to appear before a court in which he professes to practise, to accept any instructions and to act for any person on whose behalf he is briefed or instructed 'irrespective of (i) the party on whose behalf he is briefed or instructed (ii) the nature of the case and (iii) any belief or opinion which he may have formed as to the character, reputation, cause, conduct, guilt or innocence of that person'.[34] It is the advocate's duty, as Lord Irvine QC has explained, 'to appear for the Yorkshire Ripper or any other defendant against whom there may be a hostile climate of public opinion. In civil cases, it is also his duty to appear not only for a particular interest group with which he might prefer to identify but for every interest group; for plaintiffs or insurers in personal injury cases; for employers or trade unions in labour law cases; for the citizen or the State in judicial review cases.'[35] This is an obligation imposed only in respect of 'any field in which he professes to practise' but it is 'irrespective of whether his client is paying privately or is legally aided or otherwise publicly funded'.[36]

In 1990, the House of Lords gave further recognition to this principle by approving an amendment to the Courts and Legal Services Bill. The amendment,[37] which was proposed by Lord Alexander, became section 17(3)(c) of the Courts and Legal Services Act 1990. It states, as part of the general principles to be applied when considering whether a person is qualified to practise advocacy in any court or proceedings, that he must be a member of a professional body which requires the advocate not to withhold his services on the ground that the nature of the case is objectionable to him or to any member of the public, or that the conduct, opinions, or beliefs of the prospective client are unacceptable to him or to any section of the public, or on any ground relating to the source of the financial support which may properly be given to the prospective client for the proceedings in question (for example, on the ground that the case is legally aided). This cab-rank rule is, as Lord Hutchinson QC stated in the debate on the clause, 'the very basis of advocacy in this country'.[38] To include the principle in the Bill was, as Lord Ackner explained, 'a point of great constitutional importance'.[39]

Of course, there are exceptions to the principle. The rule does not require a barrister to accept instructions when, for example, he lacks sufficient experience to handle the matter competently or when his other professional commitments leave him inadequate time to prepare the case.[40] The point of the rule is not affected by these exceptions: the barrister still has a professional duty to accept instructions irrespective of the popularity or acceptability of the cause for which his client is contending.

A similar rule applies in Australia.[41] However, some other legal systems do not apply the same ethical standards as the English Bar. John W. Davis, who argued over one hundred cases before the Supreme Court, 'conceive[d] it to be the duty of the lawyer, just as it is the duty of the priest or the surgeon, to serve those who call on him unless, indeed, there is some insuperable obstacle in the way'.[42] But it is well settled as a matter of professional ethics in the USA that 'no lawyer has a duty to represent any client, except perhaps those who are unable to obtain counsel'.[43] The Comment attached to the American Bar Association Model Rules of Professional Conduct states that a 'lawyer ordinarily is not obliged to accept a client whose character or cause the lawyer regards as repugnant'.[44] This is one of the fundamental differences between advocacy in England and in the United States. Indeed, in the latter, much more frequently than in the former, counsel act only on behalf of the prosecution or only on behalf of the defence and, in civil cases, tend to act only for plaintiffs or only for defendants.

Many foreign lawyers, especially from the USA, do

not understand how an English advocate can act for different sides on similar issues (whether it be landlord and tenant disputes, or employment cases, or in immigration law) on different days. In England, the advocate may be prosecuting in a criminal case on a Monday, defending on a Tuesday, and acting in a civil case for either plaintiff or defendant for the rest of the week. In the trial of Kit on a charge of theft in *The Old Curiosity Shop*, prosecuting counsel being 'in dreadfully good spirits (for he had, in the last trial, very nearly procured the acquittal of a young gentleman who had the misfortune to murder his father) he spoke up you may be sure; telling the jury that if they acquitted this prisoner they must expect to suffer no less pangs and agonies than he had told the other jury they would certainly undergo if they convicted that prisoner'.[45]

American courts have feared that for the advocate to represent different clients on opposite sides of the legal net on different days may impede the cause of justice. It has, in particular, been suggested that, where the advocate holds a part-time appointment as a government lawyer, it might well be impermissible for him to act, in different cases, for clients on the opposing side. 'The incongruous appearance of a lawyer changing hats for the occasion of a court appointment is', according to one of the leading commentators on legal ethics in the United States, 'underscored by the danger that the lawyer's responsibilities and opportunities in public employment will lead to a less than vigorous defence.'[46] In 1974, the Supreme Court of California reversed a conviction because the defendant had been represented by counsel who was, at the time of the trial, a prosecuting City Attorney. The court thought that there was a serious risk that he did not produce 'vigorous and determined advocacy' and 'public confidence in the integrity of the criminal justice system could be adversely affected'.[47] But as the English experience shows with advocates who hold appointments as Crown counsel (in the field of civil or criminal law), the system of acting for different sides in different cases does not lead to the problems feared by American courts. The advocate is well able to do his best for his client even though he was doing his best for a client with a different interest on the previous day.

Indeed, understanding how the matter must look from the other side assists counsel to argue cases for their clients. It is the experience of many barristers that the most competent representation of a client comes from those who are objective, and are not politically or emotionally involved in any cause being championed by their client. Preserving objectivity in the interests of the client is not an easy task to accomplish. As Alan M. Dershowitz has explained, many clients are unwilling to hear the truth. 'They want to know how wonderful they are and how certain it is that they're going to win the case. Unless the lawyer becomes a cheerleader, he risks being replaced by a more upbeat attorney.'[48] But it is vital in the interests of the client that he is given an objective assessment of the position so that he can make informed choices in relation to the litigation.

Not all observers of the English legal system have been entirely convinced of the propriety of the cab-rank rule. In one of John Mortimer's tales, Rumpole reminds his wife that the principle of the Bar is that 'I will accept any client, however repulsive'. She replies, unconvinced, 'That's not a principle, that's just a way of making money from the most terrible people'.[49] It would undoubtedly be more popular for the Bar to adopt the principle expressed by the radical American lawyer William Kunstler in 1970: 'I'm not a lawyer for hire. I only defend those I love.'[50] In fact, the Bar has imposed the cab-rank rule upon itself not because its members are greedy, insensitive, selfish brutes, but because they recognize the cab-rank rule as a moral basis of advocacy and are fearful of the consequences for justice if such a principle were to be abandoned. The purpose of the cab-rank rule is, as the Bar's Code of Conduct states, 'to acknowledge a public obligation based on the paramount need for access to justice'.[51]

If counsel were entitled to pick and choose between potential clients on the basis of the acceptability of their conduct, the advocate would necessarily become identified with the causes of those for whom he does agree to act. If he may select clients in this way, why should the public not perceive him as endorsing those for whom he chooses to act? The Model Rules of the American Bar Association are hypocritical in denying a cab-rank principle while asserting that a 'lawyer's representation of a client . . . does not constitute an endorsement of the client's political, economic, social or moral views or activities'.[52] Lord Eldon was right to contend that without the cab-rank rule, observers of the legal system would find it even more difficult to understand the ethic of advocacy that the advocate is, 'however he may be represented by those who understand not his true situation, merely an officer assisting in the administration of justice'.[53] If the advocate claims the right to refuse to act for those whose conduct he finds reprehensible, he asserts his approval of those for whom he acts, and he cannot expect the public to accept that, when he makes his submissions in court, he is speaking on behalf of his client, and not on behalf of himself.

Once we identify the advocate with his unattractive

client, and criticize the former for choosing to lend his skills to promoting the legal interests of those of whom society (or a part of it) disapproves, there is a serious risk that unpopular people would be unable to obtain competent representation, causing a real risk that injustice would thereby occur.

Without a cab-rank rule, few advocates would accept instructions from those accused of rape or child molestation, either because they would find it distasteful to be associated with such persons, or because of the pressure from society directed against those who choose to act for such clients, especially if they win the case. 'If counsel is bound to act for such a person', Lord Reid explained, 'no reasonable man could think the less of any counsel because of his association with such a client, but, if counsel could pick and choose, his reputation might suffer if he chose to act for such a client, and the client might have great difficulty in obtaining proper legal assistance.'[54] Unpopular people would be unable to obtain competent representation, and serious injustice would result because, as Lord Pearce noted, it is 'easier, pleasanter and more advantageous professionally for barristers to advise, represent or defend those who are decent and reasonable and likely to succeed in their action or their defence than those who are unpleasant, unreasonable, disreputable and have an apparently hopeless case'.[55] In the House of Lords in 1840, Lord Brougham explained that 'if once a barrister is to be allowed to refuse a brief, and to say that he will no defend a man because he is in the wrong, many will be found who will refuse to defend men, not on accoun of the case, but because they are weak men, under the pressure of unpopularity, against whom power has se its mark, because they are the victims of oppression, o are about to be made so, or because it will not be convenient for parties at all times to beard power on behalf of individuals in the situation of prisoners'.[56] Once it became known that the advocate was refusing to act for the client, 'the suitor would be prejudiced in proportion to the respectability of the advocate . . .'.[57]

It would be an inadequate substitute for the cab-rank rule to require a barrister to act for a client only when that client cannot otherwise obtain representation. This would have all the disadvantages of ensuring that counsel is associated with the cause of any client, other than one for whom he acts because no one else will. In any event, the client wants, and is entitled to have, representation by a skilled practitioner. In a legal system which often magnifies the inequities in society, it is a major contribution to the rule of law and to a fair society that the cab-rank rule truly does ensure that indigent sections of society benefiting from legal aid are able to secure representation by the most qualified barristers to enable their legal rights to be fully protected.

It is far from fanciful to recognize the risk of minority or unpopular interests going undefended and therefore to devise a legal system that does its best to ensure that advocates are protected from pressure to conform to the wishes of the State or popular feeling. It should be recalled that over the centuries, barristers have suffered from the hostility of those who resent their acting on behalf of certain causes. Some of those barristers have put up more resistance than others in this respect.

During the seventeenth-century Interregnum, a litigant lamented how 'Serjeant Conyers took a fee of me to move in Chancery and kept it for several days . . . yet this Serjeant just as he came to the bar gave me my fee and ran into the court and told me that the Attorney-

General was against me and he durst not, nor would meddle in the cause; so I was forced to move the commissioners myself'.[58] Conyers' caution was understandable: when the high commission court sent two people to prison, a counsel called Fuller moved the court for a writ of habeas corpus (to secure their release) on the ground that the high commissioners had no legal power to impose such a sentence; Fuller himself was arrested and 'lay in gaol to the day of his death'.[59] In the early eighteenth century, Charles Talbot (a future Lord Chancellor) made a promising start to his career, until he 'publicly avowed his principles by appearing counsel for' those of whom his Tory patrons disapproved. Solicitors 'from that time deserted him and were very active in doing him prejudices'.[60] Showing the 'uncommon virtue of courage to stand by his principles at any cost',[61] Malesherbes (then over the age of 70) paid with his life, and that of members of his family, for defending Louis XVI against the revolutionary Government of France.[62] When Carson, though a prominent Unionist politician, appeared professionally in 1913 for Liberal Ministers in legal actions arising from the Marconi scandal he was severely criticized by members of his own party.[63] Lord Hailsham recalled that after he had successfully obtained a remedy from the court for three Pakistani immigrants to the United Kingdom who had been detained by the authorities, he received (as a Conservative Member of Parliament) 'an enormous hate mail from members of my own party and even adverse questions at public meetings for some time thereafter'.[64] When Lord Hooson defended in the Moors Murders case, 'some of my political opponents—not the candidates—could not resist using that fact against me in the election campaign'.[65] It would be foolishly complacent now to abandon or weaken the cab-rank principle, an aspect of legal practice which helps to distance advocates from their clients and so makes it easier to ensure that the political, moral, or social dissident is effectively represented in court.

There are disturbing signs from within the Bar that some sets of chambers do not understand the importance of the cab-rank rule. Either overtly or by the use of lies (such as instructing their clerk to pretend that they are otherwise engaged or requiring a fee far higher than they would normally expect), there are some barristers who will not act for landlords, or for employers accused of race or sex discrimination (unless, of course, the client is a trade union). Some barristers will not prosecute in criminal cases. Lord Hooson regretted that he had heard some young barristers say that they would not defend an alleged rapist.[66] Since all such advocates refuse to act for these categories of clients because of a moral or social or political judgment on them, they necessarily associate themselves with those clients whom they are prepared to represent. Such a practice is inconsistent with the morality of advocacy and threatens the very survival of an independent profession dedicated to ensuring that all those who appear in court—no matter how serious or offensive the allegations made against them—are entitled to have their case determined on the evidence by an independent judge under the rule of law, rather than by the political purity of their motives or by the emotional reaction to the charge against them. If the advocate is unwilling to act for the alleged rapist, why is he willing to act for the alleged drug-dealer, or baby-batterer, or drunken driver? Once the principle of acting for all those in court is sacrificed, there is no logical stopping place other than a subjective test of representing only those whom the advocate does not find too reprehensible in the light of the charge which they face and upon the strength of which it is the task of the court to adjudicate. No one suggests that barristers have to like or admire their clients or to enjoy acting on their behalf. But counsel should acknowledge and respect the professional duty to represent all clients to the best of their professional ability.

Equally unprincipled and reprehensible are those chambers which have declined to act for clients on legal aid. Such a refusal hinders the ability of vulnerable sectors of society to obtain effective legal representation in relation to proceedings which affect their welfare. It thereby weakens the contribution which an independent Bar makes to the rule of law and it subverts the moral basis of advocacy. The Code of Conduct for the Bar now clearly states the obligation to comply with the cab-rank rule, in legal aid as well as other cases.[67] The Bar should enforce the Code strictly in this respect.

The Courts and Legal Services Act requires solicitors who wish to practise as advocates in the superior courts to comply with the cab-rank rule.[68] Solicitors should not resent the application of this rule to them as an inconvenient obligation. They should welcome it as the guarantee of the integrity of the advocate: if entitled to choose his clients and to express his personal opinions to the court, the advocate would lose his professional independence and deserve to attract the moral obloquy which belongs to his less attractive clients. Solicitors will appreciate that because it helps to ensure that all persons, especially the less popular, are competently represented, the cab-rank rule supports features of our courts which are fundamental to the rule of law: freedom of expression and equality of arms for all litigants, whoever they may be. Any lawyer who does not understand this really has no business being an advocate.

Concern to improve access to justice for all similarly

suggests that the cab-rank rule should apply to the services of lawyers out of court, as well as in court. The Code of Conduct of the Bar applies to advisory work, as well as advocacy.[69] It is difficult to see why the same obligation should not extend to solicitors. Efforts to explain their conduct by solicitors who decline to act for men accused of rape[70] fail to grapple with the central issue.[71] Once they refuse, on moral or analogous grounds, to provide legal services for a client in an area (such as criminal law) in which they practise, they are implicitly but necessarily encouraging other firms to act likewise by suggesting that such a stance is proper for the profession, with the result that clients whose causes are unpopular may be denied access to the best legal services, and may thereby be impeded in securing their legal rights. The first to suffer will be the underprivileged sections of society. It is no answer to these criticisms for such solicitors to assert that the client is able to find elsewhere a competent lawyer to represent him. The criticism is not directed only to the consequences for the individual client, though he is entitled to the best representation, or to have acting for him the lawyer whom he chooses, not just a lawyer whose conscience does not trouble him. The criticism is also directed to the damage done by such a stance to the ideal of a legal system which protects the rights of all. Nor is it any answer for these lawyers to say (correctly) that all solicitors specialize in particular areas of law and so turn away considerable quantities of work: the issue is not specialization, but offering services in an area (such as criminal law) in which the lawyer does specialize but only to those clients deemed politically or socially acceptable.

The cab-rank rule, with the objective and dispassionate role it requires the advocate to play, may, perhaps, be a fortunate consequence of the phlegmatic, reserved character of the English, and so difficult to transplant into other legal cultures. Whatever the causes of this legal phenomenon, it is one of the central elements of our legal system and should remain so.

Other legal systems, though not necessarily adopting the cab-rank principle, do depend for their efficacy on the independence of the lawyer. The Seventh United Nations Congress on the Prevention of Crime and the Treatment of Offenders stated in its 1985 Resolution on the Role of Lawyers that 'adequate protection of the rights of citizens requires that all persons have effective access to legal services provided by lawyers who are able to perform effectively their proper role in the defence of those rights', and that counsel should be able to 'represent their clients in accordance with the law and their established professional standards and judgment without any undue interference from any quarter'. It therefore recommends to States that they protect 'practising lawyers against undue restrictions and pressures in the exercise of their functions'. Such protection is essential for the preservation of the rights of all citizens to live in a society governed by the rule of law.

Regrettably, however, in many countries of the world lawyers are harassed, prevented from practising their profession, ill-treated, and, on occasion, murdered, either by Governments or with the complicity of the State, because they have dared to act on behalf of clients whose views or conduct the Government deplores or fears. The Centre for the Independence of Judges and Lawyers, part of the International Commission of Jurists, publishes a depressingly long list of such violations of basic standards of legal independence.[72]

It would be idealistic to think that such States respect basic principles of civilized conduct. Nevertheless, lawyers are better placed to argue their case against such Government oppression, and more able to draw on support from other countries, if they can say that they have represented the relevant client not because they chose to do so, but because they have a professional obligation to act on behalf of any client, irrespective of his political views, to ensure that his legal rights are protected. If, as is the case in many parts of the world, advocates have a right to choose for whom they act, it is perhaps understandable (though in no way excusable) that Governments mistakenly associate the lawyer with the client for the purposes of punishment. In any event, those English lawyers who refuse to act for potential clients because of political considerations should have well in mind that in many parts of the world brave advocates are being punished for providing representation to those who are out of favour with the Government and society. It is regrettable that where the legal profession has the opportunity to act for all classes of client without any fear of adverse Government action, lawyers should decline to act for those of whom they disapprove. They should, if criticized for representing the unpopular, repeat the words of John Mortimer's Rumpole: 'I defend murderers. Doesn't mean I approve of murder.'[73]

The central principles of the ethics of advocacy—that the advocate does not express his own views, but those of his client, and that the advocate has a professional duty to act on behalf of any client, irrespective of his opinion of the litigant's conduct or opinions—are inextricably linked with a conception of justice that recognizes advocacy as essential to the protection of the rights and duties of those who appear in court. Advocacy exemplifies the principles of freedom of expression. Advocates are required to believe little for the purposes of their profession. They frequently suspend their critical faculties and present submissions which they know have little chance of being accepted by judges and juries. But they do believe that, in general, the truth will be more likely to be revealed, and error and bias avoided, if all of the issues are rationally debated by the presentation of divergent points of view. Unless there exists a profession of lawyers prepared to accept instructions to argue cases on behalf of any client, no matter how unpopular, the court might not hear all that can properly be said on behalf of such people, and the quality of judgments will be reduced, with detrimental consequences for those whose civil rights would be at risk. To help ensure that cases are decided on the evidence and the relevant law, not on prejudice, and because the only alternative is a system in which the unpopular run an unacceptable risk of being condemned without competent representation and without a fair trial, Lord Hutchinson QC was justifiably proud to state that he had 'spent so many hours in defence of alleged child abusers, rapists, traitors and even terrorists. . . . To cross-examine children and unhappy women or even corrupt policemen . . . is but painful work.'[74]

Those lawyers who vet their clients for political or moral acceptability fail to understand three essential points. First, that often we cannot know who is right and who is wrong until the case has been argued. Second, that it is the task of the judge to make that decision, not the task of the advocate. And third, that the judge can only perform this function adequately if he has the assistance of counsel to present the competing arguments for each side.

For the barrister to select his clients on the basis of

whether he thinks they are heroes or villains would be especially productive of injustice given the inherent difficulty of knowing, on the basis of the material available to one side in advance of court proceedings, what will be revealed at the trial. As Mr Justice Megarry appreciated, the 'path of the law is strewn with examples of open and shut cases which, somehow, were not; of unanswerable charges which, in the event, were completely answered; of inexplicable conduct which was fully explained . . .'.[75] It is, therefore, very far from unknown that, as Lord Pearce observed, 'the unpleasant, the unreasonable, the disreputable and those who have apparently hopeless cases turn out after a full and fair hearing to be in the right'.[76]

Were barristers to choose clients on the basis of the acceptability of their conduct they would be ignoring the wise words of the American lawyer, Lloyd N. Cutler: 'The essence of the adversary process is that judgments of right and wrong are to be made after the process is completed, not before it begins.'[77] It is the task of the judge, not the advocate, to make such judgments. As Dr Johnson explained to Boswell, 'if lawyers were to undertake no causes till they were sure they were just, a man might be precluded altogether from a trial of his claim, though, were it judicially examined, it might be found a very just claim'.[78] In his defence of Tom Paine on the charge of seditious libel in 1792, Thomas Erskine explained that he would

> for ever, at all hazards, assert the dignity, independence and integrity of the English Bar, without which impartial justice, the most valuable part of the English Constitution, can have no existence. From the moment that any advocate can be permitted to say that he *will* or will *not* stand between the Crown and the subject arraigned in the court where he daily sits to

practice, from that moment the liberties of England are at an end. If the advocate refuses to defend from what *he may think* of the charge or of the defence, he assumes the character of the judge; nay, he assumes it before the hour of judgment; and in proportion to his rank and reputation puts the heavy influence of perhaps a mistaken opinion into the scale against the accused, in whose favour the benevolent principle of the English law makes all presumptions, and which commands the very judge to be his counsel.[79]

Erskine wrote to the King explaining that it was an 'invaluable part of that very constitution' which Paine attacked that there was an 'unquestionable right of the subject to make his defence, by any counsel of his own free choice'. But the King still required Erskine to resign from his office as Attorney-General to the Prince of Wales.[80]

There is much authority in English legal history to support the principle of the cab-rank rule, but that does not prevent the issue being addressed to each generation of advocates. In 1989, the Courts Martial Appeal Court quashed a conviction because a member of the court had asked a question of defence counsel at lunchtime on the first day of the trial and counsel had answered, unaware of the identity of the questioner. The question was, as the Court accurately noted, one that 'every practising barrister at some stage of his career was asked by a curious lay person at a social occasion, "How can you defend a person when you know he is guilty?" Every barrister worth his salt knew the answer.'[81] The answer known by all competent barristers—and explained whenever the issue is raised by laymen—is that articulated by Dr Johnson when Boswell asked him whether it was proper for a barrister to support a cause which he knew to be bad:

Sir, you do not know it to be good or bad till the judge determines it. . . . An argument which does not convince yourself may convince the Judge to whom you urge it; and if it does convince him, why, then, Sir, you are wrong, and he is right. It is his business to judge; and you are not to be confident in your own opinion that a cause is bad, but to say all you can for your client, and then hear the Judge's opinion.[82]

The defence of advocacy is not just that it is to gaze into the crystal-ball and a confusion of roles for the advocate to refuse to act for clients whose conduct is objectionable.[83] It is also that a foundation of liberty would be lost were barristers to judge their potential clients. The court can properly perform its task of deciding the issues before it only if each party has someone to speak on his behalf to put his side of the case. The advocate believes that he is contributing to the pursuit of justice because he accepts the theory propounded by Lord Chancellor Eldon in 1822, that 'truth is best discovered by powerful statements on both sides of the question'[84] (though it has to be acknowledged that many of the rules of evidence impede rather than promote the search for truth). Sydney Smith preached an assize sermon to similar effect in 1824: 'justice', he suggested, 'is found, experimentally, to be most effectually promoted by the opposite efforts of practised and ingenious men presenting to the selection of an impartial judge the best arguments for the establishment or explanation of truth. It becomes, then, under such an arrangement, the decided duty of an advocate to use all the arguments in his power to defend the cause he has adopted, and to leave the effects of those arguments to the judgment of others.'[85] In this respect, as Mr Justice Megarry explained in a 1968 decision, 'argued law is tough law'. Citing from a judgment in 1409, he concluded that 'today, as of old, by good disputing shall the law be well known'.[86]

Although the advocate is obliged to present the case for any client, no matter how unattractive, and although he is constrained from offering the court his personal opinions, this does not require him to be morally neutral. Before the court hearing, counsel's role is to advise his client about all matters relevant to the case. This should include advice about the wisdom or propriety of the course adopted by the litigant, and its implications, so long as the lawyer remembers that it is for the client to make the decision and the lawyer does not suggest or imply that he has any professional expertise which accords his view of morality a higher status than the opinion or judgment of others on such questions. Louis Brandeis (thereafter a distinguished Justice of the US Supreme Court) was unusual amongst legal advisers at the beginning of this century in inquiring into 'the justness' of his client's position.[87] The American Bar Association Model Rules of Professional Conduct now provide that in 'rendering advice, a lawyer may refer not only to law but to other considerations such as moral, economic, social and political factors that may be relevant to the client's situation'.[88] It is, as observed by Felix Frankfurter (another eminent Justice of the US Supreme Court), 'one of the gravest shortcomings of lawyers to be content to give their clients merely the advice of whether this is or is not within the law'.[89] Whether the client accepts broader advice is a matter for him to decide.

During the hearing, the client may expect the professional obligations of the advocate to extend to showing enthusiasm for the case. Quintilianus in the first century AD suggested that the advocate must not merely say all that can reasonably be said. In presenting the case, he contended, the advocate should 'adopt a confident manner and should always speak as if he thought his case admirable'.[90] He should, in short, look as if he means it. One of the strengths of the advocacy of Sir Patrick Hastings KC was that 'he managed at all times to convey the impression that he was in earnest, and was not simply playing a part'.[91] When a defendant briefed Sir Edward Marshall Hall 'he did not merely buy the lawyer or even the advocate in Marshall Hall, but the whole man. He had the gift of throwing the whole of his personality into the case: by the fire of his rhetoric he threw a cloak of romance and drama round the sorry figures in the dock, convincing the jury that he believed passionately in every word he said—and for the time he really did.'[92]

Since not all clients are angels pursuing causes which are entirely just, to require the advocate invariably to rise (or descend) to such theatrical standards would be wholly inappropriate. The morality of advocacy requires the advocate to say all that the client would wish to say for himself, but it does not require him to imply by his performance that he personally subscribes to the views which he is propounding. However, although personal commitment is not required, the advocate must be careful not to dissociate himself from his client. He should avoid suggesting, by weakness of presentation, that he does not believe a word of what he is saying and that he would not be making these ridiculous submissions but for the insistence of the client and the generosity of the fee. It was said of the young Francis Bacon that

> When engaged in some cause célèbre—the Queen and the Court coming to hear the arguments or taking a lively interest in the result—Bacon no doubt exerted himself to the utmost, and excited applause by his display of learning and eloquence;

but on ordinary occasions, when he found himself in an empty court, and before an irritable or drowsy judge, he must have been unable to conceal his disgust—and eager to get home that he might finish an essay or expose some fallacy by which past ages had been misled—if he stood up for his client as long as he felt there was a fair chance of success, we may well believe that he showed little energy in a hopeless defence, and that he was careless about softening defeat by any display of zeal or sympathy.

The consequence was that Bacon 'was no favourite with the [solicitors]'.[93] As Proust observed, there are many 'whose consummate professional experience inclines them to look down upon their profession, and who say, for instance: "I know I'm a good advocate, so it no longer amuses me to go through the motions"'.[94]

The advocate has to observe fine distinctions in this context. If he indicates too great an enthusiasm for infamous clients, he will be justly criticized. The biographer of F. E. Smith recognized that a barrister must act for anyone prepared to pay his fee, and 'evil men must have the same right to legal representation as good men to make the best case they can for them and force the prosecution to prove guilt against them.' So 'F. E.'s association with [the rogue, Horatio] Bottomley is technically unimpeachable. Yet in reality', he pointedly observed, 'there must be an ethical question mark against the frequency and evident relish with which he defended Bottomley.'[95]

After the conclusion of a case, the advocate is not obliged to maintain public support for the position of his client or indeed to maintain impartiality on the issues raised in the case (so long as he does not betray any confidences and complies with the professional rule that he may not in relation to any current matter in which he is or has been briefed or instructed comment to or in any news or current affairs media upon the facts of or the issues arising in that matter).[96] Indeed, the morality of advocacy depends, to some extent, on counsel not associating themselves out of court too closely with the interests of their clients. To the extent that the barrister is understood as the general representative of the client, sharing his beliefs and goals, it becomes more difficult to make the public understand that an advocate represents in court any client, whatever his views and conduct. Charles Fried rightly criticizes the fact that 'lawyers in the United States—unlike English barristers—too often consider it good business to identify personally and totally with their clients. . . . Lawyers for liquor companies feel they must drink and lawyers for tobacco companies feel they must smoke.'[97] It causes harm to the public understanding of advocacy for counsel to tell a judge who has just made a ruling in his favour (in that case granting leave to move for judicial review of the decision of a magistrate that the crime of blasphemy did not protect the feelings of Muslims), 'you have made a most remarkable decision through which we will find a peaceful solution for years to come'.[98] It similarly implies too close a connection between the advocate and the cause for counsel to give a radio interview to explain and justify the submissions he has been making in court, as did counsel in the blasphemy case.[99]

III

Few advocates would deny that the practice of advocacy can pose profound ethical dilemmas. The difficulty for the lawyer is that such problems occur 'suddenly and unlabelled for easy analysis'.[100] So difficult, and so sensitive, are the moral questions which may be raised by advocacy that it is quite inexcusable that the professional training of the advocate has, until very recently, given so little attention to the subject. It is of interest to note that the accreditation standards for American law schools were amended to require courses in legal ethics or professional responsibility in 1974, soon after 'the involvement of many lawyers in the Watergate scandal'.[101]

The morality of advocacy requires the lawyer to make submissions on behalf of those he thinks would richly deserve the harshest punishment. In 1923 the Calcutta High Court reprimanded defence counsel for speaking to the judge privately to 'apprise him that in his opinion the man, whose fate has been entrusted to his care, has no defence to make'.[102] Similar principles have been expressed by American courts. The US Court of Appeals stated in 1977 that counsel should not disclose to the court his 'private conjectures about the guilt or innocence of his client. It is the role of the judge or jury to determine the facts, not that of the attorney.'[103] So, in 1959, a man convicted of murder was held to have been denied his constitutional right to due process because his trial attorney 'candidly admit[ted] that his conscience prevented him from effectively representing his client according to the customary standards prescribed by attorneys and the courts'.[104]

A fundamental dilemma concerns the steps which counsel may properly take on behalf of a defendant who has told his lawyer that he is guilty of the crime alleged against him, yet declines to plead guilty. In such circumstances, the barrister must 'advise that all that can be done is to enter a plea of not guilty and rely on the failure of the prosecution to prove its case, but that the accused must not give evidence or call witnesses to prove his innocence, such, for example, as witnesses to prove an alibi'.[105] But it would be quite wrong for the defendant to be left undefended. This is not simply because the prosecution must prove guilt. It is also because, notwithstanding the confession, the defendant may, in fact, be innocent. For a number of reasons, people confess to crimes which they have not committed: they may be deluded, or seeking to shield another, or expressing moral guilt where no legal liability exists, or simply worn down by the strain of resisting the conclusion which the prosecution is urging on the court.

In 1840, Lord Russell was murdered in his bed. His Swiss servant, Courvoisier, was charged with the murder. He pleaded not guilty and was tried at the Old Bailey.[106] During the trial the defendant told his counsel, Charles Phillips, 'I committed the murder' but 'I expect you to defend me to the utmost'.[107] Phillips (whose eloquence in an earlier case was said to have been the model for the speech of Serjeant Buzfus in Charles Dickens's *Pickwick Papers*)[108] privately sought the advice of Baron Parke, one of the judges (though not the presiding judge) hearing the case. Baron Parke told Phillips that, in the circumstances, it was his duty to continue to represent the defendant 'and to use all fair arguments arising on the evidence'.[109] In those days, a man charged with a felony could not give evidence on his own behalf. Nor did Phillips call any other evidence for the defence (other than witnesses as to good character). But he submitted to the jury that they should acquit his client on the evidence before them. Courvoisier was convicted, and was hanged.

Opinions have differed on the propriety of Charles Phillips's conduct in the Courvoisier case. Richard du Cann QC concluded that Phillips acted properly because his submission was addressed to whether the jury could be sure that the prosecution had proved the case on the evidence before them.[110] Others have focused on the language used by Phillips in his closing speech to the jury. Unless the prosecution had proved its case, he urged the jury, 'I beseech you to be cautious how you imbrue your hands in this man's blood. The Omniscient God alone knows who did this crime'.[111] As David Mellinkoff has commented, 'there were those who thought that God had company'.[112]

A similar case arose in Australia in 1934. The High Court of Australia heard an appeal from a murder conviction which led to a sentence of death. After discussing the prosecution evidence with his client, and before beginning his cross-examination of a prosecution witness, counsel appearing for the defendant had told the trial judge, in front of the jury, that he 'was in a predicament, the worst predicament that he had encountered in all his legal career'. After the jury had convicted his client, the defence lawyer explained to the judge that the predicament was caused by the fact that the defendant confided that he had, as the prosecution evidence asserted, confessed that he was guilty of the offence. The High Court was unsympathetic. 'Why he should have conceived himself to have been in so great a predicament it is not easy for those experienced in advocacy to understand. He had a plain duty . . . to press such rational considerations as the evidence fairly gave rise to in favour of' his client who, 'whether he be in fact guilty or not . . . is, in point of law, entitled to acquittal from any charge which the evidence fails to establish that he committed'.[113]

It may, then, be proper for counsel for the defence to cross-examine prosecution witnesses for the purpose of discrediting their reliability or credibility even though the lawyer has good reason to think (because of what his client has told him) that the witness is telling the truth. Monroe Freedman gives the example of an old lady wearing glasses who is a prosecution witness and testifies (accurately, as the defendant has told his counsel) that the defendant was near the scene of the crime at the relevant time.[114] The problem arises in reconciling the duty to test the evidence with the duty not to present, on behalf of the client, a case which falsely suggests that the defendant was elsewhere. Because the client *may* have been elsewhere, notwithstanding what he has told his lawyer, and because it is for the prosecution to prove its case, it may be appropriate to cross-examine such a witness to assess whether the old lady can see well even with her glasses, what the lighting conditions were, how far away she was from the man she claims to have seen, what she remembers him to have been wearing. If the witness has some reason for exaggerating her evidence—a previous animus against the defendant, perhaps—this should be brought out by way of cross-examination.

It would be improper to put on the witness-stand to give evidence a witness who the advocate knows (because the witness has confided in him) will commit perjury. But what is the advocate to do if a client who is charged with a criminal offence insists on giving evidence which, he tells his advocate, will be perjured?[115] One solution is for the advocate to seek to withdraw from the case, preserving client confidentiality by telling the judge only that irreconcilable conflicts have arisen between him and his client. If the judge declines to allow counsel to withdraw, perhaps because of the stage which the trial has reached, then counsel should permit the client to give evidence, but should not lend any assistance to the perjury. He should not ask the client any questions by way of examination-in-chief, other than to invite him to make his statement to the court. Nor would it be proper to refer to this evidence when counsel makes his closing submissions.[116] A better view is that the advocate should not assist the client to produce evidence which the lawyer knows (because the client so informs him) is perjured. The advocate should simply decline to lend any assistance to the client who wishes to commit perjury and so should refuse to call him to give evidence. The US Court of Appeals has held that such a refusal cannot amount to a breach of the defendant's constitutional rights.[117] The practical difficulty, of course, is that the advocate will normally only suspect, not know, that the evidence is going to be perjured. In such circumstances, it is a matter for the court, not the lawyer, to decide on its veracity and so the advocate should not prevent the client from giving such evidence.

Similar problems arise where the client informs his advocate, after giving evidence, that he has perjured himself. Again, one solution is for the advocate to seek to excuse himself from the trial. If this is not allowed, he should make no use of the perjured testimony. But there is authority for the proposition that he should go further and make a full report to the court of the criminal acts of his client.[118] Again, such ethical dilemmas only arise where the advocate *knows* that perjured evidence has been given.

The answers to the moral dilemmas faced by the trial lawyer must be founded in a principled conception of the function of the advocate. His task is to present to the court the case for one party, so as to ensure that legal rights and duties are determined by reference to all the relevant facts and law. But it is not the function of the advocate to assist his client to mislead the court. To draw a dividing line between what is proper, and what is improper, is not an easy task. Geoffrey Hazard has pointed to the essential paradox involved in such dilemmas of legal ethics: lawyers are trained to focus on what the rules actually say and they are skilled in assisting their clients to avoid inconvenient applications of the regulations by making fine distinctions; to ask lawyers to apply to themselves principles of ethics which they should operate by reference to their spirit and not seek to distinguish by creative reasoning therefore requires of them something outside their normal mode of professional operation.[119]

Until very recently, certain rules of the barrister's code of conduct expressly required the barrister to mislead the court on matters of fact and so could not be justified. The 1989 Code of Conduct stated that 'defending counsel is not under any duty to correct any misstatement of fact made by the prosecution'. So, if the prosecution erroneously led the court to believe that an accused had no previous convictions, 'defence counsel is under no duty to disclose facts to the contrary which are known to him, nor correct any information given by the prosecution if such disclosure or correction would be to his client's detriment'. In such circumstances, the defence counsel must merely 'take care not to lend himself to any assertion that his client has no convictions or no more than a limited number of convictions or to ask a prosecution witness whether there are previous convictions against his client in the hope that he will receive a negative answer'.[120] As late as 1989, the Code of Conduct surprisingly suggested that in a criminal case, once the judge has begun to sum-up to the jury, 'a defence barrister is under no duty to draw matters of fact or law to the court's attention unless he considers that to do so would be to the advantage of his lay client'.[121] Presumably such statements were included in the Code because they were thought consistent with the prosecution duty to prove the case against the defendant. In relation to details of previous convictions, it was presumably thought that to require defence counsel to provide information supplied to him by his client would unjustifiably breach confidence. Without such principles, it may have been thought, no informed defendant would confide in his counsel or entrust him with such information.

But there should be limits to such principles. It is wrong to impose on counsel a duty to conceal from the court matters of legal record upon which there is no dispute but which the judge and the prosecution have simply misunderstood or not appreciated. Whether they relate to previous convictions, or to errors by the judge, such rules have no moral basis. They require defence counsel to participate in deception of the court or to further the maladministration of justice on false premisses. They make much more difficult the task of the advocate in seeking to persuade the public that his function contributes to justice. Such unprincipled rules have no place in the ethics of the profession.

Important though it is to maintain the confidentiality of discussions between the lawyer and his client, lawyers cannot justify the absolute nature of the duty of confidence asserted by some American courts. In 1976 the Supreme Court of Arizona held that the judge in a murder trial was correct to exclude evidence which the defence wished to call from two lawyers. Those lawyers were willing to tell the jury that another man, their client (who was dead), had confessed to them that he was guilty of the murder which the defendant was accused of committing. That legal confidentiality should be valued more highly than material evidence when a man is on trial for murder will understandably strike laymen as a quite astonishing proposition. (The defendant's conviction was reversed on other grounds.)[122] By contrast, in a 1981 ruling the Bar Council of New South Wales demonstrated greater wisdom by regarding human life as a higher value than client confidentiality. It decided that when a barrister was acting for the wife in a case concerning the custody of her children, and that client told the lawyer that if she lost the case she would shoot the children (and the lawyer believed that his client was capable of this act), it was the duty of the barrister to inform the judge, counsel for the husband, and (through his instructing solicitor) the police.[123]

IV

The reality is that there is a conflict between the professional and the lay approach to the ethics of advocacy. The lawyer addresses the issue from the legal perspective. Competent advocacy, performed within the confines of professional duties not to mislead the court, will further the objectives of the law by helping to ensure that the correct legal result is achieved, or that the judge or the jury have been provided with the information required to make the best legal decision possible.

By contrast the layman is not so interested in the ethics of the legal system. His main concern is that the law should achieve morally and socially acceptable results. To the extent that the answer reached in court is perceived to be unfair or unjust, or a villain escapes the punishment or the liability which he richly deserves, the advocate who has contributed to that end is considered to be earning his fee from morally dubious practices. The layman is not convinced by the contention that the advocate would be taking the place of the judge were he to assess whether his client has a good case. Many advocates act for defendants who they have every reason to believe are guilty, and represent clients in civil litigation when they have no real doubt that the law requires a particular result or that the submissions which they are making would lead to a result which is morally and socially undesirable.[124] The weakness of the defence of advocacy advanced by Dr Johnson is that, whatever his legal ability, the advocate may be as well equipped as the judge to assess whether the interests of society are going to be advanced by success for the cause for which the advocate is pleading. If wrongdoing would be promoted by the triumph of that cause, whatever the legal rights and wrongs as determined by the judge, the advocate has to recognize that he is contributing to the furtherance of a social mischief.

The advocate knows that whether or not the system of advocacy has a moral basis will not prevent him from reflecting on the social consequences of his oratory. He will often find it difficult to reconcile his conscience with his professional mask of indifference to the result of his submissions. He appreciates that, depending how competently he performs his work, a wrongdoer may escape the punishment he merits, or the sum total of human happiness may be reduced, for no good purpose. Advocacy does result in offensive, objectionable, and, on occasion, evil people gaining benefits to which the law entitles them, or avoiding detriments from which they have a legal immunity. Powerful advocacy may persuade the court to reach an erroneous conclusion on the facts or the law, giving a litigant something to which he has no legal right (such as an acquittal from a criminal charge). As the US Court of Appeals has recognized, 'in our complex society, the accountant's certificate and the lawyer's opinion can be instruments for inflicting pecuniary loss more potent than the chisel or the crowbar'.[125]

The advocate cannot avoid adopting some responsibility for what he has helped to secure. The future happiness of people—all those involved in the case, not merely his client, and sometimes other people who may be affected by the precedent established by the judgment—can depend on what he says and does in court. The decision, as he is told by his profession and as he constantly repeats to himself in hard ethical cases, is made by the judge, not by the advocate who therefore bears no responsibility for it. His advocacy may be even less persuasive in this private respect than it was in court. No advocate of sensibility wholly resists the temptation to agonize over the consequences of his work. No amount of professional balm can completely heal a moral vacuum in the nature of advocacy as diagnosed by Tolstoy in *Resurrection*. A man 'was expatiating on the remarkable way a celebrated lawyer had handled his case, whereby one of the parties, an old lady who was entirely in the right, would have to pay a huge sum to the other side. "A brilliant lawyer!", he said.' Tolstoy describes how

> During a recess the old lady came out whose property that genius of a lawyer had succeeded in getting hold of for his sharp-witted client, who had not the slightest right to it—which the judges knew, and the plaintiff and his counsel knew even better; but the case had been so presented that there was nothing for it but to take the old lady's property and hand it

over to the sharp dealer. The old lady was a stout woman in her best clothes with enormous flowers in her bonnet. Coming through the door she stopped in the corridor and, making a helpless gesture with her hands, kept repeating, 'But what will happen? I beg of you, what does it mean?', as she turned to her lawyer. The lawyer was looking at the flowers on her bonnet and not listening to her, preoccupied with something else.

Following the old lady out of the doors of the Civil Court, starched shirt-front resplendent under his low-cut waistcoat, a self-satisfied look on his face, hurried the famous advocate who had fixed matters in such a way that the old lady with the flowers lost all she had, while the smart fellow, his client, for a fee of ten thousand roubles, had got his hands on over a hundred thousand. Aware that all eyes were directed upon him, his whole bearing seemed to say: 'Please, I don't need any acts of homage', and quickly made his way through the crowd.[126]

The reality is that advocates have to recognize that the ethics of their profession are not so plain and obvious. There is a real moral conflict which they need to explain to laymen. The practice of advocacy on behalf of the evil, the dangerous, and the simply unpleasant elements in our society *may* advance the interests of such bad causes. Advocates cannot continue plausibly to suggest that advocacy does only moral good. But, we need to explain to the public, the absence of a profession of advocates, with a duty to represent to the best of our ability all clients irrespective of their merit, would cause much more moral harm to occur within the legal system. Advocates need to remind the layman that we have adopted, as the best available method of government, a system dependent on the rule of law, one in which rights and duties are determined not by the exercise of discretion on the facts of an individual case, or by reference to the popularity of the litigant, but by the application of general rules announced in advance. So long as we maintain such a system as preferable to any other, and so long as we continue to enjoy the democratic right to change those laws when they are considered to be unjust or inappropriate, the advocate contributes to a just society by performing his professional function of arguing the case for his client as part of the process by which an independent judge assesses what those general rules permit or demand. The role of the advocate in Nazi Germany, or any other totalitarian society, obviously poses very different questions. Since advocacy is an indispensable part of a democratic society based on the rule of law, the unfairness which advocacy can promote is a fair price to pay for the maintenance of such a political structure. And it should not be forgotten that it is the client, not the advocate, who decides whether—and how—to enforce his legal rights in a democratic society. If such conduct causes unfairness to others, it is the client, not the advocate, who should be criticized.

The moral defence of advocacy has important consequences for the nature of the legal services provided to the community. If 'to promote justice the adversary procedure involves advocacy of contrary contentions by representatives with special gifts and training',[127] it is essential to ensure that the case for each side is indeed presented by an advocate who is at least competent to raise for the consideration of the judge or jury all relevant facts and matters. To the extent that one party is represented by an advocate who is incompetent, the function of advocacy (to assist the court to see the strengths of the competing arguments on both sides) is frustrated. The legal profession and the judiciary have a responsibility to ensure that only those advocates who are competent are allowed to offer their services to the public. Lawyers also have a duty to ensure that all sectors of society have access to skilled advocates who can present their case in court. The importance of an effective legal aid system, providing specialist advocates for those members of the community who could not otherwise afford the fees, is thus vital to the proper administration of justice. At present, the legal aid system is creaking badly. Any Government must make expenditure on legal aid a high priority in defence of the rule of law.[128] The advocate has a duty, not least because of the considerable benefits he obtains from the legal system, to provide a part of his services on a voluntary basis *pro bono publico* (for the good of the public) where necessary to help ensure that access to justice is not denied to those who lack financial resources. It must be for each individual to decide what charitable activities he is willing to undertake to support the rule of law. But it is desirable that the advocate's Code of Conduct should encourage such philanthropy. The American Bar Association Model Rules of Professional Conduct provide a useful precedent. Rule 6.1 states:

> A lawyer should render public interest legal service. A lawyer may discharge this responsibility by providing professional services at no fee or a reduced fee to persons of limited means or to public service or charitable groups or organizations, by service in activities for improving the law, the legal system or the legal profession, and by financial support for organizations that provide legal services to persons of limited means.[129]

Such activities may help to persuade the public of the essential truth that advocacy is a force for moral good in a democratic society.

CHAPTER 6

Reform

I

THE morality of advocacy depends on the judge receiving the best possible argument from each side to assist him to decide what the law allows, requires, or prohibits. Until recently, the Bar and the Bench applied a series of antiquated practices which hindered the furtherance of this goal. Rights of audience in the higher courts were unjustifiably confined to barristers, limiting the number of advocates from whom the client could choose, and preventing competition which would help to raise standards. The Bar maintained professional rules in relation to advertising and conduct which restricted the publication of important information about the nature of the services on offer and thereby detracted from, rather than advanced, the ability of the lawyer effectively to serve his clients.

Few laymen doubt, and only the most complacent of lawyers would dispute, that such restrictive practices have been a serious impediment to providing a quality service to meet the demands of the community. By the application of those practices, some of which would bring envious tears to the eyes of the toughest trade union official, the legal profession has defied the laws of competitive gravity and angered its customers. Lawyers are resented for their closed shops, inefficient procedures, and general self-satisfaction. Those who use the system complain about the delays, the expense, and, on occasion, the poor quality of the service. Public resentment of those practices is such that not even the combined powers of advocacy of all lawyers could begin to persuade a lay audience that the administration of the law is consistent with the public interest. Since the appointment of Lord Mackay as Lord Chancellor in 1987, much necessary progress has been made in these and other respects.

In 1840, the Court of Common Pleas held that the Serjeants at Law (a small group of barristers) were entitled to the exclusive right of audience in that court. During the delivery of the judgment, so the law reporter noted, 'a furious tempest of wind prevailed, which seemed to shake the fabric of Westminster Hall, and nearly burst open the windows and doors of the Court . . .'.[1] A century and a half later, the restrictive practices governing rights of audience in the law courts remain a sensitive subject productive of much wind, as demonstrated by the difficult passage through Parliament of the Courts and Legal Services Act.

The Government understandably wished to apply to the legal system the elementary truths elsewhere accepted: that free competition, buttressed by the minimum of necessary regulation, is good for the consumer. This was the framework of the Green Paper, *The Work and Organisation of the Legal Profession*, published in January 1989, which proposed fundamental reforms of the profession, in particular to allow some solicitors rights of audience in the Crown Court and the High Court.[2] Virginia Woolf observed in the 1930s that the daily toil of the barrister 'leaves very little time for friendship, travel or art. . . . That explains why most successful barristers are hardly worth sitting next [to] at dinner—they yawn so'.[3] The dinner-table conversation of lawyers was considerably enlivened by their opposition to the proposed reforms.

Lord Chief Justice Lane condemned the Lord Chancellor's Green Paper as 'one of the most sinister documents ever to emanate from Government'.[4] He warned, with an astonishing disregard of the inappropriate nature of the analogy, that 'oppression does not stand on the doorstep with a toothbrush moustache and a swastika armband'.[5] Lord Ackner (a Law Lord) suggested, extravagantly, that the Government was 'hell-bent on the destruction of the Bar'.[6] Lord Donaldson (Master of the Rolls) told the Lord Chancellor, 'in the terms reportedly employed by a distinguished former Prime Minister to a distinguished former president of the AUEW . . . "Get your tanks off my lawn"'.[7] The Government was 'thinking with its bottom and sitting on its head', according to the former Lord Chancellor, Lord Hailsham.[8] 'Dog licences', as Lord Rawlinson QC (the former Attorney-General) contemptuously suggested in a letter to *The Times*,[9] would have to be sought by anyone who wished to practise as an advocate. Lord Alexander QC felt 'bound to say that if the language of [the proposals for reform] had emanated from the Government of South Africa, there would have been howls of cynical protest throughout the civilized world'.[10] Lord Chancellor Mackay had evidently touched some very raw nerves.

What was it about this proposal to extend rights of audience in the Crown Court and the High Court to qualified lawyers other than barristers which provoked such an outraged response? The distinction between the lawyer who represents another for the purposes of litigation and the lawyer who speaks for him in court was 'fundamental in early law'.[11] Although based on a premiss of great antiquity, and although in some respects it may have 'greatly contributed not only to the dignity of the Bar but to the improvement of English jurisprudence',[12] the division of labour between barristers and solicitors is far from logical. The solicitor had long enjoyed a right of audience in the County Court; in the Magistrates' Court; and in High Court proceedings heard in chambers, but not those conducted in open court, other than in certain bankruptcy applications or in wholly exceptional circumstances (for instance when counsel had to leave court and the client would otherwise be unrepresented).[13] The solicitor could represent his client in the industrial tribunal and on appeal to the Employment Appeal Tribunal. But, however satisfied the client might be with his services, the solicitor could not appear on a further appeal to the Court of Appeal. Perhaps one should not expect too much sense from a legal system in which, according to the Master of the Rolls, the Treasury Solicitor 'being in fact a member of the Bar, is incapable of obtaining a practising certificate'[14] (though the position may be held by a solicitor),[15] and in which (by constitutional convention) the Solicitor-General must be a barrister.

But even by the standards of the legal system, it was an obvious anachronism—and the most sensitive nerve for the Bar—that the barrister enjoyed an exclusive right of audience in the High Court and in the Crown Court in relation to trials on indictment (though not in other circumstances), however eager the client was to have his solicitor speak for him, and however competent the solicitor was to represent the interests of that client in court as well as out of court. In 1867, Mr Justice Byles held that a solicitor could not, on behalf of his client, even assent to a verdict in a case in the High Court. This was, said the judge (in a refreshingly frank statement of the basis of the monopoly interest involved) 'for the sake of members of the Bar'.[16] The litigant had to brief counsel, irrespective of his wishes. In 1889, a solicitor at Quarter Sessions for the Borough of Oswestry told the Recorder that 'he was instructed to defend a prisoner, his instructions being expressly not to instruct counsel'. The court declined to hear him.[17]

An important reason for the offended tone of the judicial response to the Green Paper was that the judiciary had jealously guarded its right to determine who appeared as an advocate in various courts. As Mr Justice Parke stated in 1831, 'no person has a right to act as an advocate without the leave of the Court, which must of necessity have the power of regulating its own proceedings in all cases where they are not already regulated by ancient usage'.[18] Even the successful attempt by a solicitor to represent his client by presenting written submissions to the court has excited judicial concern. This was, said Lord Justice Danckwerts in the Court of Appeal in 1966, 'wholly irregular and contrary to the practice of the court and . . . should not be allowed as a precedent for future proceedings'.[19] Indeed, the exercise by solicitors of the rights of advocacy which they enjoyed in County Courts was subject to the criticism of many judges. When, in 1885, a solicitor who was sued for negligence explained that he was employed by the firm to act as an advocate in County Court and other cases where solicitors had a right of audience, the judge in Warwick County Court, His Honour Sir Richard Harington, said that 'he never allowed that sort of thing in his Courts. It was a most reprehensible practice, and he wished there was some penalty for it. Such a system was unjust to the client and unfair to the Bar. It was much better that gentlemen who had entered as solicitors should keep to their own duties instead of undertaking those which should be properly discharged by counsel'.[20] Barristers were accustomed to getting their own way, even when they travelled abroad. When the first English barristers arrived in New South Wales, Australia, in 1824, they successfully persuaded the Supreme Court to compel 'the gentlemen at present practising as solicitors and acting as barristers . . . to retire from the Bar'.[21]

The width of the monopoly on High Court advocacy enjoyed by the Bar, and its absurdity, had been demonstrated in 1985. The Bar foolishly opposed the modest suggestion that a solicitor (Mr Alastair Brett) be allowed the right of audience in the High Court to read out on behalf of his client (Mr Cyril Smith MP) an agreed statement in settlement of a libel action. There was no rational reason why the client should be obliged to pay a barrister to read such a statement. No skills of advocacy were required, the case having already been resolved, with the terms of settlement having received the approval of the judge. This was no more and no less than a restrictive practice working to the undoubted advantage of members of the Bar but based on no conceivable public interest. Yet the then Chairman of the Bar, Robert Alexander QC, wrote to *The Times* in support of the status quo, pleading that 'it is open to the parties . . . to read the statement for themselves. If they do not choose to do so, it is surely reasonable that the barrister should see the case through to the end.'[22] The matter was considered by the Court of Appeal. The Master of the Rolls (Sir John Donaldson) explained that the judges meeting collectively had the power to decide whether, in the public interest, established general practices relating to rights of audience should be modified.[23] Less than five months later, after such collective consideration of the issues by the judiciary, the rights of audience of solicitors in the High Court were extended to cover proceedings—such as the reading out of libel statements—where by reason of agreement between the parties there is unlikely to be any argument and the court will not be called upon to exercise a discretion.[24] In their judgments in the 1985 case, Sir John Donaldson and Lord Justice May emphasized that what mattered in this context was to ensure that the public interest was being served. Lord Justice May (perhaps generously) had 'no doubt that both branches of the profession have this well in mind'.[25]

As a result of the Courts and Legal Services Act 1990, the parties will no longer be told by the Bar, or the judiciary, that the public interest requires a monopoly on advocacy for barristers. Lawyers (solicitors as well as barristers) who are fully trained and licensed in advocacy will be permitted to address judges on behalf of their clients in the higher courts of the land. The Bar, surprisingly for a profession whose expertise is advocacy, was slow to tell the public that the reforms do not question the need for the continuance of a specialist independent Bar and would not threaten the survival of the barrister's profession. Barristers always have been briefed to represent clients in courts and tribunals where solicitors already had a right of audience (such as Magistrates' Courts, County Courts, Industrial Tribunals, Planning Inquiries, arbitrations, and hearings before the Judge in Chambers). This is for three reasons: because solicitors think (correctly) that barristers have special skills of advocacy; because solicitors recognize, as do their clients, that it is to their advantage to obtain the services of someone objective to give independent advice and to present those points which truly have weight; and because solicitors often find that it is cheaper for the client, and more convenient to the solicitor, to brief a barrister than to conduct the case themselves. There is every reason to think that the same will be true now that some solicitors will have extended rights of audience in the Crown Court and the High Court.

Most important of all, the Bar ought to be reminding the public that it neither wants, nor needs, restrictive practices to prove its worth. Barristers should be prepared to be judged by their performance. They are confident that they do meet a need, that (in general) they provide a good service, and that they will survive as a profession. If the Bar cannot prosper in an atmosphere of competition, then it needs to improve its standards.

A few (but not many) solicitors will wish to undertake advocacy training and then subject themselves to the daily ritual of performing before unpredictable and irritable judges. Some barristers will be offered, and even fewer will accept, partnerships in large City firms. Why should solicitors' firms seek to recruit skilled barristers when it is in the interests of their clients to have access to the various talents of an independent Bar rather than to a limited number of in-house advocates? Why should leading barristers accept such appointments when they so value their independence and their freedom from the chore of constant contact with the client? At a more junior level, some young lawyers and students who aspire to advocacy will opt for the security of salaried life as a solicitor, but many will remain who will risk the independence, detachment, and potential rewards of a career at the Bar. The life of the barrister will continue much as before, save that the monopoly which understandably brought ridicule and scorn on the legal system will have been removed, lawyers will have an expanded career choice, competition will rightly have been encouraged, and standards ought to rise.

II

For decades the Bar Council imposed on lawyers medieval standards of conduct and etiquette which made no contribution to the public interest and created a popular perception of barristers as out of touch with the modern world.

The rules of the profession demonstrated an idiosyncratic preoccupation with irrelevancies. What barristers wore in court under their wigs and gowns was, for reasons that could be comprehensible only to psychologists, of especial interest to those who regulated the profession. In the sixteenth century, the Benchers of Lincoln's Inn prohibited barristers from having beards.[26] In 1910, it was regarded as 'improper and disrespectful to the Court for a barrister to appear in Court robed and at the same time arrayed in a white waistcoat, or in any coat or waistcoat not black or very dark in colour (the allowance claimed in some quarters for blue garments is to be deprecated), or to wear any but a white tie beneath the bands or to "sport" a flower in his button-hole. Fancy buttons on the garments and coloured shirts or collars should be avoided.'[27] It was not long ago that a magistrate refused to listen to the submissions of an advocate wearing brown suede shoes because 'your footwear is more suitable for the golf course than for [a] court of law'.[28] The 1980 edition of the Code of Conduct for the Bar of England and Wales advised that 'suits and dresses should be of dark colour. Dresses or blouses should be long-sleeved and high to the neck. Men should wear waistcoats. Shirts and blouses should be predominantly white or of other unemphatic appearance. Collars should be white and shoes black.'[29] And it is remarkable that, in 1983, a barrister author should advise beginners in the art of advocacy that 'ideal wear—unless you are utterly determined to make a political statement—is still the black jacket and waistcoat with striped trousers'.[30]

The Bar also maintained an extraordinary interest in regulating minor matters of personal conduct. Many of the most ridiculous rules imposed by the Bar Council were a statement of a devout belief in a professional status that would be demeaned and destroyed by any vulgar manifestation of trade. Self-promotion was the mark of the tradesman, and so any publicity was anathema to the professional. In his standard work on advocacy, written in 1946, Sir Malcolm Hilbery emphasized, with a sense of priorities which is astonishing viewed from the 1990s, that the 'first commandment which [the barrister] finds he must obey is, "Thou shalt not advertise or solicit work". . . . [This] is in the highest degree improper. It is beneath the dignity of the Bar. . . . This rule . . . protects the public by helping to ensure that their work is obtained and done by men for no other reason than that they are competent.'[31]

It was thought that if the barrister were to come into too close a proximity with others, he would be tempted to mention his occupation, with disastrous consequences for the wellbeing of the legal system. In the nineteenth century, 'a barrister on the Norfolk Circuit was forbidden to travel directly to a circuit town in a private conveyance accompanied by [a solicitor] or in a public coach, to enter a circuit town before the opening of the assizes there, and until the 1850s to lodge in public hotels in most of the circuit towns'.[32] In 1968, the Bar Council made the pompous pronouncement that there was no longer any objection (it is extraordinary that there ever had been) 'to practising barristers associating freely with solicitors and other professional persons, e.g. accountants, who are in a position to send work to counsel, either socially or in the course of attending professional conferences'.[33] In 1984, the Bar solemnly announced that 'it is inappropriate for chambers to use compliment slips on which the names of all members of chambers are printed' but that 'there is no objection to chambers informing regular solicitor clients that a facsimile machine has been installed'.[34] As late as the February 1989 edition, the *Code of Conduct* for the Bar still purported to specify what information a barrister's visiting card might contain, to forbid the use of the description 'barrister' or 'barrister-at-law' on chambers' or private stationery, and to regulate when solicitors could be invited to chambers' parties.[35] It was ironic, to say the least, that the Bar Council should greet the Lord Chancellor's proposals for reform of the legal profession in 1989 by warning that the application of supervisory control from outside the Temple would threaten the lawyer's 'independence'.

There was no excuse, other than an inability to think logically and progressively, for the Bar Council to have maintained an obsession about the advertising of the services of a professional man. The only restraints which are required are those expressed by the British Code of Advertising Practice of the Advertising Standards Authority: that advertising should be legal, decent, honest, and truthful. It was always an insult to the care with which almost all solicitors look after the interests of their clients for the Bar Council to imply that solicitors could be bribed or misled into providing work to barristers by an invitation to a chambers' party or by the contents of a barrister's visiting card.

More fundamentally, the standards imposed by the Bar ignored the vital interests of legal consumers in knowing what services were available, who could expertly provide them, and at what price. It was undoubtedly in the interests of a lazy profession, untroubled by competition and disinclined to consider how it could improve standards and reduce costs, to prohibit the supply of information which might lead intelligent laymen to ask critical questions about the manner in which legal services were organized and distributed.

The US Supreme Court and the European Court of Human Rights have recognized that freedom of expression extends to advertising, which is to the advantage of the consumer in the context of legal services as elsewhere. The citizen's 'interest in the free flow of commercial information . . . may be as keen, if not keener by far, than his interest in the day's most urgent political debate'.[36] In 1977, the US Supreme Court held unconstitutional as a violation of freedom of expression a State Bar rule which prohibited attornies from advertising the scale of their fees. The Court explained that 'commercial speech serves to inform the public of the availability, nature and prices of products and services, and thus performs an indispensable role in the allocation of resources in a free enterprise system'.[37] Such compelling reasoning is much to be preferred to the complacent platitudes expressed in 1979 on the same subject by the Royal Commission on Legal Services: 'information about the services provided by individual barristers may be obtained by those who require it without resort to individual advertising'.[38]

The US Supreme Court was correct to note that 'cynicism with regard to the [legal] profession may be created by the fact that it long has publicly eschewed advertising, while condoning the actions of the attorney who structures his social or civic associations so as to provide contacts with potential clients'.[39] Barristers have always had 'acceptable' ways of advertising their services. The future Lord Chancellor Camden found, as a young barrister in the mid-eighteenth century, that 'not inviting [solicitors] to dine with him, and never dancing with their daughters, his practice did not improve'.[40] In modern times, as the US Supreme Court recognized, since 'the belief that lawyers are somehow "above" trade has become an anachronism, the historical foundation for the advertising restraint has crumbled'.[41] It has, for a long time, been obvious that a good advertisement for the legal system would be to abandon all rules that prevented lawyers from telling the public the truth about their fees and their services. It is a disgrace that the legal profession, whose very existence is inextricably linked with the merits of freedom of expression,[42] should for so long dedicate itself to prohibiting and punishing the supply of information about its practices to those it purports to serve.

The intensity of the legal reaction to some of the reforms proposed by the Lord Chancellor in 1989 was partly explicable by the inherent conservatism of lawyers and by the fact that most judges are, in the words of Oliver Wendell Holmes (the great US Supreme Court judge of the early decades of this century), 'elderly men, and are more likely to hate at sight any analysis to which they are not accustomed, and which disturbs repose of mind, than to fall in love with novelties'.[43] But the reaction was also the inevitable consequence of the extent to which lawyers were cocooned from changes in their working practices for most of the 1970s and 1980s. While other aspects of society were subjected to critical analysis which resulted in fundamental change to their structure and conduct, the legal profession was protected from reform by Lord Chancellor Hailsham during his periods of office from 1970 to 1974 and 1979 to 1987.

From the time of his appointment as Lord Chancellor in 1987, Lord Mackay abandoned the ridiculous rules that prevented judges from speaking on the radio and television.[44] He refrained from condemning any press criticism of judicial decisions as a threat to judicial independence. He imposed the discipline of competition on the practices of the Bar. The breadth of the reforms, and the pace of the change, are the result of trying to make up for lost time. The Bar and the judiciary have found, for the first time in decades, that the Lord Chancellor does not have the same values as them. The novelty of fresh air has made the occupants of the stuffy Inns of Court feel distinctly queasy. What is so extraordinary is that, in the wake of the Government's proposals for reform of the legal profession, the Bar Council has been forced to reassess its standards and has suddenly appreciated that many of the restrictions, such as those on advertising, so long retained as vital to the integrity of the legal system, were in fact pointless relics of a bygone age which damaged the image of the lawyer and hindered his ability to serve the public.

Barristers are now permitted to advertise, subject to conformity with the British Code of Advertising Practice. Such advertising or promotion may include photographs of the barrister, statements of rates and methods of charging, details of the nature and extent of the barrister's services, and, with the express written consent of a client (though it is impossible to see why such consent should be required when the fact that the barrister has acted in a leading case is already public knowledge from newspaper or law reports), the name of any client.[45] By 1989, the only rule regulating dress in court simply stated that a barrister must dress 'in a manner which is appropriate for appearance in Court and which will be unobtrusive and compatible with the wearing of robes'.[46] By 1990, the Code wisely thought it unnecessary to make any mention of couture, save that a barrister's 'personal appearance should be decorous and his dress, when robes are worn, should be compatible with them'.[47] It will not be long before the absurd anachronism of wearing wigs and gowns in court is abandoned.[48]

Save for the duty not to betray confidences, public comment by barristers about their own cases is now restricted only in relation to observations to or in 'news or current affairs media upon the facts of or the issues arising' in relation to 'any current matter'.[49] This would appear to allow barristers to write about their own current cases in scholarly journals. And they may write or speak about their own cases once they cease to be current (so long as confidences are respected).

The creation, by section 21 of the Courts and Legal Services Act, of a Legal Services Ombudsman to investigate the manner in which a professional body has considered a complaint against an advocate should help to maintain high standards and reassure the public that complaints will receive independent assessment. It may, in the future, depending on the success of the Ombudsman, be appropriate to move towards the more open procedures adopted by many US States for the consideration of complaints alleging lawyer incompetence. Because lawyers have no monopoly of wisdom on the content of proper ethical standards, and because of concern to maintain objectivity, 'several State Bar associations have relinquished to independent bodies their authority to discipline lawyers and issue ethical opinions'.[50]

There have always been barristers—their shirts not predominantly white, their visiting cards containing unauthorized material—who have resented the controls imposed by the Bar Council as a wholly unjustified interference, contrary to the public interest, by an overpowerful regulatory body in matters which are no concern of theirs. Until recently, that was a dissident view. The reforms introduced by Lord Chancellor Mackay have precipitated changes in the English legal system so fundamental as to render almost incredible that we tolerated so meekly and for so long as arbitrary and as conservative a regime as that imposed by the Bar Council.

III

The Legal Aid and Advice Act 1949 aimed, as its long title explained, to make legal representation 'more readily available for persons of small or moderate means' in criminal and civil cases. The Act recognized that access to law may be as important as access to education and health services, for without access to law we are unable to enforce the other civil rights to which we are entitled.

Considerable strains are now being imposed on the maintenance of this worthy principle. Legal rights and remedies are ever developing in their sophistication and scope. To the constant surprise of lawyers, most of whom would avoid personal involvement in litigation at almost any cost, laymen are increasingly eager to litigate problems which would once have been resolved more or less amicably outside court. As Lord Mackay, the Lord Chancellor, lamented, the result of this demand for lawyers is that the cost of legal aid is increasing rapidly. 'Resources are finite', the Lord Chancellor has warned.[51]

Despite the cost, defects in the structure of legal aid are in need of urgent repair. The financial criteria for receipt of legal aid now leave a large number of people ineligible for the benefit, but insufficiently wealthy to pay for litigation out of their own pockets. The result is the frustration of the principle expressed by the Attorney-General, Sir Hartley Shawcross, when introducing the Bill in 1948: that it was 'the charter of the little man' which would 'open the doors of the courts freely to all persons who may wish to avail themselves of British justice without regard to the question of their wealth or ability to pay'.[52]

The problem is to find ways to provide the funds for legal aid. The cost can be reduced, in part, by seeking to deter litigation which would not occur if the parties were paying for it themselves. Lawyers are very familiar with civil cases in which wholly unreasonable clients refuse to resolve differences sensibly because they are not contributing towards their day in court. Lawyers and judges should take more seriously their obligations to inform the legal aid fund of circumstances which may justify the removal of legal aid. The minds of those who are tempted to abuse legal aid would be focused by the introduction of an 'excess' of £100 for legal aid, that is a contribution to be paid by all those in receipt of the benefit (with an exception for litigants on income support) unless the judge awards costs in their favour at the hearing.

We rightly take for granted a legal aid system which a leader of the American Bar Association condemned in 1951 as 'part of an increasing menace' by which 'communists have made great efforts to infiltrate their own kind into the profession'.[53] What was once politically controversial, and remains so in other parts of the world, is now rightly recognized in this country as an essential aspect of social justice. The need to finance legal aid in the 1990s should be seized as an opportunity to implement, for reasons of economic efficiency, the major structural reforms for which progressive thinkers have long argued in the interests of equity.

Lower legal aid bills may be helped by cutting legal costs through such measures as the greater use of small claims courts, the transfer of business to the County Courts, and the operation of pre-trial reviews. The removal of restrictive practices relating to advertising and rights of advocacy should reduce costs to the consumer by promoting competition and increasing knowledge of where a good service can be obtained at a cheaper price. If compensation for victims of accidents could, at last, be made dependent on need rather than on an assessment of fault, the legal system would cease to consume resources that could be better spent on meeting the requirements of the afflicted.

The continuing limitations of legal aid make essential the search for other methods of financing litigation. The recognition that lawyers should ease, rather than inhibit, access to the courts also justifies the removal of the ban on fees which are conditional on the result of the litigation. English law has traditionally condemned the contingent fee as 'contrary to public policy'.[54] The prohibition of such fee arrangements was needed, said Lord Esher MR in 1896, 'in order to preserve the honour and honesty of the profession'.[55] Because a lawyer's duty is to advise his client 'with a clear eye and an unbiased judgment' and because he has a duty to the court 'to ensure that his client's case . . . [is] presented and conducted with scrupulous fairness and integrity', Lord Justice Buckley concluded that the lawyer must not have any financial interest in the outcome of the legal proceedings.[56] The opposition to contingent fees has focused on the undesirability of lawyers agreeing to receive a high percentage of any damages which might be recovered by their client, this being thought to encourage the promotion and settlement of actions on a basis valuable to the lawyer but not to the client or to society.

The idea that the validity of any form of conditional fee would lead to lawyers abandoning their objectivity and misleading the court is insulting to the integrity of those who practise at the Bar and dismissive of the abilities of the judiciary and the professional bodies to impose sanctions on those who might be tempted by financial gain to breach their professional duties to the client and the court. In any event, whatever harm it is feared *may* be done by conditional fees has to be weighed against the solid reality that there are many people unable to afford litigation to assert their legal rights who would be able to secure legal remedies if only their lawyers were able to agree a conditional fee with them. Furthermore, the arguments against certain types of contingency fees do not apply to the speculative fee. This means that the lawyer is paid only if the case succeeds, and is paid no greater amount than the proper professional fee (possibly with an uplift to take account of the risk he is running that he may receive no fee if the case is lost). The fee (apart from any uplift) will come out of the costs to be paid by the other, unsuccessful party to the litigation (or the sums paid by way of settlement of the action).

The Green Paper *Contingency Fees* published by the Lord Chancellor's Department in January 1989 observed that 'in Scotland there is a long tradition of the lawyer acting on a speculative basis'. The Green Paper concluded that 'there does not appear to be any substantial argument against the introduction of speculative actions in England and Wales'.[57] The White Paper *Legal Services: A Framework for the Future* stated that although there was a consensus that a contingent fee system in which the lawyer received a share of the proceeds recovered by his client was unacceptable, there was 'little objection' to the Scottish model of the speculative fee arrangement.[58] As promised in the White Paper, section 58 of the Courts and Legal Services Act 1990 makes lawful such conditional fees, save in certain types of cases (primarily those concerning children and other family matters), subject to an implementing order being introduced by the Lord Chancellor. Conditional fee arrangements should promote access to justice for those who have found it difficult to fund litigation. Those who use a conditional fee arrangement will still be at risk as to the costs of the other side if the case is lost, but the knowledge that they will not have to pay their own lawyers if they lose may well make it possible for them to bring litigation to protect their legal interests which previously they would have been unable to afford.

IV

Quintilianus explained in the first century AD that one of the central principles of good advocacy was to confine yourself to essential submissions: 'we must not always burden the judge with all the arguments we have discovered, since by so doing we shall at once bore him and render him less inclined to believe us'.[59] Here, the interests of the client are entirely consistent with the interests of the judge, opposing counsel and the administration of justice, none of them benefiting from lengthy submissions from the advocate. As Lord Reid said in

1967, 'most experienced counsel would agree that the golden rule is—when in doubt stop. Far more cases have been lost by going on too long than by stopping too soon.'[60] Lord Pearce agreed that 'one of the merits of great advocates has often been that . . . where ten possible points were available they would often ruthlessly select the best, sacrifice nine, and thereby win on the tenth'.[61] It was simply wrong for the US District Court to suggest in 1964 that 'experienced attorneys' should act on the principle that 'it is never wise to assume that any judge . . . will remember and apply all of the points in favour of his client without having them called to his attention'.[62]

Judges find it especially difficult to control the verbosity of litigants in person. In 1888, Mr Justice Wills complained that in listening to such a litigant 'our time was taken up for two hours and a half by arguments founded largely on legal solecisms of the wildest kind'.[63] In 1975, the Supreme Court of New South Wales complained in its judgment that the litigant in person had

> spent some time reading to the court disconnected statements as to the law from a series of cards, some of which statements it was impossible to understand and most of which had no significant relationship to the issues in the proceedings. Indications from individual members of the court that these readings were of no assistance in determining the appeal appeared to have no effect upon the manner of his conducting the proceedings.[64]

In one recent burglary trial, in which the defendant represented himself, 'the manner in which the [defendant] chose to conduct his defence caused intense difficulty for the very experienced trial judge and grossly prolonged the proceedings. . . . It is estimated that the evidence-in-chief given by the witnesses on behalf of the prosecution lasted little more than an hour, after an opening of the case for the prosecution which lasted six minutes. The trial, however, extended over 38 days.' The defendant was convicted. When he appealed to the Court of Appeal, he submitted a 'notice of appeal [which] sets out 53 grounds and numerous sub-grounds of appeal and extends to 100 pages . . . '. His appeal was dismissed.[65]

There are limits to what the court will tolerate even from the amateur advocate. At the end of the last century a Magistrates' Court convicted some defendants of disobeying an order that they have their children vaccinated. The defendants complained in the Divisional Court that the Magistrates had refused to listen to the Revd Arthur Graham, who had represented them at the hearing. The Divisional Court was unsympathetic when it realized that the Revd Graham had 'addressed the Justices at great length on the subject of vaccination in general . . . telling the Justices that they were bound to sit to listen to anything he might choose to say or read.' The Justices had adjourned the case 'in order that the defendants might have the opportunity of appearing by someone not quite so reverend and not quite so abusive'. But the Revd Graham had again appeared and continued to use 'disrespectful and abusive language'. The Justices had refused to hear his submissions in other cases on the same subject. The Divisional Court had no difficulty in rejecting a contention that 'it was not enough for an advocate to misbehave himself in one case, but that he must have an opportunity of misbehaving himself in each case'.[66] It is doubtful whether the present-day House of Lords would permit the antics of Miss Sheddon. In 1869, she appeared in person in the House of Lords. She addressed the House for 23 days. In his judgment, Lord Chancellor

Hatherley hinted at extraordinary judicial self-control during this marathon. He referred to her argument as having been 'conducted with the greatest possible ability during the first three or four days of the discussion when all, I think, was said that fairly could be said upon the subject . . .'. He added that the sole advantage of her lengthy address was that 'we had the fullest and amplest time, even during the discussion, to consider the different propositions that were brought before us'. Miss Sheddon had not exhausted her oratorical impulses: she repeatedly interrupted the judgments. As she informed their Lordships in one such intervention, the case was 'one of life and death', and the Respondent's 'own counsel is our murderer'.[67]

Some professional advocates are almost as unwilling, or as unable, as amateurs to focus on the point at issue. Judges have therefore had cause to regret that the English legal system has proceeded on the generous assumption that advocates may occupy the court for as long as they can think of authorities to cite and submissions to make. When the aggravation becomes too intense, they may say, as did Mr Justice Harman in a 1954 tax case, 'this case has been an unconscionable time a-trying. I have listened with a patience which, I am afraid, has worn more thin as the hours succeeded one another, to a very nice exercise in dialectic by both counsel who have addressed me'.[68]

More recently, courts have begun to appreciate that although the independent advocate has an important role, there is no principle of law or justice which entitles advocates, at great expense to the State and their clients, to take days to have their say. Lord Chief Justice Lane has understandably suggested that 'judges nowadays should . . . more often . . . stop counsel from indulging in prolixity, unnecessary questions and repetition'.[69] Because barristers have not always been prepared voluntarily to obey the essential principle of effective advocacy—keep it short and to the point—changes have been made in the regulation of advocacy which will have the welcome effect of cutting down the amount of court time occupied by oral argument. The procedure of the English courts is, slowly, moving in the direction of recognizing that court time is too valuable to be made available to advocates in unlimited quantities.

In March 1989, Lord Donaldson, Master of the Rolls, handed down a Practice Direction concerned with the presentation of argument in the Court of Appeal.[70] In all civil appeals, skeleton written arguments were made compulsory. At the commencement of the appeal, 'counsel for the appellant will be expected to proceed immediately to the ground of appeal which is in the forefront of the appellant's case'. The object of these changes, the Master of the Rolls explained, was 'to reduce the amount of time spent in court whilst at the same time adhering to our long established tradition of oral argument in open court. Time spent in court is costly both to the nation and the parties. It is therefore vital that it is used economically and effectively.' The Commercial Court and the Divisional Court also expect skeleton arguments to be provided. In other courts, it is becoming common practice for counsel (with the assistance of their word processor) to hand in and argue from skeleton written representations. Judges do much more pre-hearing reading than their predecessors ever contemplated.

These changes are designed to reduce the amount of oral advocacy required at any hearing. They rightly recognize that it is more efficient (as well as less tedious) for judges to read the documents and the authorities to themselves in chambers rather than have the materials read out to them by counsel in court. But the reforms do not impose any time limit on the loquacious advocate. There are signs that some judges are questioning the utility of unlimited amounts of oral advocacy and are contemplating confining the advocate to a set period of time for his submissions. Lord Templeman complained in 1989 that for the conduct of a set of appeals before the Appellate Committee of the House of Lords there had been 'locked in battle 24 counsel supported by batteries of solicitors and legal experts, armed with copies of 200 authorities and 14 volumes of extracts, British and foreign, from legislation, books and articles. Ten counsel addressed the Appellate Committee for 26 days. This vast amount of written and oral material tended to obscure [the] fundamental principles. . . . In my opinion the length of oral argument permitted in future appeals should be subject to prior limitation by the Appellate Committee'.[71] In another recent appeal, Lord Templeman repeated his concern that the consequences of unlimited advocacy 'not infrequently are torrents of words, written and oral, which are oppressive', and he restated his suggested remedy of a limit to the time allowed for oral advocacy.[72] Another Lord of Appeal, Lord Griffiths, has complained that barristers were 'drowning the judge in a torrent of words' and has suggested a considerable reduction in the quantity of oral argument.[73]

Foreign lawyers tend to be surprised at the willingness of the English judge to spend his professional life listening (or at least appearing to listen) to the lengthy submissions of counsel. They rightly find it bizarre that legal authorities are read out to judges whose own ability to read is not in doubt and who could therefore more efficiently acquaint themselves with the material in private in a fraction of the time, leaving the advocate to draw attention to particular passages on which especial reliance is placed. When the US Supreme Court hears argument on fundamental issues of constitutional law, the advocates are (in accordance with the practice in that Court) allocated less than one hour for oral submissions. The European Court of Justice in Luxembourg and the European Court of Human Rights in Strasbourg similarly confine advocates to less than one hour for their oral argument. In all of these courts, extensive written submissions are provided on behalf of the parties in advance of the hearing. English lawyers who appear in Luxembourg or Strasbourg are thereby encouraged to think in advance about what they really want, and need, to say to the Court at an oral hearing. There is no reason why the English advocate should not be able to organize his submissions so as to make them effectively and efficiently were English courts to confine the quantity of advocacy to be heard. An American professor, Robert J. Martineau, who recently conducted a study of advocacy in the Court of Appeal, observed that the English advocate spent no more time than his American counterpart in arguing the central point in the case, usually no more than fifteen to thirty minutes on each side. The extra length of the hearing in the English court was occupied by preliminary submissions which could much more efficiently be made in writing.[74]

It is, as Lord Pearce explained in 1967, 'important to justice that it should not get bogged down in irrelevant details. The judge in this is often at the mercy of the advocates . . .'.[75] Consideration ought now to be given to what would be gained, and whether anything of value would be lost, if the Court of Appeal and the House of Lords were to confine counsel's submissions to a specified amount of time, only to be exceeded at the discretion of the court. Such a change in procedure would have the advantages of freeing some judges from sitting in court for five hours a day, giving them more time to read the documents and the authorities to themselves, and focusing the hearing more precisely, and concisely, on the relevant legal points. There is no doubt that oral argument can, and does, direct attention to the real issues and help to identify the strengths and weaknesses of the opposing contentions. But there is no reason why the preliminary facts and background law should be slowly read by counsel to the judge in open court rather than being quickly read to himself by the judge in his chambers.

In 1989, the Divisional Court quashed the order of a Crown Court Judge that because of the manner in which the case had been conducted, counsel should personally bear part of the costs of an appeal against a decision of Justices.[76] Limiting the amount of advocacy judges are required to endure should be considered before judges acquire the habit of looking for such alternative remedies.

V

Should the advocate have an immunity from liability for negligence in the performance of his duties? In 1967, the House of Lords concluded that 'the present independence of counsel is a carefully considered part of a great legal system which has commanded admiration from various parts of the world'[77] and that if counsel were to be 'subject to actions for negligence, it would make it quite impossible for him to carry out his duties properly'.[78] Therefore, despite the fact that 'all other professional men . . . are liable to be sued for damages if loss is caused to their clients by their lack of professional skill or by their failure to exercise due care',[79] public policy required that barristers (and solicitors when acting as advocates) should have an immunity from such an action.[80] The 1979 Royal Commission on Legal Services agreed that such an immunity was in the public interest.[81]

Immunity from liability could not be justified by the fact that 'it is most unpleasant for a barrister to have to fight an allegation that he has been negligent', for 'such an experience is no more unpleasant for a barrister than it is for a physician or a surgeon, an architect or an accountant'.[82] In case something does go wrong, all barristers have a professional duty to insure against professional negligence.[83]

Nor could the immunity be explained by the fact that, as Lord Wilberforce observed in a 1978 judgment, 'much if not most of a barrister's work involves exercise of judgment' and so 'is in the realm of art not science'. Even if a barrister owed a legal duty of care, the fact that he exercises judgment would mean that 'an action against a barrister who acts honestly and carefully is very unlikely to succeed'.[84] The advocate 'is under no duty to be right'.[85] As Chief Justice Abbott remarked, 'God forbid that it should be imagined that a [solicitor], or a counsel, or even a judge is bound to know all the law'.[86] It is well established that the common law does not impose 'any liability for damage resulting from what in the result turn out to have been errors of judgment, unless the error was such as no reasonably well-informed and competent member of that profession could have made'.[87] In California, where there is no immunity for legal negligence, 'the attorney is not liable for every mistake he may make in his practice; he is not, in the absence of an express agreement, an insurer of the soundness of his opinions or of the validity of an instrument that he is engaged to draft; and he is not liable for being in error as to a question of law on which reasonable doubt may be entertained by well-informed lawyers'.[88] Similarly, the common law well appreciates that professional decisions are often taken urgently. And, as Lord Diplock has observed, the absence of an immunity from negligence has not 'disabled members of professions other than the law from giving their best services to those to whom they are rendered'.[89]

Of course, disgruntled clients may bring misconceived actions. But that is something which other professional men have to withstand. 'There are', as Lord Diplock has pointed out, 'other and more specific means of disposing summarily of vexatious actions'.[90] Under the Rules of the Supreme Court, frivolous or vexatious claims can be struck out at an early stage. And, unlike other professional defendants, barristers would have the very considerable 'protection that the judge before whom the action for negligence will be tried is well qualified, without any need of expert evidence, to make allowance for the circumstances in which the impugned decision fell to be made and to differentiate between an error that was so blatant as to amount to negligence and an exercise of judgment which, though in the event it turned out to have been mistaken, was not outside the range of possible courses of action that in the circumstances reasonably competent members of the profession might have chosen to take'.[91]

Five main reasons were advanced by the House of Lords in 1967 for the existence of a special immunity for advocates. None of them, on analysis, is a convincing basis for denying an action to the client who is a victim of negligence.

First, it was pointed out that the advocate owes a duty

to the court as well as to his client. The House of Lords feared that liability for negligence in the performance of advocacy might make the lawyer less willing to perform his duty to the court when it conflicted with the interests of his client. It would, said Lord Reid, 'be a grave and dangerous step to make any change which would imperil in any way the confidence which every court rightly puts in all counsel who appear before it'.[92] But the advocate appreciates that every court would immediately accept that 'any refusal to depart at the behest of the client from accepted standards of propriety and honest advocacy would not be held to be negligence'.[93] The Supreme Court of California has held that to found an action for negligence, 'the attorney's choice to honour the public obligation must be shown to have been so manifestly erroneous that no prudent attorney would have done so'.[94] The advocate also knows that any lapse from professional standards, in particular his duties to the court, would be met with disciplinary sanctions. The advocate already has the difficult task of explaining to the client why his duties to the court prevent him from taking steps which the client wishes, or instructs, him to take but which conflict with professional standards.[95] There is no logical reason to think that the theoretical possibility of a negligence action is going to make any difference to the advocate's behaviour in this respect. And, as pointed out by Krever J in the Ontario High Court of Justice, there is no empirical evidence to support the assertion that the imposition of liability for negligence would cause advocates to ignore their duties to the court.[96] Moreover, other professional men have duties other than to their client (doctors have duties to medical ethics, for example), and this does not confer on them immunity from liability for negligence.

Second, it was said by the House of Lords that the removal of immunity from suit in negligence would 'at least subconsciously lead some counsel to undue prolixity'[97] so as to avoid an allegation that they had omitted to make a point. 'Prudence will always be prompting him to ask every question and call every piece of evidence that his client wishes' in order to avoid the risk of a negligence action.[98] But is there really any appreciable risk that the existence of legal liability would encourage prolixity in counsel? It is important to remember that the advocate would know that 'in most cases it would be an effective answer to an allegation of negligence to say that the course that had been followed in litigation was that which the advocate in the honest exercise of his discretion had deemed it advisable to follow'.[99] Lord Upjohn emphasized that he was 'not, of course, suggesting for one moment that the fact that counsel does or does not call a witness, or does or does not ask a question or does or does not ask to amend his pleadings could possibly by itself be a cause of action for negligence, even if . . . on mature reflection it had been better if counsel had pursued an opposite course'.[100] The vague possibility of a negligence action is no more likely to cause advocates to change their style than is the existing sanction of discipline by their professional body after a complaint by a dissatisfied client. Furthermore, even if there were some basis for the concern that liability in negligence might cause defensive advocacy, it is difficult to understand why this argument should suffice to confer immunity on advocates, but not on other professionals (such as doctors) in respect of whom similar arguments would seem to have as much (or as little) force.

Third, is the fact (which Lord Diplock in 1978 thought of significance)[101] that for reasons of public policy, the law gives broad immunities to all those who participate in court proceedings. For example, counsel cannot be sued for defamatory statements about the opposing party[102] and judges have a similar immunity.[103] But it is easy to understand the public policy which seeks to encourage freedom of speech in court by preventing legal actions resulting from what is said. Any such legal liability might well deprive the court of full information about the issues in the case. This has little, if anything, to do with the alleged public policy which requires immunity from legal action for negligent acts.[104] That immunity has no role to play in furthering freedom of expression in court.

Fourth, the House of Lords was concerned that permitting an action for negligence against an advocate would have the undesirable consequence of requiring a reconsideration of the merits of the original trial. It would, thought Lord Morris, be 'a sort of unseemly excrescence' upon the legal system if a man who was convicted of a criminal offence, and whose appeal was dismissed, could seek to re-open the issue by contending that but for the incompetence of his counsel he would have been acquitted.[105] It is, indeed, not a happy prospect to contemplate, years after the alleged negligence, requiring 'a court of co-ordinate jurisdiction to try the question whether another court reached a wrong decision and, if so, to inquire into the causes of its doing so'.[106] But it is unlikely in the extreme that courts would tolerate attempts by disappointed litigants to revive failed lawsuits through negligence actions unless there were some prima facie basis for their complaint. Unless it thought that there was a firm factual foundation for the allegation that the result of the lawsuit was due to the advocate's incompetence, the court would conclude that the plaintiff 'has no reasonable chance of success in this action on the facts alone and that consequently his claim is truly frivolous and vexatious and should be struck out'.[107] If the litigant could, in an extreme case, show that he had a prima facie case that he was convicted, or failed in civil litigation, because of the incompetence of his lawyer, then it is far from obvious that the law should adopt a policy of refusing to consider whether the first court came to an erroneous conclusion, should require the victim to bear the loss, and should render the advocate immune from liability. It is true that, in such (hopefully rare) cases, there will need to be a reconsideration of the original issues, and this may well pose substantial difficulties (for example, because the other party to the original civil action will not be a party to the negligence action).[108] Although the English law does have an understandable bias against allowing such re-litigation, issues already decided can be re-opened for sufficient cause, for example if a conviction has been due to the incompetence of counsel,[109] or when the Home Secretary refers back to the Court of Appeal for further consideration (under section 17 of the Criminal Appeal Act 1968) the conviction of a particular person for a criminal offence. Furthermore, it is not necessarily more difficult to re-open, years after the event, the circumstances involved in a legal trial than it is to reconstruct what happened during a medical operation or any of the other incidents which may form the background to a claim for negligence against a professional man. Such a difficulty does not lead to an immunity from negligence liability for professionals other than lawyers. Indeed, the same problems of investigating complex matters years after the relevant events occurred may well arise in litigating a negligence claim against a lawyer under existing English law, that is where the negligence did not involve advocacy, or matters incidental to the presentation of the case in court, and so already there is a cause of action.

Fifth, it was said by the House of Lords that it would be unfair to make counsel liable in negligence since they were obliged to accept instructions from anyone who wished to engage their services for a proper professional fee in an area of law in which they practised. Although it is true that the role of the advocate can be distinguished from that of the doctor in that the latter does not act on the instructions of the client,[110] there are many similarities between the position of the doctor and that of the advocate. The doctor owes a duty to medical ethics as well as to the interests of his patient, yet still the law thinks it appropriate to impose liability in negligence. There are, as Lord Denning appreciated, 'many people—taxi-drivers, inn-keepers, and so on—who cannot refuse to take "clients"',[111] but who have a liability in negligence. In any event, although the cab-rank principle may oblige the barrister 'to accept instructions on behalf of an obstinate and cantankerous client who is more likely than more rational beings to bring proceedings for negligence against his counsel if disappointed in the result of his litigation', nevertheless, as Lord Diplock observed, 'the existence of this risk does not . . . justify depriving all clients of any possibility of a remedy for negligence of counsel, however elementary and obvious the mistake he has made may be'.[112]

The true position is that 'the pressures and special demands of trial practice are merely a circumstance, perhaps an important one in a particular case, for the fact finder to consider along with other evidence in determining whether a lawyer has acted reasonably'.[113] It was accurately submitted by Louis Blom-Cooper on behalf of the aggrieved client in *Rondel v. Worsley* in the House of

Lords in 1967 that 'the peculiar characteristics of the professional work of a lawyer . . . are relevant to the issue: what *standard* of duty of care does the law impose? But these characteristics do not constitute, either singly or cumulatively, any denial of the *existence* of a duty to take care.'[114]

Even if there is substance in some of the arguments presented by the House of Lords for giving advocates immunity from actions in negligence, those factors have to be weighed against the arguments for liability. There are three.

First, it is wrong in principle that the victims of flagrant incompetence should have no remedy. Mr Justice Deane, dissenting from the majority judgment of the Australian High Court that advocates have this immunity from suit in negligence, rightly said that even if the arguments adopted by the House of Lords in *Rondel v. Worsley* have some force, they do not 'outweigh or even balance the injustice and consequent public detriment involved in depriving a person, who is caught up in litigation and engages the professional services of a legal practitioner, of all redress under the common law for "in court" negligence, however gross and callous in its nature or devastating in its consequences'.[115]

Second, the existence of legal liability is likely to raise standards. Lord Pearce thought that it was 'unnecessary' to provide such 'a spur to the advocate', since counsel 'are always keen to win a case and, incidentally, to give satisfaction to their clients so far as this is compatible with their duty to the court and to their professional standards'.[116] Lord Justice Salmon similarly suggested that 'apart from the high traditions of the Bar, strong materialistic motives are always acting as a sharp spur for him to take great care to do his very best'.[117] But the law does not make doctors immune from liability for negligence on the ground that medical men are already sufficiently eager to save lives (and that providing extra, legal, inducements might encourage them to cut the corners of medical ethics). There is always room for improvement.

Third, the reputation of the legal system is of importance. The immunity of lawyers from actions for negligence for their performance in court contributes to the cynicism and distrust expressed by laymen for lawyers. The removal of the immunity might help to persuade the layman that, in the vast majority of cases, lawyers do a good job for him in court and have no need of legal immunities to protect them from actions for negligence. As Louis Blom-Cooper submitted for the aggrieved litigant in *Rondel v. Worsley*, 'perpetuating an anomalous privilege' may well erode the confidence of laymen in the legal system.[118] It is difficult to find non-lawyers who are persuaded that the advocate should be immune from liability for negligence.

A strong case needs to be made out before public policy can justify an exception to the normal principles of liability for negligence. No such case has been established in respect of the performance of the duties of advocates. When, in 1791, Lord Kenyon CJ dismissed a claim for negligence brought against a barrister, he said he 'believed this action was the first, and hoped it would be the last, of the kind'.[119] This issue will not go away. English law will, in the future, have more to say on this topic.

CHAPTER 7

Success (and Failure)

I

At one extreme of the Bar was James Scarlett (later Lord Abinger), of whom it was said at the beginning of the nineteenth century that 'he had invented a machine by the secret use of which in court he could always make the head of a judge nod assent to his propositions; whereas his rivals, who tried to pirate it, always made the head of the judge move dissentingly from side to side'.[1] His secret was, in fact, more mundane: he 'disdained to adopt the vicious practice of some barristers, then far too common, of wandering about from court to court, and taking contemporaneous briefs in all'.[2] Unlike so many of his colleagues, then and since, he 'invariably mastered every brief delivered to him and . . . refused to accept more retainers than he could really attend to'.[3] As late as the turn of the last century, C. F. Gill was unusual as a King's Counsel in that he 'adopted the somewhat rare practice of never accepting a brief which would be likely to clash with any other he was holding'.[4]

Other mortals who earn their living by attempting to exercise the skills of persuasion find the task less mechanical in its precision and reliability than did James Scarlett, and more difficult in the pitfalls which daily have to be avoided. After all, as Lord Justice Salmon appreciated, 'advocacy is not an exact science. It is an art.'[5] Although it has been suggested that 'anybody with the patience to work at it can become a competent advocate by learning the principles',[6] some practitioners never acquire the necessary technique, however long they labour. Norman Birkett, sitting as a Judge at the Nuremberg War Crimes tribunal in 1946, was not the first judge (or the last) to feel that 'with complete murder in my heart I am compelled to sit in suffering silence, whilst the maddening, toneless, insipid, flat, depressing voice drones on in endless words which have quite lost all meaning'.[7]

II

To become a successful barrister requires, in addition to the necessary skill, considerable patience, perseverance, and not a small portion of luck. Little has changed since James Boswell recognized, in the 1780s, that to pursue a career at the Bar would 'involve me in expense and in dependence on [solicitors]'.[8]

The aspiring barrister must negotiate a pupillage. Twelve months spent with one or more practising barristers, watching and learning the trade, is not necessarily the most productive use of time or the most effective method of preparing lawyers to argue cases in court. In the middle of the nineteenth century, James Stephen was the pupil of the leading junior on the Midland Circuit 'but it was on the distinct understanding that he was to receive no instruction from his tutor'.[9] At around the same time, the future Lord Bowen (a Lord of Appeal) was sitting in what he later recalled as 'the white-washed misery of the pupil's room. . . . So bitter is the thought of it that death itself can hardly be more bitter.'[10] In the early years of this century, Charles Gill, one of the Treasury Counsel at the Old Bailey, 'never allowed his pupils to ask him questions'.[11] Unlike Mr Pickwick, barristers do not need to be reminded 'what fine places of slow torture' barristers' chambers are for the pupil: 'the waiting—the hope—the disappointment—the fear—the misery—the poverty'.[12]

Once pupillage has been overcome, the enthusiastic and promising advocate who wishes to practise at the Bar must find a seat in chambers—by no means an easy task. Many are called to the Bar, but few are chosen to join Chambers. Much still depends on being in the right place at the right time.

If that hurdle can be overcome, work must be found and a reputation made. There is, as Dr Johnson warned Boswell, a real risk that 'a man might pass half a life-time in the courts, and never have an opportunity of showing his abilities'.[13] Boswell himself was 'very happy to get business the second week I was at the bar, when many able men stand for years unemployed'.[14] Trollope's Mr Younglad 'was a promising common-law barrister, now commencing his career, of whom his friends were beginning to hope that he might, if he kept his shoulders well to the collar, at some distant period make a living out of his profession. He was between forty and forty-five years of age, and had already overcome the natural diffidence of youth in addressing a learned bench and a crowded court.'[15] When Serjeant Snubbin advises Mr Pickwick, the junior counsel is Mr Phunky. He is, the solicitor explains, 'a very young man' who was only called to the Bar 'the other day. Let me see—he has not been at the Bar eight years yet.' Serjeant Snubbin acknowledges his junior counsel's youth 'in that sort of pitying tone in which ordinary folks would speak of a very helpless little child'. Phunky—'although an infant barrister, he was a full-grown man'—not surprisingly 'had a very nervous manner, and a painful hesitation in his speech; it did not appear to be a natural defect, but seemed rather the result of timidity, arising from the consciousness of being "kept down" by want of means, or interest, or connection, or impudence, as the case might be'.[16] Because of the barriers to be surmounted before the young lawyer could become a successful advocate, Blackstone lamented that 'we must rarely expect to see a gentleman of distinction or learning at the bar'.[17]

Since advocacy cannot be learnt by studying theory, only by actual practice, the young advocate needs to attract clients. A lucky break, perhaps the consequence of the misfortune of another, can help. In the 1740s, Charles Pratt (later Lord Chancellor Camden) was dispirited by his failure and contemplating leaving the Bar. He was the junior in an important case. 'Just as it was about to be called on, the leader was suddenly seized with an attack of gout.' Pratt's eloquence won the case, he was 'complimented by the judge, was applauded by the audience, and received several retainers before he left the hall'.[18] Erskine made his reputation in 1778 in a case in which he acted on behalf of Captain Baillie. Erskine had been briefed after expounding at a dinner on the injustice done to the Captain, not knowing that Baillie was one of the other guests. Erskine spoke as the fifth counsel for Baillie and won the case. When asked how he had the courage to stand up to the Chief Justice, Lord Mansfield, he replied that he contemplated his children pulling at his robe, and saying to him, 'Now, father, is the time to get us bread'.[19] Soon after his call to the Bar in 1829, Alexander Cockburn (later Lord Chief Justice) appeared in the court of Lord Chancellor Brougham. The judge 'was engrossed with his correspondence, and took no notice of the argument except to say curtly at the conclusion of counsel's speech, "Motion refused"'. Thereafter, Cockburn was surprised to receive a number of briefs from a solicitor who had not previously instructed him. The solicitor explained that he had been in court when Cockburn made the motion before Brougham 'and when I saw the Chancellor taking down every word you said, I made up my mind that . . . you were the man for my money'.[20] In 1884, Marshall Hall was 26 years old, only a moderately successful barrister, 'and was thinking of trying his fortune elsewhere, when one of those romantic pieces of luck came to him which fortunately are not uncommon at the Bar'. Lacking any work, he had gone to the Old Bailey to watch some trials, and was in the robing room when a busy junior asked him to assist. A brief and a seat in chambers followed.[21] At the end of the First World War, Rayner Goddard (later Lord Chief Justice) had 'one of those strokes of luck'. He was sitting in Chambers on a Saturday morning, lacking work to occupy him. Some representatives of the Midland Bank called, looking for a counsel to take a brief. They said that they had already tried three sets of chambers without success. 'They put to him a question of a kind that had been thoroughly answered in the law report he had been browsing through the day before.' He was briefed, and developed a substantial banking practice. 'Yet before I read the law report by chance', Goddard later reflected, 'I knew almost nothing about banking.'[22]

Many lawyers, as well qualified and as hard-working,

never have such luck. They struggle unheroically through their first cases, as did Travers Humphreys. His 'client confessed to stealing three books . . . and a detective went into the witness box. I heard nothing of what he said, or if I did I failed to take it in, being engaged in a strenuous and fortunately successful effort to avoid being sick.'[23] Unlike Humphreys, some of those called to the Bar find that their suitability for practising as an advocate does not improve with experience and that their luck does not change.

III

Sir Patrick Hastings explained that the inexperienced barrister is 'travelling in a foreign country amid a hostile population' but that he will, if he remains unscathed, discover, as the years go by, that 'no case is new to him'.[24] This does not guarantee that the job of persuading judges and juries becomes any easier.

The task which the advocate has undertaken may be a formidable one. As Cicero appreciated, 'often he who is to adjudge the victory is ill-disposed and angry, or even friendly to the other side while hostile to yourself', so 'every impressive reflection, every weighty word must be employed. There must be added a delivery that is free from monotony and forceful and rich in energy, animation, pathos and reality.'[25] When such exacting standards need habitually to be met, however humble the setting and inadequate the factual or legal material with which the lawyer has to work, it is hardly surprising that the advocate is usually grateful if he can escape from court without having disgraced himself or his client.

Since they are only human, 'the greatest of advocates are not immune from grave errors of judgment'.[26] None of us is infallible. Failure to persuade the judge may be especially embarrassing if the advocate has previously advised his client that he will succeed in court. In 1845, Lord Campbell recalled that when he 'had the honour of practising at the Bar of England', he had 'repeatedly given erroneous opinions'. It would, he thought, 'be utterly impossible that you could ever have a class of men who would give a guarantee, binding themselves, in giving legal advice and conducting suits at law, to be always in the right'. It was, he recollected Mr Justice Heath saying, 'a very difficult thing for a gentleman at the Bar to be called upon to give his opinion, because it was calling upon him to conjecture what . . . other persons would say upon some point that had never before been determined'.[27] For that reason, and no doubt for others, 'we have', confessed Lord Justice Salmon, 'all given wrong advice'.[28] But it is little comfort, either to the advocate or to his client, that everybody makes mistakes.

The advocate's 'livelihood depends upon his public reputation'.[29] But, as he is well aware, any fame is likely to be transient, whereas notoriety tends to have a greater degree of permanence. As Chief Justice Cardozo of the New York Court of Appeals appreciated, 'reputation in such a calling is a plant of tender growth, and its bloom, once lost, is not easily restored'.[30] The lawyer knows that, like a sportsman or an actor, he is as good, or as bad, as his last performance. No one except Rumpole remembers his success in the Penge Bungalow Murders, 'alone and without a leader'.[31]

Often the judge has 'had the utmost assistance from counsel on both sides. If I have come to the wrong conclusion on this by no means simple case, I have no one but myself to blame.'[32] But ineffective advocacy is more memorable than a persuasive submission. Disaster can strike the advocate in many forms. When F. Lee Bailey began his closing speech for the defence in the trial of the American heiress Patty Hearst, 'he swept his arm up in a gesture, [and] knocked a glass of water off the podium. The water dribbled down the front of his pants. Several members of the jury tittered. The judge smiled. But F. Lee Bailey went on talking, disregarding the ignobility of having wet his pants.'[33] The question posed to the jury by Mervyn Griffith-Jones, prosecuting counsel in the *Lady Chatterley's Lover* obscenity trial in October 1960—'Is it a book that you would even wish your wife or your servants to read?'[34]—was 'the famous question which will for ever be associated with his name'[35] and is likely to be remembered longer than any more successful oratorical display by that, or almost any other, advocate. Griffith-Jones, though to be applauded for respecting the ethics of the British prosecutor that you 'do not pull out all stops to obtain a conviction',[36] had plainly forgotten the advice given by Cicero: 'in oratory the very cardinal sin is to depart from the language of everyday life, and the usage approved by the sense of the community'.[37]

Who now remembers the career at the Bar of Sir Thomas Inskip (Attorney-General 1928–9 and 1932–6) other than for his act of informing the Law Lords during the course of argument in an appeal that 'roulette was played with cards'? He had the indignity of 'suffering a devastating monosyllabic correction from the Woolsack',[38] the recollection of which not even his later rise to office as Lord Chancellor and, thereafter, Lord Chief Justice could expunge in the history of advocacy. If the advocate's comment is sensible at the time he makes it, progress in social conditions can make him look very silly thereafter. At the 1935 Rattenbury murder trial, prosecuting counsel, Mr Croom Johnson, asked a medical witness for the defence whether 'regular sexual intercourse with a member of the opposite sex by a boy of eighteen or onwards would be likely to do him good or harm'.[39]

Poor advocacy may be heard on mundane occasions, as well as in *causes célèbres*. That one of the first lawyers to appear before the Immigration Appeal Board (created to help administer the Aliens Act 1905) 'raised the Board to a high pitch of irritation' causing his client to lose the appeal will come as no surprise to those who have experience of the serious inadequacies of some advocates.[40] Tom Wolfe imagines how, in the Bronx Criminal Court, 'emotional crescendos were beyond' the defence counsel. 'His posture was so bad that every woman on a jury, or every good mother, in any case, was aching to cry out, "Hold your shoulders back!" As for his delivery, it wasn't that he didn't prepare his summations, it was that he obviously prepared them on a yellow legal pad, which lay on top of the defence table.'[41]

However crass the mistakes which the advocate may make, and however appalling his performance, he knows, on standing up in court to make his submissions, that judges usually resist the temptation to humiliate counsel. Gone are the days when Sir Thomas Egerton 'sharply rebuked' counsel (in 1596) 'with such words as these—"you must go to school to learn more wit . . ."'.[42] It is a very unfortunate advocate who encounters a judge who concludes that he has made a 'submission [which] is so far removed from reality, from even the most rudimentary notions of justice and fair play, that one has no more than to state it for it to be abundantly obvious that it cannot be maintained. Yet here was the Solicitor-General, whom we all know as one of the most amiable of men, voluntarily casting himself in the role of Count Dracula.' In that case, Mr Justice Walton described suggestions made by counsel in the course of argument as 'fantastic' and 'laughable'.[43] On appeal to the House of Lords, Lord Wilberforce said, 'Less genially, I agree'.[44]

Indeed, although many judges may think it, they rarely pronounce, as did Lord Justice Russell in a judgment in 1972, that 'I have dealt rather briefly with the extensive arguments that were put before us . . . because, in my perhaps not very humble opinion, there is absolutely nothing in the case at all and nothing in the appeal'.[45] If the judge wishes to cause especial pain to the feelings of the advocate, he may indicate, with varying degrees of politeness, that he is not assisted by the argument (conscientiously prepared though it may have been) advanced before him. Even so skilful an advocate as Erskine could complain that in one case Lord Mansfield (Chief Justice 1756–88) 'put me aside with indulgence, as you do a child when it is lisping its prattle out of season'.[46] In a 1923 case, Lord Justice Scrutton expressed his 'regret that counsel who argued this case would probably not recognise any part of the judgments as having any relation to the arguments they addressed to us'.[47]

As Sir John Donaldson, Master of the Rolls, has explained, 'presenting the contentions of the parties in a concise and logical form, deploying and testing the evidence and examining the relevant law demands professional skills of a high order'.[48] Judges are occasionally provoked to remind counsel that it is their duty to try to avoid making a submission which has 'no foundation in sense, reason or law'.[49] The advocate should do his best not to present arguments which 'were . . . plainly fallacious [and] . . . demonstrated the contrary of what he sought to prove'.[50] If he cites an authority, the advocate should ensure that the court cannot conclude that 'the facts were so far away from the present case that I feel it is not helpful to refer to them, save to mention the name of the case out of courtesy to [counsel] who cited it to us'.[51] He should resist arguing 'hopeless appeals' and making an 'incomprehensible' submission which 'fail[s] to recognise that every word of this court's decision in [an earlier case] wholly contradicts the argument which he has presented to us'.[52] If the advocate is going to place reliance on a book which he has written, he may find the judge concluding that 'there was no support for [counsel's] argument in authority, or in the writing of distinguished legal authors other than in [counsel's] own book, or in logic, or in reason, or in any principle of public policy'.[53]

Occasionally, the advocate is guilty of rank incompetence. In 1978, Mr Justice Bouck in the British Columbia Supreme Court declared a mistrial after two days of a civil action because 'the nature of this case is far beyond the ability of counsel for the plaintiff' and 'an obvious travesty of justice is taking place'. He ordered counsel personally to pay the costs which had been wasted.[54] An appeal against conviction was allowed by the Court of Appeal in England in 1977 because the unfortunate defendant 'had been led into a trap by his own counsel' who had failed to see the danger in the line of questioning he was pursuing in the examination of his client. In the opinion of the Court of Appeal, the trial judge should have intervened to warn counsel. 'It had long been a principle that judges should protect the accused,' said the appeal court. 'It was rare that they had to protect them from their own counsel.'[55] In 1982, Mr Justice Montgomery in the Ontario High Court criticized defence counsel who had 'indulged in miles and miles of cross-examination' which was largely 'repetitive' and 'prolix'.[56] In 1984, the Supreme Court of Victoria, Australia, allowed an appeal against a conviction for murder and ordered a retrial, on the ground of the errors of defence counsel at the original trial.[57] In 1988, the Court of Appeal concluded that the solicitors should personally pay the costs of hearings in which a mother was appealing against a decision to refuse her access to her child. The solicitors had briefed counsel who was incompetent, and they had failed to withdraw instructions from him when this became obvious. It was reported that on more than one occasion the exasperated judges had asked him, 'What is your best point?', to which he had replied, 'I'm not prepared to disclose that'. The solicitor, said Lord Justice May, was 'not entitled to rely blindly on counsel's views'.[58]

The advocate may be temporarily incapacitated from arguing the case effectively. As a matter of principle, 'no court should countenance the appearance before it of an intoxicated attorney'—in particular one whose inebriation caused him to be arguing a case in the wrong courtroom.[59] In 1981, the Supreme Court of Indiana suspended an attorney from practice for 90 days for attending a trial in an intoxicated state. 'He staggered when walking before the jury, and he fell asleep several times during the course of the morning proceedings.' He failed to return to court after lunch and was discovered in his car outside the court building: he was 'either asleep or had passed out'.[60] In 1983, the New Zealand Court of Appeal allowed an appeal by a man convicted of rape and ordered a new trial when he alleged that his counsel was suffering from alcoholism at the time of the trial.[61] In a strange case heard in 1957, the Transvaal Provincial Division of the Supreme Court of South Africa set aside the conviction of an advocate for contempt (and the fine of £10) imposed by a magistrate on the ground of drunkenness during a trial. The advocate's appeal was allowed on natural justice grounds because, although he accepted that 'he was thoroughly exhausted on that day', the magistrate had not 'suggested to [him] that he was under the influence of liquor and unfit to proceed with the trial. He was apparently stopped in his cross-examination and informed that the court was imposing upon him a fine for £10 for being under the influence of liquor.'[62]

Counsel's advocacy may be unsuccessful because he has failed to make himself understood. Lord Justice Scrutton observed in a judgment in 1929 that 'there was also a third point, which [counsel] said was difficult to express in words, but which, as he never made me understand what it was, I cannot deal with'.[63] Sometimes, the advocate may not understand the judge. I remember, a few years ago, a young female barrister being bemused by the formal question posed to her by a Chancery Division judge, 'Do you move?' (She seemed to be wondering if he was putting in a request for personal information or, perhaps, making an improper suggestion.)

The advocate's difficulty may be that, having made the judge understand what the point is, there is no doubt that it is a hopeless one. The court may conclude that, despite the rhetorical efforts of counsel, the point 'was born and lived and flourished and died . . . in the course of Mr Beyfus' argument';[64] or that 'were it not for the very able and ingenious argument of Mr Dingle Foot, I should consider this a thoroughly impudent application';[65] or that the submission was 'with all respect to Mr Beloff's forensic prowess, talking in the air'.[66] When a barrister unsuccessfully objected to the use of the term 'blackmail' in the charge brought against his client in an Old Bailey trial as being a 'derogatory stigma' against black people, Judge Lipfriend explained that the term was to be found in section 21 of the Theft Act 1968 and so could justifiably be used in court.[67] 'Wives' cannot be construed to include 'husbands' in section 1(5) of the Immigration Act 1971, as the Court of Appeal held in 1988.[68]

By contrast, if an advocate finds that he has no difficulty persuading the judge to accept the submission he is making, the advocate may have cause to doubt that the point is of much force. Serjeant Shee confidently submitted in 1845 that 'the Court will take judicial notice that rain falls from time to time'.[69] Counsel appearing in 1989 for a bank robber who used a cucumber wrapped in binliners to imitate a gun was on strong ground when he suggested that the judge 'may not have heard before of a man choosing a cucumber to commit this type of offence'.[70] The defendant was jailed for seven years.[71]

Counsel may have missed the real point at issue. When an appeal was brought in 1926 by a doctor who had been fined for contravening the Dangerous Drugs Act 1925, the Court of Criminal Appeal realized that the Act had not been brought into force.[72] In 1921, the Appellate Committee of the House of Lords was very cross that counsel had failed to direct its attention to a material section in the relevant statute. Counsel had 'studiously ignored its existence'.[73] One of the Law Lords had discovered the section after oral argument had been heard. Lord Birkenhead accepted the embarrassed apologies of the various shamefaced counsel, including Sir John Simon (who had been Attorney-General and would later become Lord Chancellor), that they 'were unaware of the existence of the section'.[74] In 1932, Viscount Dunedin for the House of Lords 'regretted that neither the County Court judge nor the Court of Appeal had their attention directed by the Bar before them to . . . recent cases in this House . . . without a consideration of which it is impossible to determine the present question'.[75] In July 1989, the Court of Appeal announced that a judgment given earlier that year was erroneous because counsel had not drawn the court's attention to a relevant provision of the governing statute.[76]

As Lord Justice Stephenson has observed, 'the history of judicial decisions is littered with cases in which points that appear later to be obvious have not been taken, even by the most eminent counsel, for reasons which are not clear—it may be from mere human fallibility'.[77] One such example was provided by Lord Justice Denning who regretted in a judgment that it was 'unfortunate that the principle which I have enunciated was not drawn to the attention of the court in [an earlier case] but that was my fault, because I was counsel in the case'.[78] Error may infect particular proceedings. In a Court of Appeal judgment in 1904, Lord Justice Romer compared the case to 'a comedy of errors'. Neither party had seen the vital point, and 'the plaintiff's evidence supported the defendant's case and the defendant's evidence supported the plaintiff's case'.[79]

There may be many reasons why counsel has not seen the vital point. In 1979, a journalist, Marcel Berlins, spent time listening to advocacy in criminal trials in Crown Courts and Magistrates' Courts and assessing its quality. He was far from impressed. It was bad enough when counsel were 'unaware of the leading relevant case or the relevant piece of legislation' or when they made 'mistakes about the detail and circumstances of the crime and, in pleas in mitigation, about the defendant's age, occupation and personal circumstances'. Even less excusable were the occasions 'when counsel managed to forget the crime with which his client had been charged'.[80] Ten years later, still a glutton for punishment, he repeated the experience. He concluded that standards had 'improved a little' in that 'most of the barristers I saw were competently mediocre, and in a few years some of them might graduate to becoming competent'.[81] In 1973, Chief Justice Burger of the US Supreme Court suggested that 'from one-third to one-half of the lawyers who appear in the serious cases are not really qualified to render fully adequate representation'.[82] After studying appellate proceedings in the USA and in England, an American professor, Robert J. Martineau, recently concluded that 'only a small percentage of appellate advocates in either country can be classified as highly competent, with the remainder ranging from adequate to incompetent'.[83]

Defective advocacy may result from inadequate instructions. It is a rule of etiquette, though not a rule of law, that a barrister must normally be instructed by a solicitor.[84] Not all solicitors appreciate that, as Chief Baron Pollock held in 1849 in a successful claim against a solicitor for the negligent conduct of a case, the act of 'instructing counsel cannot mean merely putting a piece of paper into his hands. . . . It must mean the putting him into such a situation, both with respect to the information which is given him and the means of making that information available, as will enable him to conduct the cause properly. . . . Instructing counsel means properly instructing him.'[85]

With or without the aid of adequate instructions, the advocate may be required, on behalf of his client, to profess expertise in subjects of which he knew nothing prior to receiving his brief—occasionally remaining in the same state of blissful ignorance on beginning to address the court. The advocate's lack of preparation is occasionally and embarrassingly revealed. Serjeant Vaughan was 'utterly ignorant of the rudiments of the law of real property and terribly alarmed lest he should commit some absurd blunder'. Arguing before Chief Justice Gibbs a property case 'of which he knew no more than the usher . . . he laid down Preston's proposition that "an estate in fee simple is the highest estate known to the law of England"'. The judge, wishing to frighten him, 'pretended to start, and said, "What is your proposition brother Vaughan?", when, thinking he was quite wrong and wishing to get out of the scrape, he observed, "My Lord, I mean to contend that an estate in fee simple is *one of* the highest estates known to the law of England—that is, my Lord, that it may be under certain circumstances—and sometimes is so'.[86]

Judicial rebukes for 'numerous submissions, many of a trifling nature'[87] or for presenting a claim which is 'trivial and banal even when topped up with much legalistic froth'[88] are not necessarily the result of defective advocacy or inadequate preparations. When an advocate exceeds the limits of judicial tolerance, it may be as much—if not more—the fault of the judge for any of the occupational diseases associated with chronic irritability to which some judges have been known to fall victim.[89] Sometimes, the advocate—and his client—may be afflicted by injudicious expansions of the law. Who would not have sympathy with Crown counsel faced with Lord Denning at the height of his law-making powers and reprimanded for reminding the judge that legislating was for Parliament: 'In the course of his submissions, [counsel] said at one point—and I made a note of it at the time—that if the court interferes in this case, "it would not be long before the powers of the court would be called in question". We trust that this was not said seriously, but only as a piece of advocate's licence.'[90] Harry Woolf (now Lord Justice Woolf) was Treasury devil (counsel to the Crown in common law matters) when, as Master of the Rolls, Lord Denning 'was setting about government departments with an irrepressible enthusiasm. When I die there may be found burnt on my heart the names *Laker, Congreve, Tameside,* and *Crossman,* just to name a few of my defeats when acting for the Government.'[91] Treasury counsel may be criticized for the unattractive position adopted by his clients. In 1941, Lord Atkin complained (admittedly in a dissenting speech) of having listened to 'arguments which might have been addressed acceptably to the Court of King's Bench in the time of Charles I'.[92]

The uncertainty of the law may defeat counsel's efforts. Treasury counsel may have the impossible task of seeking to make sense of an obscurely worded immigration rule. As the Master of the Rolls, Sir John Donaldson, observed in one case, 'at this point the impartial observer asks Mr Simon Brown to explain how paragraph 70 is intended to operate, and Mr Brown says that he will have to take instructions'.[93] Counsel may be frustrated by the judicial habit of changing the law in the judgment, something judges do not always acknowledge with the frankness of Lord Russell in a 1982 case in the House of Lords in which he expressed 'considerable sympathy for counsel . . . when he was told that he had all the law on his side, but was (in effect) facing the prophets'.[94] If he finds a clever point, the advocate may hear the judge respond, as did Mr Justice Danckwerts to a formidable argument by Crown counsel in a tax case, 'it always is rather a discouraging pursuit to endeavour to find consistent principles in the statutes relating to income tax'.[95] Or the judge may sidestep the carefully constructed argument of an advocate by observing, as did Mr Justice Cave, that 'doubtless no form of words has ever yet been framed by human ingenuity with regard to which some ingenious counsel could not suggest a difficulty'.[96] A judge in Alberta, Canada, is said to have dismissed a lengthy legal argument for an appellant with the judgment, 'Bullshit, costs to the respondent'.[97]

Some lawyers are simply not designed to be advocates. This may be for the best of reasons. When acting as Treasury counsel in the early nineteenth century, Charles Abbott (later Chief Justice) displayed 'the most marvellous inaptitude for the functions of an advocate and almost always lost the verdict. This partly arose from his power of discrimination and soundness of understanding which, enabling him to see the real merits of the cause on both sides, afterwards fitted him so well for being a Judge'.[98]

The inability of the lawyer adequately to perform the role of advocate may be for less worthy reasons. It was apparently said by his contemporaries of Charles Phillips (who died in 1859 after an eventful career which included acting as the unfortunate defence counsel for Courvoisier, the client who confessed to his lawyer that he had committed the murder but insisted on pleading not guilty)[99] that his style was 'pitiful to the last degree. He ought by common consent to be driven from the Bar.'[100] The aspiring advocate may possess all the necessary qualities, but for judgment. The career of an otherwise competent advocate may be destroyed by an obsession on behalf of a particular client who he thinks has been unjustly treated, or by a grievance against an opponent or a judge who he is sure has behaved improperly. An extreme example was Edward Kenealy. In 1873, he acted as leading counsel for Orton, the Tichborne claimant. 'He made groundless imputations against witnesses and against various Roman Catholic bodies, insulted and trifled with the Bench, and mercilessly protracted the case into the longest trial [on circuit] on record. The jury appended to their verdict a censure of the language he had employed.' His conduct after the trial, which included founding a newspaper to champion Orton's cause in which he 'menaced the chief justice . . . and the solicitor-general . . . with threats of revelations affecting their private lives and morals', led to him being disbarred.[101] Young barristers should ensure that (unless drafting a notice of appeal) they immediately forget all about their defeats in court.

IV

Great advocacy is more difficult to describe than the mediocre variety. The biographer of Norman Birkett suggested that 'the model advocate should be alert, courteous, of impressive bearing and possessed of a melodious speaking voice'.[102] There are many barristers with all those qualities whose submissions are far from compelling. By contrast, there are some very persuasive counsel who are lazy, inattentive to detail, rude, undistinguished in appearance, and whose voices tend to squeak. Much may depend on the audience: jury, magistrate, tribunal, trial judge, or appeal court. It was said of the successful nineteenth-century Chancery practitioner Sir Horace Davey (afterwards a Lord of Appeal) that 'the intellectual effort necessary to follow his utterances was always considerable; and the absence of anything like animation in his voice and delivery was so ostentatious that one sometimes wondered how he had forced himself into prominence at all'.[103]

The best advocates have learnt the lesson taught by Quintilianus that 'a timid witness may be terrorised, a fool outwitted, an irascible man provoked, and vanity flattered'.[104] They have a command of language, empathy for the conduct of others, an appreciation of what will persuade the tribunal, and a knowledge of the law. When appearing before a jury, the latter is less important than the former qualities. Marshall Hall 'was the first to acknowledge his ignorance of law'.[105]

So dependent is advocacy on mood, tone, and gesture that it cannot be appreciated by a mere reading of the transcript of legal proceedings. Its power inevitably vanishes into the air. It is difficult to say more of the greatest advocates than that they enjoyed a simplicity, directness, and brevity of approach that merits imitation by those who consider that only lengthy submissions and protracted cross-examination of hostile witnesses can earn their brief fee on behalf of their client.

When Oscar Wilde unsuccessfully prosecuted the Marquess of Queensberry for criminal libel for accusing Wilde of sodomy, Carson (on behalf of Queensberry) destroyed Wilde in cross-examination. Carson asked, in respect of a servant of Lord Alfred Douglas, 'Did you ever kiss him?' He drew the incriminating answer, 'Oh dear no. He was a peculiarly plain boy.' The trial judge, Mr Justice Henn Collins, sent a message to Carson congratulating him on his cross-examination and 'on having escaped the rest of the filth'.[106] Rufus Isaacs, as prosecuting counsel cross-examining the poisoner Seddon, having established that the defendant had lived with the murdered woman for over a year before she suffered her cruel fate, asked the devastating question, 'Did you like her?'[107] Norman Birkett QC demonstrated the ignorance of two witnesses claiming technical expertise by asking them, 'What is the co-efficient of the expansion of brass?'[108]

For eloquence it would be difficult to improve on Brougham's 1820 speech in defence of Queen Caroline: that 'the evidence before us is inadequate even to prove a debt; impotent to deprive of a civil right; ridiculous for convicting of the pettiest offence; scandalous if brought forward to support a charge of any grave character; monstrous if to ruin the honour of an English Queen'.[109] Sir Samuel Romilly (who died in 1818) was said to have 'marshalled his premises, and deduced his conclusions with mathematical precision, and his diction was as chaste as his logic was cogent. The unerring instinct with which he detected and the unfailing felicity with which he exposed a fallacy, united to no small powers of sarcasm and invective, made him formidable in reply, while the effect of his easy and impressive elocution was enhanced by a tall and graceful figure, a melodious voice, and features of classical regularity.'[110]

The successful advocate, of any generation, is the one who has the power, by persuasion, to move the mind or the heart of the judge or jury. Many techniques may be available. It may be by cool logic or by rigorous analysis of the legal materials. It may be by a naked appeal to the emotions. In a personal injuries case brought by a man who had both hands amputated in an accident, an American jury was impressed by an advocate whose entire closing argument consisted of slowly telling the jury that he had had lunch with his client and 'He . . . eats . . . like . . . a . . . dog'.[111]

Judges are human, and, just as was the case nearly two thousand years ago in the observations of Quintilianus,

> as soon as they begin to be angry, to feel favourably disposed, to hate or pity, they begin to take a personal interest in the case, and just as lovers are incapable of forming a reasoned judgment on the beauty of the object of their affections, because passion forestalls the sense of sight, so the judge, when overcome by his emotions, abandons all attempt to enquire into the truth of the arguments, is swept along by the tide of passion, and yields himself unquestioning to the torrent.[112]

Proust remarked that 'the first time one listens to a barrister . . . one is surprised by his tone, so different from the conversational'.[113] M. de Charlus' voice 'continued to rise, as piercing, as different from his normal voice, as that of a barrister grandiloquently addressing the court'.[114] But fashions in advocacy are not immutable. As recently as 1946, the standard practitioner's guide to the principles of advocacy lamented that 'day by day in the courts you will see barristers addressing the court as if they were engaged in a casual conversation in a club smoking room with a fellow member for whom they had little regard'.[115] Today, the conversational style of advocacy has effectively replaced the oratory previously practised by lawyers. What is considered necessary in one generation will be thought old-fashioned or radical in another. In 1907, Marshall Hall told the jury, 'I do not merely ask for a verdict of not guilty—I demand it'.[116] Embarrassed laughter, rather than applause, would greet the defence counsel who today imitated that example or modelled his advocacy on Marshall Hall's successful plea in 'the first great case which he fought on his own', in 1894: 'Look at her, gentlemen of the jury. Look at her. God never gave her a chance—won't you?'[117] By 1949, Sir Patrick Hastings explained that 'the days of flatulent oratory are gone'. Juries were no longer impressed by defence counsel with 'waving arms and streaming eyes. At one time it was thought effective to refer at repeated intervals to the blind Goddess of Justice sitting above the Central Criminal Court, and no advocate of any value was not fully equipped with a heart-breaking and totally irrelevant peroration'.[118] Since then, Hastings's observation that the great advocates 'possessed a personality which seemed to dominate the court'[119] has become dated. There will, nevertheless, always be room for the unconventional. In one

1956 libel trial, a great modern advocate, Fearnley-Whittingstall QC, began his final speech to the jury with the words, 'Yo-ho-ho and a bottle of rum' as a criticism of the tactics of the other side.[120] Because there are no absolute standards, no immutable rules, little more can be said of the great masters of advocacy than that 'they succeeded in their day, and that their contemporaries acclaimed them as masters'.[121]

Important though the advocate is, his influence should not be exaggerated. Sir Patrick Hastings was 'satisfied that at least ninety per cent of all cases win or lose themselves, and that the ultimate result would have been the same whatever counsel the parties had chosen to represent them'. He was sure that 'a case can be lost by bad advocacy'. And, on 'rare occasions . . . so rarely that perhaps they can be counted on the fingers of one hand', brilliant advocacy may win a case that would otherwise have been lost.[122] Infrequently does great advocacy persuade judges to accept what they would otherwise reject. As Sir John Donaldson MR commented in his judgment in a 1984 case, 'only Mr Blom-Cooper could have made such a submission attractive and even he could not make it remotely plausible'.[123] It is by advocacy before a jury that counsel can make a real difference.

V

The English barrister who is best known to the legal and lay world, both in England and abroad, is John Mortimer's creation, Horace Rumpole. It is a tribute to Mortimer's skill as an author (and Leo McKern's ability as an actor in the television version of Rumpole's adventures) that on a visit to the robing room of any Crown Court in south-east England it is impossible to tell whether the barristers to be found there served as the raw material for this work of supposed fiction or whether they have modelled their professional performance on Rumpole's example.

Mortimer's literary achievement is to have made a popular hero out of a barrister. It is a feat which would have surprised Dickens and Trollope and, I think, has only otherwise been performed—though with less credibility—by Terence Rattigan in his play *The Winslow Boy* and by John Cleese in the film *A Fish Called Wanda*. The stories Mortimer has written about Rumpole are already classics of legal literature, at least in the same class as A. P. Herbert's *Uncommon Law* and Theo Mathew's *Forensic Fables*, and much more widely read.

Rumpole is, and takes pride in being, an Old Bailey hack barrister. He practises, and enjoys practising, crime on behalf of the defence. 'Give me a murder on a spring morning with a decent run and a tolerably sympathetic jury, and Rumpole's happiness is complete.'[124] He adopts the ethics of the barrister's profession, considering it his 'duty to be as difficult as possible'[125] on behalf of his client. But he does so not from philosophical or political principles, but out of self-interest. He 'will stand up in Court for absolutely any underprivileged person in the world. Provided they've got legal aid . . . . My motivation is the money.'[126] His approach is resolutely unacademic. He has 'always found knowing the law a bit of a handicap for a barrister'.[127] He views the members of the Appellate Committee of the House of Lords with no great respect as judges who make his life more difficult by 'always having something to say; they're a lot of old chatterboxes up there'.[128] When Rumpole 'applied a torn-off page of the *Criminal Law Review* to the electric fire and lit the small cigar',[129] the limited influence of the academic lawyer on the practitioner is effectively demonstrated.

Other members of the cast of legal London are portrayed in wickedly accurate caricatures: the ambitious prosecuting counsel, marking his notes with ten differently coloured pencils for reference purposes; the eager young advocate from the Crown Prosecution Service 'who spoke very fast, as though he wanted to get the whole painful ordeal over as quickly as possible';[130] the radical instructing solicitor convinced that the case will be won by producing in evidence an article from a left-wing magazine to show that the police are racist; the bullying judge who can be tamed by 'the fear of being criticized by that august assembly . . . the Court of Appeal';[131] the token female member of chambers, assertive of her own rights but determined to prevent any other woman from threatening her monopoly.

An arrogant legal profession is put in its place, firmly but humorously. Mortimer displays for all to see the pomposities and pretensions of a service industry that is not always industrious and only sometimes serves the interests of the public. Irritable judges 'suffer from a bad case of premature adjudication'.[132] Sanctimonious barristers give talks on 'the Christian approach to the Rent Acts'.[133] Court lists are arranged by discussions at the local amateur dramatic society. John Mortimer is concerned to remind us that the gap between the lawyer and the litigant is not so wide as the professional would like us to believe. The domestic and business crises of Rumpole and his colleagues mirror and reflect the legal predicaments of his clients, whether in the context of confidentiality, matrimonial relations, or alcoholic consumption.

But Rumpole remains an enigma. He has his off days, but he frequently displays remarkable powers of advocacy. He is a barrister of exceptional wit and considerable charm, whose eloquence has juries eating out of his hand and whose powers of deduction would do credit to

Sherlock Holmes, Miss Marple, and Hercule Poirot. It is Rumpole who, 'by an unaided process of deduction',[134] solves the crimes when he is paid to defend the accused. Admittedly (and understandably) he does not always see eye to eye with members of the judiciary. But in important criminal cases it is the jury which makes the vital decision as to whether the defendant is convicted or acquitted. You would expect to see a man of Rumpole's ability at the top of his profession, much in demand from high-class criminals anxious to stay out of prison and prepared to pay large fees to a lawyer with the necessary skills to charm juries on their behalf. Yet he is, we are asked to believe, an underpaid hack barrister, attempting to make a meagre living from the legal aid fund, desperately asking his clerk if there is 'any chance of a small brief going today, perhaps a spot of indecency at the Uxbridge Magistrates Court',[135] and pathetically seeking to entertain his friends 'with a complete account of my cross-examination of the pathologist'[136] in a rare triumph he enjoyed long ago.

There is much of the fairy tale about the legal world inhabited by Rumpole. Under a rigorous cross-examination, the prosecution witness 'swayed and fell crumpled at the side of the witness-box'.[137] The Lord Chief Justice, Lord Wantage, allows Rumpole to ridicule him in court. The innocent are always acquitted and the guilty are usually convicted. By the end of his cases, Rumpole *knows* (most barristers can do no more than guess, often erroneously) what really happened in the events leading up to the commission of the crime. The adversary process of a real trial more often leaves the truth mysteriously, and sometimes conveniently, hidden, covered over by the evasions, half-truths, and plain lies embedded in the conflicting contentions of the hostile witnesses.

Rumpole conducts his private life according to the basic principles of defence advocacy. He does not tell lies on his own behalf but he feels entitled to require those persecuting him to prove their case without his assistance. When he declines to admit to some minor infraction of the domestic rules, his wife despairs of his intransigence, is unconvinced by his defence that arguing has 'been my life', and becomes a stern judge who 'looked at me, weighed up the evidence and summed up, not entirely in my favour'.[138] Although he has had many successes at the Bar, he recognizes that he has 'never, when all the evidence has been heard and the arguments are over, secured a verdict' in a dispute with his wife.[139] So, when Mrs Rumpole learns the truth about a domestic issue, he 'had no alternative but to come clean and throw myself on the mercy of the court'.[140] Despite the inadequacies and the imperfections of the legal system, so pointedly exposed by Mortimer, the message is far from a revolutionary one: the law, Rumpole tells us, can provide reassuring principles by which a good man can live until he is 'called to account by the Great Benchers of the Sky'.[141]

If the Rumpole stories, and the advocacy of their main protagonist, occasionally fail to convince, they are never less than a delight. Rumpole fears that 'soon we'll be replaced by a couple of chartered accountants and a good computer'.[142] They could not possibly provide the same quality of information or entertainment concerning the life of the advocate.

VI

It is one of the regrets of Horace Rumpole that his profession inhibits him from being able to 'say exactly what I thought'.[143] He reflects that he 'had spent my whole life being other people, safe blowers, fraudsmen, a few rather gentle murderers. I'd had remarkably little time to be Rumpole.'[144] His son is concerned that acting for others means that 'you must forget your own voice sometimes'.[145]

The advocate spends much of his working life as a cipher who is required to appear for anyone, pleading their case however reprehensible and hopeless, and professionally obliged *not* to give the court his opinions. There is a real danger that while seeking to satisfy the often irreconcilable demands of his client, the court, and his conscience, the advocate will make the serious mistake of believing all his submissions, fail to maintain a professional detachment from the case, and cause himself to become an object of ridicule once he takes off his wig and gown. Occupying his professional life speaking on behalf of others, he may find that he has nothing to say for himself, no values which he holds dear, no firm opinions in opposition to which he is not prepared to perceive and to argue the competing contention. Cynicism about right and wrong is an occupational disease of the barrister. As Charles W. Wolfram has observed, 'putting one's emotions out for hire to someone whose objectives the lawyer despises is the sort of professional debasement that may predictably lead to professional burnout and withdrawal and stagnation in law practice. Or, if pressed, it may lead to profound moral scepticism, an utter insensitivity to the human qualities of persons—clients and opponents alike.'[146] The advocate who still aspires to be a human being must retain his independence, objectivity, and beliefs. Sir Edward Marshall Hall was a great advocate but a less fulfilled, and less attractive, human being. He 'was without settled convictions on any subject, but . . . might be convinced in all sincerity of anything in the world for a moment'.[147] As John Mortimer QC has observed, 'perhaps, in taking on so many lives, Marshall Hall had little time for his own'.[148]

It would be wrong to think that an ability to represent others in court connotes any necessary qualities as a human being. As Proust observed of the medical profession, ability as a lawyer 'does not imply any superiority in the other departments of the intellect, and a person of the utmost vulgarity, who admires the worst pictures, the worst music, who is without the slightest intellectual curiosity, may perfectly well possess' great expertise in his professional capacity.[149] Indeed, for Swift, 'in all points out of their own trade, [lawyers] were usually the most ignorant and stupid generation among us, the most despicable in common conversation, avowed enemies to all knowledge and learning . . .'.[150] The advocate should aspire, out of court, to cleanse himself of the dirt which proximity to his unattractive clients may have caused to attach to him. In court, Trollope's Mr Chaffanbrass 'is a little man, and a very dirty little man . . . [who] has all manner of nasty tricks about him'. But at home 'he is one of the most easy, good-tempered, amiable old gentlemen that ever was pooh-poohed by his grown-up daughters, and occasionally told to keep himself quiet in a corner. . . . He is charitable, too, and subscribes largely to hospitals founded for the relief of the suffering poor.'[151]

What is the advocate to do as he grows older? After a while, his eagerness or willingness to ingratiate himself with judge and jury may recede. He may conclude that trying to understand and explain the conduct of his clients is work for an enthusiastic young man or woman. He may be unable to disguise his desire for promotion to the Bench. When a vacancy occurred in the Appellate Committee of the House of Lords in 1909, Thomas Shaw was arguing a case in a Scottish court. He 'abandoned his client at a critical stage of the proceedings, and departed to London in order [successfully] to urge personally upon the Prime Minister his claims to the vacant office'.[152] Or he may contemplate with horror the prospect of a judicial appointment. Rumpole could not 'imagine a worse way of passing your life than having to actually listen to the speeches of the learned friends'.[153]

If he accepts an appointment as a judge, the advocate may, like Norman Birkett, find that 'there is no satisfaction in work on the Bench at all comparable with the work one used to do at the Bar' and that he enjoyed 'the limelight and cannot bear now to be in obscurity'.[154] He may prove a disastrous appointment. Lord Campbell explained that there can be many reasons for this. 'The celebrated advocate, when placed on the Bench, embraces the side of the plaintiff or of the defendant with all his former zeal, and—unconscious of partiality or injustice—in his eagerness for victory becomes unfit fairly to appreciate conflicting evidence, arguments and authorities.' It may be equally unsatisfactory to appoint to the Bench 'the man of a naturally morose or impatient temper who has been restrained while at the bar by respect for the ermine, or by the dread of offending [solicitors], or by the peril of being called to a personal account by his antagonist for impertinence'. If he is made a judge, he may become 'puffed up by self-importance, and revenging himself for past subserviency, is insolent to his old competitors, bullies the witnesses, and tries to dictate to the jury'. It may be unwise for the Lord Chancellor to accede to the claim of 'the selfish practitioner, who, while struggling to advance himself, was industrious and energetic, [but] having gained the object of his ambition, proves listless and torpid, and is quite contented if he can shuffle through his work without committing gross blunders or getting into scrapes'. To raise to the Bench the barrister who has been 'more laborious than discriminating' may result in a judge who 'hunts after small or irrelevant points, and obstructs the business of his court by a morbid desire to investigate fully and to decide conscientiously'. Counsel 'who constantly complained of the interruptions of the court' may, when promoted, 'himself become a by-word for impatience and loquacity'. The enthusiastic, reforming lawyer 'may, with the best intentions, be led astray into dangerous courses, and may bring about a collision between different authorities in the state which had long moved harmoniously, by indiscreetly attempting new modes of redressing grievances, and by an uncalled-for display of heroism'.[155]

Felix Frankfurter said of Mr Justice Jackson that, when at the Bar,

> his aims increasingly groped beyond that of mere advocacy. . . . Deeper insight made him aware that the best of phrases may be less than the truth and may even falsify it.[156]

In moments of depression, the advocate may, like Sir John Simon (himself one of the great advocates of this century), conclude that advocacy does not come within 'the higher ranges of human achievement . . . Advocacy as practised at the Bar is just a way of earning a living; and a man's livelihood ought not to be the whole of a man's life.'[157] Like Lord Macmillan (a Lord of Appeal from 1930 to 1939 and again from 1941 to 1947, the intervening period being spent as Minister of Information), he may persuade himself that advocacy has an adverse effect on the mind of the practitioner so that the more skilful he becomes the less qualified he will be 'for other spheres of intellectual or practical activity'.[158] And he may, as did Sir

Patrick Hastings, lament the fact that 'a barrister builds up nothing that he can leave behind him, his practice dies with him, even he himself is soon forgotten'.[159] Who (with the exception of other advocates) looks in the volumes of old law reports to read the arguments of counsel?

Such sentiments are unworthy of the function of the advocate. For all its absurdities and ambiguities, and despite its equivocal moral basis, advocacy makes an indispensable contribution to the maintenance of the rule of law in a free society.

CHAPTER 8

Conclusion

I

IN his *History of English Law*, Sir William Holdsworth commented that it is difficult to know if there was ever a time when the law did not permit a man to plead in court on behalf of another. 'Certainly he was allowed such assistance as early as the laws of Henry I [1110–35], unless he was charged with felony.'[1]

Some societies, real and fictional, have abolished advocates. Thomas More's *Utopia* contained no advocates at all 'to be over-ingenious about individual cases and points of law. They think it better for each man to plead his own cause, and tell the judge the same story as he'd otherwise tell his lawyer. Under such conditions, the point at issue is less likely to be obscured, and it's easier to get at the truth . . .'[2] Article 70 of the 1669 Constitution of Carolina prohibited the profession of barrister, stating it to be 'a base and vile thing to plead for money or reward'.[3]

Some legal systems have, on occasion, jealously confined the right to act as an advocate, preventing particular people (by reason of their characteristics or conduct) from having such power and responsibility. In 1810, Mr Sheridan MP presented a petition to the House of Commons containing what he described as 'a grave and serious charge against a respectable body of men, the Benchers of Lincoln's Inn', alleging that 'they have committed an act of grievous and unwarrantable oppression'. The petition complained of a bye-law made in 1807 which stated that 'no person who has written for hire in the newspapers shall be admitted to do exercises to entitle him to be called to the bar'.[4] Women have struggled to gain acceptance as advocates. In 1872, the US Supreme Court held that a woman had no constitutional right to practise law. Justice Bradley (in an opinion joined by two other Justices) explained that the 'paramount destiny and mission of woman [is] to fulfil the noble and benign offices of wife and mother. This is the law of the Creator.'[5] In 1903, the refusal of Gray's Inn to call Bertha Cave to the Bar because she was female was upheld by a tribunal consisting of the Lord Chancellor, the Lord Chief Justice, and five other judges.[6] In 1945, the US Supreme Court (by a majority of 5–4) upheld the refusal of the Supreme Court of Illinois to allow a conscientious objector to be admitted to the Bar because his moral beliefs would prevent him from taking an oath to support the State constitution.[7] In 1950, the British Columbia Court of Appeal held that the Benchers of the Law Society of British Columbia were entitled to conclude that a Communist was not a fit person to be called to the Bar.[8] The Supreme Court of New York, Appellate Division, concluded that obstruction of the due administration of justice while serving as the President of the United States rendered a man unfit to remain as an attorney.[9] But the Supreme Court of Florida has concluded that 'private noncommercial sex acts between consensual adults are not relevant to prove fitness to practise law'.[10]

No modern society which values human rights could survive without professional advocates. No modern society which understands the central role of advocacy in the legal system would confine its practice by reference to irrelevant criteria.

It is a fundamental rule of natural justice that a man shall be heard before he is condemned in any respect. As Mr Justice Fortescue noted in 1723, even God himself applied such a principle before passing sentence on Adam in the Garden of Eden.[11] But the right to be heard would often be of little use if it did not include the right to counsel. For those who are less than articulate, the importance of the hired voice is obvious. The role of the independent advocate, speaking for those who cannot (because of inability) or should not (because of unpopularity) address the court on their own behalf, is an indispensable aspect of the rule of law. Freedom of expression in court, especially for those whose liberty or property is endangered, cannot depend on an ability personally to present your case, or to find someone prepared to assist without reward.

As Mr Justice Sutherland explained on behalf of the US Supreme Court in 1932:

> Even the intelligent and educated layman has small and sometimes no skill in the science of law. If charged with crime, he is incapable, generally, of determining for himself whether the indictment is good or bad. He is unfamiliar with the rules of evidence. Left without the aid of counsel he may be put on trial without a proper charge, and convicted upon incompetent evidence, or evidence irrelevant to the issue or otherwise inadmissible. He lacks both the skill and knowledge adequately to prepare his defence, even though he have a perfect one. He requires the guiding hand of counsel at every step in the proceedings against him. Without it, though he be not guilty, he faces the danger of conviction because he does not know how to establish his innocence. If that be true of men of intelligence,

how much more true is it of the ignorant and illiterate, or those of feeble intellect.[12]

The US Supreme Court has noted that 'lawyers to prosecute are everywhere deemed essential to protect the public's interest in an orderly society' and 'there are few defendants charged with crime, few indeed, who fail to hire the best lawyers they can get to prepare and present their defences'.[13] For such reasons, it has been generally recognized that, as Viscount Maugham stated for the Judicial Committee of the Privy Council in 1944, 'the importance of persons accused of a serious crime having the advantage of counsel to assist them before the courts cannot be doubted'.[14] The Irish Supreme Court has stated a similar rule.[15] The High Court of Australia, in an unconvincing judgment in 1979, dismissed an appeal by a man convicted of rape at a trial in which he had represented himself. His barrister had ceased to act for him owing to the absence of legal aid and the trial judge had refused to grant an adjournment to enable the defendant to find other counsel. Mr Justice Murphy, dissenting, complained that 'even an experienced lawyer would be regarded as foolish to represent himself if accused of serious crime'.[16] When a wife tried to speak for her husband in a case in 1850, Lord Campbell CJ told them that it would be better if he were represented by counsel than that she should 'come into court to . . . engage in scenes inconsistent with the character of her sex'.[17]

Where an indigent individual loses his liberty, it has been held by the US Supreme Court to be a breach of his fundamental rights to deny him representation by counsel,[18] even where the offence is a minor one carrying a short period of imprisonment, 'absent a knowing and intelligent waiver'.[19] This constitutional right to counsel includes the right to have counsel make a closing speech to the judge or jury.[20]

Article 6 of the European Convention on Human Rights guarantees legal assistance in criminal cases to anyone without sufficient means to pay for it, if the interests of justice so require (though this does not necessarily extend to appeal proceedings).[21] Article 14.3 of the International Covenant on Civil and Political Rights is in similar terms. The layman involved in civil litigation, suing for damages, concerned about being deported, or fighting for custody of a child, may well have a similar need for an advocate to represent his interests. The European Court of Human Rights has therefore recognized that in civil cases there will, on occasion, be a right to 'the assistance of a lawyer when such assistance proves indispensable for an effective access to court . . . by reason of the complexity of the procedure or of the case'.[22]

II

During the debates on the Contempt of Court Bill in 1981, Lord Hailsham, the Lord Chancellor, recalled a decision made by the Court of Appeal in 1980. It was, the court had decided, not unreasonable behaviour justifying a divorce for a wife to ration her husband to sexual intercourse once a week.[23] This had caused considerable interest in certain newspapers. Lord Hailsham said that he had no complaint about headlines which announced, 'Once a week is enough'. But he did object to the fact that 'three newspapers tried to interview the wives of the judges concerned'.[24] Freedom of speech will, on occasion, inconvenience those in authority. Its exercise may cause pain to other citizens. All rights have their cost. Of course, we recognize that freedom of expression is not absolute. We tolerate restrictions, such as the laws of libel and obscenity. But we apply a principle (expressly stated in Article 10 of the European Convention on Human Rights) that no limitation on free speech is to be applied except where necessary. This means, according to the European Court of Human Rights, except where there is 'a pressing social need' for a restraint on free speech.[25] Applying a similar test, Mr Justice Brandeis explained in the US Supreme Court in 1927 that it is only a 'clear and present' danger of a 'relatively serious' nature that could justify a limitation on free speech. For 'if there be time to expose through discussion the falsehood and fallacies, to avert the evil by the processes of education, the remedy to be applied is more speech, not enforced silence. Only an emergency can justify repression.'[26] The onus of proving the necessity for an impediment to freedom of expression is firmly placed on those who wish to impose fetters on what we may read or write.

Freedom of expression is central to a liberal, democratic society. Only by exercising the right to discuss, dispute, and dissent can we hope to understand what is true and to identify what is prejudice, confusion, or plain error. Without the liberty to impart and receive information and ideas, we cannot take full advantage of our potential as autonomous individuals. And it is futile to boast of democracy if we are prevented from learning and then criticizing what those who govern us are doing on our behalf.

Advocacy adopts and asserts the primary value of freedom of expression. It is a practical manifestation of the principle of freedom of speech which developed western societies hold so dear. Advocacy displays to advantage the premiss that freedom of expression produces the benefits claimed by John Milton in *Areopagitica*, by John Stuart Mill in *On Liberty*, and thereafter by various constitutional courts. Free speech in the courts helps the truth to emerge. It aids the revelation of corruption, bias, and mistakes. It assists stability by permitting the articulation of grievances and by promoting the peaceful resolution of conflicts. It encourages the development of individual dignity, autonomy, and equality. And it plays its part in helping to secure the protection of other fundamental human rights.[27] In these respects, legal procedure illuminates how free speech 'constitutes one of the essential foundations of a democratic society',[28] and is 'one of the basic conditions for its progress and for the development of every man'.[29]

Though it may (at times) be embarrassing to many, in court as well as out, the principle of freedom of expression is vital to the maintenance of a free society. It is essential to the rule of law and the liberty of the citizen that as few fetters as possible are imposed on the advocate in the exercise of his important function. In both the criminal and the civil context, it is, as Mr Justice Bayley stated in 1825, 'for the advantage of the administration of justice that [the advocate] should have free liberty of speech'.[30]

According to Talmudic learning, when the Prophet Elijah returns, he 'will resolve all unsolved legal questions'.[31] Until that time, legal disputes will continue to be settled by judges who require the assistance of counsel appearing for the competing sides to put the opposing points of view. Freedom of expression for the advocate does not ensure that justice will be done. But without such a freedom, the prospects for a fair trial, a just result, and the protection of an individual's rights under the rule of law, are immeasurably reduced.

III

In some circumstances the advocate truly has, as Edward Marjoribanks contended, a 'high and responsible calling'[32] which makes him responsible for the reputation, the welfare, sometimes even the life of his client. It is, however, important for the advocate to keep his feet on the ground. What he says in court will not always sound, or be, sensible. Nor will it habitually win him friends. The honest advocate also knows that there are limits to the glory of which he, and his profession, can boast. As Quintilianus observed in his epic study of advocacy written in the first century AD, 'others besides orators persuade by speaking or lead others to the conclusion desired, as for example harlots, flatterers and seducers'.[33]

It is, then, somewhat surprising that the profession of advocacy has, at times, involved very considerable glamour for its practitioners. At the end of the eighteenth century, Thomas Erskine occupied, by reason of his powers of advocacy in cases concerning the liberty of the subject, an extraordinary place in public life:

> his name was on every lip as the fearless defender of the citizen's rights; and he was hailed as the saviour of his country. Bonfires were lit in every part of the kingdom in his honour. After some of his great victories in the courts, the horses were taken out of his carriage by worshipping crowds, and he was drawn in triumph through the streets of London to his home in Serjeant's Inn. Portraits and busts of him were sold by the thousand; a hundred cities offered him their freedom.[34]

Earlier this century, Edward Marshall Hall 'was as well known as any man in England, and millions read of his doings with interest and awe day by day, and year by year'.[35]

Today, few advocates would aspire to public recognition and approval, let alone adulation. Their aim is a more modest one: to secure a degree of popular understanding that they perform a valuable function. They perceive, and regret, misunderstanding and consequent distrust of their role. It is becoming increasingly difficult to make intelligent people understand that it is desirable to maintain a legal system in which the lawyer has the duty, or even the right, to argue cases on behalf of those whose conduct he may find unwise, distressing, or even reprehensible. Laymen remain unclear why it is advantageous in the public interest that advocates should not be perceived as endorsing the views or actions of those they represent. Widespread cynicism, or plain abuse, is the response to the Bar Council's accurate statement that the Bar constitutes 'an important part of the system of the administration of justice, serving the needs of the public, the upholding of the rule of law and the maintenance of civil liberties'.[36]

Despite all the advances in media technology, the public knows less than ever about the principles which govern the work of the advocate. This may have something to do with the absence of capital cases in which defendants can be saved from (or, if counsel does not do his job adequately, propelled towards) the gallows, the dearth of society divorces in which dirty linen is washed in the Royal Courts of Justice, and, as Lord Rawlinson (Attorney-General 1970–4) has lamented, the fashion that 'the successful modern advocate must have the style of a chartered accountant who is accustomed to reading the lesson in church'.[37] It may also be the result of lawyers neglecting to inform the public of the reality that without a body of advocates prepared to act on behalf of anyone, irrespective of the nature of their cause, such representation constituting no endorsement of the opinions or behaviour of the client, 'it would', as Mr Justice Brennan of the Australian High Court has observed, 'be difficult to bring unpopular causes to court and the profession would become the puppet of the powerful'.[38] Advocates have not been persuasive in the cause of their own profession, but they have a very strong case.

ABBREVIATIONS

A	Atlantic Reporter (USA)
ABAJ	American Bar Association Journal
AC	Law Reports: Appeal Cases (UK)
AD	Appellate Division (South Africa)
AIR	All India Reports
ALJR	Australian Law Journal Reports
All ER	All England Law Reports
ALR	American Law Reports
	Australian Law Reports
App Cas	Law Reports: Appeal Cases (UK)
B & Ad	Barnewall and Adolphus Reports (UK)
B & Ald	Barnewall and Alderson Reports (UK)
B & C	Barnewall and Cresswell Reports (UK)
B & S	Best and Smith Reports (UK)
BCLR	British Columbia Law Reports (Canada)
Beav	Beavan's Reports (UK)
Bing	Bingham's Reports (UK)
Burr	Burrow's Reports (UK)
C & P	Carrington and Payne's Reports (UK)
Cal Rptr	California Reporter
Car & Kir	Carrington and Kirwan's Reports (UK)
CBNS	Common Bench Reports (New Series) (UK)
CCC	Canadian Criminal Cases
CD	Collection of Decisions (European Commission of Human Rights, Strasbourg)
Ch	Law Reports: Chancery Division (UK)
Ch D	Law Reports: Chancery Division (UK)
Chit	Chitty's Reports (UK)
Cl & Fin	Clark and Finnelly's Reports (UK)
CLR	Commonwealth Law Reports (Australia)
Cmnd	Command Papers (UK)
Co Rep	Coke's Reports (UK)

Cowp	Cowper's Reports (UK)
Cox CC	Cox's Criminal Law Cases (UK)
Cr App Rep	Criminal Appeal Reports (UK)
DLR	Dominion Law Reports (Canada)
ECR	European Court Reports
EG	Estates Gazette (UK)
EHRR	European Human Rights Reports
ER	English Reports
F	Federal Reporter (USA)
F & F	Foster and Finlason's Reports (UK)
Fam	Law Reports: Family Division (UK)
FLR	Family Law Reports (Australia)
FSR	Fleet Street Reports (UK)
F Supp	Federal Supplement (USA)
H & N	Hurlstone and Norman's Reports (UK)
HC	House of Commons (UK)
HL	House of Lords (UK)
HL Cas	House of Lords Cases (UK)
ICLR	Irish Common Law Reports
ICR	Industrial Cases Reports (UK)
ILR	Irish Law Reports
	Indian Law Reports
Imm AR	Immigration Appeal Reports (UK)
IR	Irish Reports
IRLR	Industrial Relations Law Reports (UK)
Jac & W	Jacob and Walker's Reports (UK)
JP	Justice of the Peace (UK)
JPL	Journal of Planning Law (UK)
Jur	The Jurist (UK)
KB	Law Reports: King's Bench Division (UK)
LJ	Law Journal (UK)
LJ Ch	Law Journal: Chancery (UK)
LJCP	Law Journal: Common Pleas (UK)
LJQB	Law Journal: Queen's Bench (UK)
LQR	Law Quarterly Review (UK)
LR Ch App	Law Reports: Chancery Appeals (UK)
LR CP	Law Reports: Common Pleas (UK)

LR Ex	Law Reports: Exchequer (UK)
LR Ir	Law Reports: Ireland
LR QB	Law Reports: Queen's Bench (UK)
LR PC	Law Reports: Privy Council Appeals (UK)
LR Sc & Div	Law Reports: Scotch and Divorce Appeals (UK)
LT	Law Times (UK)
MLJ	Malayan Law Journal
My & Cr	Mylne and Craig's Reports (UK)
NE	North Eastern Reporter (USA)
NI	Law Reports: Northern Ireland
NLJ	New Law Journal (UK)
NSWLR	New South Wales Law Reports (Australia)
NSWR	New South Wales Reports (Australia)
NW	North Western Reporter (USA)
NYS	New York Supplement (USA)
NZLR	New Zealand Law Reports
NZPCC	New Zealand Privy Council Cases
OLR	Ontario Law Reports (Canada)
OR	Ontario Reports (Canada)
P	Law Reports: Probate Division (UK)
	Pacific Reporter (USA)
PD	Probate Cases (UK)
QB	Law Reports: Queen's Bench Division (UK)
QBD	Law Reports: Queen's Bench Division (UK)
Salk	Salkeld's Reports (UK)
SALR	South African Law Reports
SC	Session Cases (Scotland)
S Ct	Supreme Court Reporter (USA)
SCR	Supreme Court Reports (Canada)
SE	South Eastern Reporter (USA)
SI	Statutory Instruments (UK)
Sid	Siderfin's Reports (UK)
SLT	Scots Law Times
So	Southern Reporter (USA)
Sol J	Solicitors' Journal (UK)
SR NSW	State Reports (New South Wales) (Australia)
Str	Strange's Reports (UK)

St Tr	State Trials (UK)
SW	South Western Reporter (USA)
Taunt	Taunton's Reports (UK)
TC	Tax Cases (UK)
TLR	Times Law Reports (UK)
TPD	Transvaal Provincial Division (South Africa)
US	United States Reports
VLR	Victoria Law Reports (Australia)
WLR	Weekly Law Reports (UK)
WN	Weekly Notes (UK)
WR	Weekly Reporter (UK)
WWR	Western Weekly Reports (Canada)

NOTES

1. Introduction

1. *Rondel v. Worsley* [1969] 1 AC 191, 216 (submission of Robin Dunn QC).
2. Plato, *Gorgias* (transl. Walter Hamilton, Penguin Classics, 1960), p. 32.
3. Felix Frankfurter, 'Mr Justice Jackson' 68 *Harvard Law Review* 937, 939 (1955).
4. Cicero, 'On Duties (II)' in *On the Good Life* (transl. with introduction by Michael Grant, 1971), p. 147.
5. Cicero, *De Oratore* (transl. E. W. Sutton and H. Rackham, Loeb edn., 1942), II. xlii. 178 at p. 325.
6. *Attorney-General v. Barker* [1990] 3 All ER 257, 261e–f (Lord Donaldson MR for the Court of Appeal).
7. *Independent* 15 Feb. 1990.
8. *Matthews v. US* 449 F 2d 985, 987n (1971) (US Court of Appeals).
9. H. Montgomery Hyde, *Norman Birkett* (1964), p. 502.
10. *The Times* 11 Apr. 1985.
11. *US v. Benn* 476 F 2d 1127, 1134n (1973) (US Court of Appeals) cited in David L. Bazelon (presiding judge of the US Court of Appeals), 'The Defective Assistance of Counsel' 42 *University of Cincinnati LR* 1, 3 (1973).
12. *Independent* 5 Jan. 1991.
13. *Re An Advocate* [1964] MLJ 1.
14. *Geiler v. Commission on Judicial Qualifications* 515 P 2d 1, 5n–6n (1973) (Supreme Court of California), cert. denied 417 US 932 (1974) (US Supreme Court).
15. *In the Matter of Marvin F. Frankel* 323 NW 2d 911 (1982) (Supreme Court of Michigan).
16. *State of Tennessee ex rel Inman v. Brock* 622 SW 2d 36, 50 (1981) (Supreme Court of Tennessee), cert. denied 454 US 941 (1981) (US Supreme Court).

17. *In the Matter of Judge William H. Heuermann* 240 NW 2d 603 (1976) (Supreme Court of South Dakota).
18. *Danzey v. Metropolitan Bank of England and Wales* (1912) 28 TLR 327, 328.
19. *Earl Beauchamp v. The Overseers of Madresfield* LR 8 CP 245 (1872) (argument of A. Wills QC). On the duty of the advocate, see ch. 4, n. 21 on this case.
20. For examples of deceptive advocacy by Hummel's law firm see ch. 2, at pp. 27–9.
21. Richard H. Rovere, *Howe and Hummel* (1947), pp. 110–11.
22. Roy Grutman and Bill Thomas, *Lawyers and Thieves* (1990), p. 56.
23. *Ex parte Lloyd* (1822) Montagu's Reports 70n, 72.
24. Above, n. 4 at p. 146.
25. Ibid., p. 147.
26. Rodney Jones, Charles Sevilla, and Gerald Uelman, *Disorderly Conduct: Real-life comedy from the courtrooms* (1988), p. 131.
27. *R v. O'Connell* (1844) 7 ILR 261, 312-3 (Crampton J in the Queen's Bench of Ireland).
28. Travers Humphreys, *Criminal Days* (1946), p. 98.
29. Alan M. Dershowitz, *Reversal of Fortune* (Penguin edn., 1991) p. 207.
30. *In Re G. Mayor Cooke* (1889) 5 TLR 407, 408 (Court of Appeal).
31. *Financial Times* 4 May 1989.
32. Peter V. MacDonald QC, *Court Jesters* (1987), p. 29.
33. *The Florida Bar v. T. David Burns* 392 So 2d 1325 (1981) (Supreme Court of Florida).
34. Above, n. 29 at p. 192.
35. *American Bar Association Journal*, Jan. 1990, p. 32.
36. See 59 George III, ch. 46 (1819), and *Ashford v. Thornton* 106 ER 149 (1818).
37. *Serville v. Constance* [1954] 1 WLR 487, 491 (Harman J).

2. Clients

1. *Independent* 4 Aug. 1989.
2. Sir William Holdsworth, *A History of English Law* (4th edn., 1936), vol. 2, pp. 314–15.

3. *R v. Walker* (c.1668), *Tremaine's Pleas of the Crown*, p. 261, cited in *The English and Empire Digest* (1978), vol. 3, p. 787.
4. David Lemmings, *Gentlemen and Barristers: The Inns of Court and the English Bar 1680–1730* (1990), pp. 146–7.
5. John Lord Campbell, *Lives of the Lord Chancellors* (5th edn., 1868), vol. 2, p. 333 n.
6. *Lord Eldon's Anecdote Book* (ed. Anthony Lincoln and Robert McEwen, 1960), p. 34.
7. Above, n. 5, vol. 4, p. 287.
8. *Butterworth v. Clapham* (1820) 1 Jac & W 673n.
9. *Re London and Manchester Direct Independent Railway Co. (Remington's Line)* (1849) 18 LJ Ch 245, 247.
10. These cases are described by Lord Chancellor Eldon in *Ex parte Lloyd* (1822) Montagu's Reports 70n, 72–3.
11. Peter Carter-Ruck, *Memoirs of a Libel Lawyer* (1990), p. 143.
12. *Pickering v. Dowson* (1813) 4 Taunt 778, 782–3.
13. *Atkinson v. Pacific Stevedoring and Contracting Co* 24 DLR 400 (1915).
14. See *The Royal Commission on Legal Services* (Cmnd. 7648, 1979), vol. 1, p. 467.
15. *Attorney-General v. Lord Advocate* (1834) 2 Cl & Fin 481.
16. Above, n. 2 (1924 edn.), vol. 6, p. 477 n.
17. Wilfrid R. Prest, *The Rise of the Barristers: A Social History of the English Bar 1590–1640* (1986), p. 295.
18. See n. 91 below on Dunning's earnings.
19. Above, n. 6 at p. 67.
20. *Weidekind v. Tuolumne County Water Co* 19 P 173 (1887) (Supreme Court of California).
21. *Re S.K.H. (Advocate)* (1907) ILR 34 Calc 72.
22. *Devi v. Singh* AIR 1917 PC 80, 84.
23. *Re Jack Martin Conflenti* 624 P 2d 253 (1981) (Supreme Court of California).
24. Roy Grutman and Bill Thomas, *Lawyers and Thieves* (1990), p. 51.
25. *Re Hobler* (1844) 8 Beav 101.
26. *In Re McL* (1903) 3 SR NSW 388, 400.
27. *R v. Woodward* [1944] KB 118, 119 (Court of Criminal Appeal).
28. *Vescio v. The King* [1949] SCR 139, 142 (Supreme Court of Canada).
29. *Faretta v. California* 422 US 806, 852 (1975) (Blackmun J, dissenting in the US Supreme Court).

30. *Re A. Graham Greenlee* 658 P 2d 1 (1983) (Supreme Court of Washington).
31. *In the Matter of Collins* 271 SE 2d 473 (1980) (Supreme Court of Georgia).
32. *Re Application of the Legal Aid Society of the City of New York* 415 NYS 2d 432, 433 (1979) (Supreme Court of New York, Appellate Division).
33. *Mercy v. Persons Unknown* 231 EG 1159 (1974) (Court of Appeal).
34. *R v. M'Gregor and Lambert* 1 Cox CC 346, 347 (1844).
35. *R v. M'Gregor and Lambert* 1 Car & Kir 429, 433 (1844).
36. *R v. Secretary of State for India in Council ex parte Ezekiel* [1941] 2 KB 169, 175n. See generally *Code of Conduct of the Bar of England and Wales* (27 Jan. 1990), para. 501(*d*).
37. *Thellusson v. Lord Rendlesham* 7 HL Cas 429, 430–1 (1858).
38. *Ahmed Hassan Saad v. Abu Tilla Mohamed Ahmed* (1966) 1 African Law Reports (Commercial) 51 (Shibeika J).
39. *Code of Conduct for the Bar of England and Wales* (4th edn., 1989), Annex 6, para. 10.
40. Section 75 and Schedule 11 of the Courts and Legal Services Act 1990.
41. *McKeown v. The Queen* 16 DLR (3d) 390, 399 (1971).
42. *People of the State of Illinois v. Ernest* 544 NE 2d 1275 (1989) (Appellate Court of Illinois).
43. Above, n. 2 at p. 314.
44. Above, n. 5 at p. 309.
45. *Horton v. Ruesby* 90 ER 326 (1686).
46. *R v. Peters* (1758) 1 Burr 568, 571.
47. *Dundass v. Lord Weymouth* (1777) 2 Cowp 665.
48. F. D. MacKinnon, *On Circuit* (1940), pp. 170–1.
49. Above n. 2 at p. 313.
50. *In the Marriage of Slender* 29 FLR 267 (1977) (Family Court of Australia).
51. *Legal Services: A Framework for the Future* (Cm 740, 1989), para. 3.23.
52. Section 70 of the Courts and Legal Services Act 1990.
53. I owe this story to my wife, Denise Sloam, who was the unfortunate defence counsel.
54. *Rondel v. Worsley* [1967] 1 QB 443, 490 (argument of Graham Swanwick QC).

55. *Re Harold Knox* 20 Cr App Rep 96, 97 (1927).
56. Patrick Hastings KC, *Cases in Court* (1949), pp. 109 and 337.
57. John Mortimer, *Rumpole à la Carte* (1990), p. 11.
58. *Rondel v. Worsley* [1969] 1 AC 191, 254–5 (Lord Pearce).
59. *Rondel v. Worsley* [1967] 1 QB 443, 453 (Lawton J).
60. *Independent* 1 Sept. 1989.
61. *Guardian* 7 Sept. 1989.
62. Ibid. 25 Oct. 1989 and *Independent* 24 Aug. 1991.
63. A. P. Herbert, *Uncommon Law* (1969 edn.), p. 100.
64. *Sunday Times* 3 Sept. 1989.
65. *Independent* 13 Dec. 1989.
66. Ibid. 28 June and 3 July 1990.
67. *The Times* 17 July 1990.
68. Lord Birkett, *Six Great Advocates* (1961), p. 14.
69. *Ferguson v. Moore* 39 SW 341, 343 (1897) (Supreme Court of Tennessee).
70. William Durran, *The Lawyer: Our Old-Man-of-the-Sea* (1913), pp. 56 and 214.
71. Richard H. Rovere, *Howe and Hummel* (1947), pp. 59–60.
72. Ibid., p. 69. Similarly at p. 132.
73. *People of the State of Illinois v. Dukes* 146 NE 2d 14, 17 (1957) (Supreme Court of Illinois).
74. *State of Arizona v. Bailey* 647 P 2d 170, 175 (1982) (Supreme Court of Arizona).
75. Marcus Fabius Quintilianus, *Institutio Oratoria* (transl. H. E. Butler, Loeb edn., 1985), VI. i. 30, pp. 401–3.
76. Above, n. 71 at pp. 57–8.
77. Above n. 75, IV. i. 49, p. 33.
78. C. P. Harvey QC, *The Advocate's Devil* (1958), p. 30. See, similarly, John Mortimer, *Clinging to the Wreckage* (1982), p. 127.
79. John Mortimer, *The First Rumpole Omnibus* (1983), p. 254.
80. Above, n. 71 at p. 71.
81. *Rondel v. Worsley* [1967] 1 QB 443, 469 (Lawton J).
82. Above, n. 5 at p. 77 n.
83. *Rondel v. Worsley* [1967] 1 QB 443, 522.
84. R. E. Megarry QC, *Lawyer and Litigant in England* (1962), p. 14.
85. *Stanley v. Board of Professional Responsibility* 640 SW 2d 210, 213 (1982) (Supreme Court of Tennessee).

86. Edward Marjoribanks, *The Life of Sir Edward Marshall Hall* (1929), p. 470.
87. *In Re Lonrho PLC* [1990] 2 AC 154, 201 (House of Lords).
88. *Rondel v. Worsley* [1969] 1 AC 191, 283 (Lord Upjohn).
89. *Dictionary of National Biography 1961–1970* (ed. E. T. Williams and C. S. Nicholls, 1981), p. 111.
90. *Morris v. Hunt* (1819) 1 Chit 544, 551.
91. *Boswell: The English Experiment 1785–1789* (ed. Irma S. Lustig and Frederick A. Pottle, 1986), p. 211.
92. *Dictionary of National Biography 1951–1960* (ed. E. T. Williams and Helen M. Palmer, 1971), p. 428.
93. John Lord Campbell, *Lives of the Chief Justices* (3rd edn., 1874), vol. 3, pp. 140–1.
94. H. Montgomery Hyde, *Carson* (1953) (paperback edn., 1987), pp. 67–8, 81.
95. Jean-Denis Bredin, *The Affair: The Case of Alfred Dreyfus* (1987), pp. 410–11.
96. Ronald Hayman, *Proust* (1990), p. 129.
97. 416 HL 386 (20 Jan. 1981, debate on the Contempt of Court Bill).
98. *Jewish Chronicle* 9 Dec. 1988, *Independent* 14 Mar. 1989, and *Jewish Chronicle* 30 June 1989.
99. *The Times* 20 Aug. 1990.
100. See ch. 5 at p. 147.
101. *French v. French* (1824) 1 Hogan 138.
102. *Estes v. The State* 6 So 2d 132 (1942) (Supreme Court of Mississippi).
103. *People of the State of Illinois v. Carr* 278 NE 2d 839 (1971) (Appellate Court of Illinois). See, generally, 'Assault on Attorney as Contempt' 61 ALR 3d 500 (1975).
104. *Bryans v. Faber and Faber*, cited in *Borrie and Lowe's Law of Contempt* (2nd edn., 1983), p. 29.
105. *Paul v. The Queen* 111 DLR (3d) 626, 629 (1980) (Supreme Court of Canada).
106. *Helen Smith v. The State* 238 SE 2d 116 (1977) (Supreme Court of Georgia).
107. I am grateful to the unfortunate counsel, Robert Griffiths, for this information.
108. *R v. Collins* [1954] VLR 46, 49, 53–4 (Supreme Court of Victoria).

109. Above, n. 86 at p. 178.
110. William O. Douglas, *The Court Years 1939–75* (1980), pp. 20 and 181.
111. H. Montgomery Hyde, *Norman Birkett* (1964), p. 88.
112. Above, n. 91 at pp. 56–7.
113. Above, n. 48 at p. 46.
114. Above, n. 56 at p. 34.
115. *In Re Dellinger* 370 F Supp 1304, 1310 (US District Court) (appeal dismissed by the US Court of Appeals: 502 F 2d 813 (1974); cert. denied by the US Supreme Court: 420 US 990 (1975)).
116. See ch. 5 on morality.
117. John Mortimer, *Clinging to the Wreckage* (1982), p. 12.
118. *Rondel v. Worsley* [1969] 1 AC 191, 274.
119. Boswell, *Life of Johnson* (1791) (ed. R. W. Chapman, corrected by J. D. Fleeman, 1970), p. 358.
120. Above, n. 93, vol. 1, pp. 248–9.
121. Above, n. 5, vol. 9, p. 142.
122. Anthony Trollope, *The Three Clerks* (1858), ch. 40.
123. Above n. 56 at pp. ix–x.
124. *Rondel v. Worsley* [1969] 1 AC 191, 276 (Lord Pearce).
125. *Saif Ali v. Sydney Mitchell & Co. (A Firm)* [1978] QB 95, 105 (Lawton LJ).
126. Richard A. Cosgrove, *The Rule of Law: Albert Venn Dicey, Victorian Jurist* (1980), p. 41.
127. 40 *Law Times* 18 (1864).
128. *Kennedy v. Broun* (1863) 13 CBNS 677, 737 (Erle CJ).
129. *Cornwell v. Myskow* [1987] 1 WLR 630, 639 (Court of Appeal).
130. *Jarvis v. Swan Tours Ltd* [1973] QB 233, 236–7 (Lord Denning in the Court of Appeal).
131. Above, n. 56 at p. 208.
132. See ch. 5.
133. E. P. Evans, *The Criminal Prosecution and Capital Punishment of Animals* (1906), pp. 18–19.
134. *Miles v. City Council of Augusta, Georgia* 710 F 2d 1542, 1544n (1983).
135. *The Times* 28 Jan. 1987.
136. *Lord v. Thornton* 80 ER 965 (1616).
137. *Nixon v. Attorney-General* [1931] AC 184, 190 (House of Lords).

138. Above n. 117 at pp. 240–1. The case was *DPP v. Jordan* [1977] AC 699.
139. *Rondel v. Worsley* [1969] 1 AC 191, 257 (Lord Pearce).
140. *Rondel v. Worsley* [1967] 1 QB 443, 513.
141. *Batchelor v. Pattison* 3 Cases in the Court of Session (4th Series) 914, 918 (1876).
142. Joseph Conrad, *The Secret Agent* (1907), ch. XI.
143. *Attorney-General v. Heinemann Publishers Australia Pty. Ltd. and Wright* [1989] 2 FSR 349, 588.
144. *Attorney-General v. Wellington Newspapers Limited* [1989] 2 FSR 691, 695.
145. Lord Oliver, 'Spycatcher: Confidence, Copyright and Contempt' 23 *Israel Law Review* 409, 410 (1989).
146. 119 HC 972 (14 July 1987).
147. Philip Agee, *On the Run* (1987), p. 115.
148. *Attorney-General v. Guardian Newspapers Ltd. and others* [1987] 1 WLR 1248.
149. *Attorney-General v. Guardian Newspapers Ltd. and others* [1987] 1 WLR 1248, 1269–70.
150. Ibid. 1277.
151. Ibid. 1321.
152. Ibid. 1286.
153. Ibid. 1306.
154. *Daily Mirror* 31 July 1987.
155. *Attorney-General v. South China Morning Post* [1989] 2 FSR 653.
156. *Daily Telegraph* 30 Dec. 1987.
157. *Attorney-General v. Guardian Newspapers and others (No. 2)* [1990] 1 AC 109, 143.
158. Ibid. 223, 227, and 232.
159. *Attorney-General v. Heinemann Publishers Australia Pty. Ltd. and Wright* [1989] 2 FSR 631.
160. Malcolm Turnbull, *The Spycatcher Trial* (1988), p. 196.
161. *Attorney-General v. Wellington Newspapers Ltd* [1989] 2 FSR 691 and [1988] 1 NZLR 129 (New Zealand Court of Appeal).
162. *Guardian* 15 June 1988.
163. *Attorney-General v. Guardian Newspapers and others (No. 2)* [1990] 1 AC 109.
164. John le Carré, *The Russia House* (1989), p. 69.

3. Judges and Opponents

1. *Great Western Railway Co. v. Waterford and Limerick Railway Co.* 17 Ch D 493, 507 (1881).
2. *Rondel v. Worsley* [1969] 1 AC 191, 283 (Lord Upjohn).
3. J. B. Atlay, *The Victorian Chancellors* (1906), vol. 1, p. 83.
4. Wilfrid R. Prest, *The Rise of the Barristers: A Social History of the English Bar 1590–1640* (1986), p. 303.
5. *Florence v. Lawson* 17 *Law Times* 260 (1851).
6. *Place v. Searle* 48 TLR 428, 429 (1932).
7. *Dimsdale Developments (South East) Ltd v. Secretary of State for the Environment* (1986) JPL 276, 277 (Macpherson J).
8. *Independent* 14 Dec. 1988.
9. *Rondel v. Worsley* [1969] 1 AC 191, 227 (Lord Reid).
10. *Berger v. US* 295 US 78, 88 (1935) (US Supreme Court).
11. *People of the State of Illinois v. Roberts* 356 NE 2d 429, 431 (1976) (Appellate Court of Illinois).
12. *Hawk v. Superior Court of the State of California in and for the County of Solano* 116 Cal Rptr 713, 727 (1974) (Court of Appeal of California), cert. denied 421 US 1012 (1975) (US Supreme Court).
13. A. P. Herbert, *Uncommon Law* (1969 edn.), p. 100.
14. *Olimpius v. Butler* 248 F 2d 169, 170–1 (1957) (US Court of Appeals).
15. *State ex rel Cary v. District Court of Hennepin County* 125 NW 1020 (1910) (Supreme Court of Minnesota).
16. *In the Matter of Owen W. Crumpacker* 383 NE 2d 36, 48 (1978) (Supreme Court of Indiana), cert. denied 444 US 979 (1979) (US Supreme Court).
17. *State v. Turner* 538 P 2d 966, 976 (1975) (Supreme Court of Kansas).
18. *Tarrant v. State of Florida* 537 So 2d 150, 152 (1989) (District Court of Appeal of Florida).
19. *In the Matter of Thomas Marshall* 55 S Ct 344 and 513 (1935) (US Supreme Court).
20. *In the Matter of Owen W. Crumpacker* 383 NE 2d 36, 40 (1978) (Supreme Court of Indiana), cert denied 444 US 979 (1979) (US Supreme Court).
21. Jan Morris, *Destinations* (1982), p. 225.

22. *Columbus Bar Association v. Riebel* 432 NE 2d 165, 166 (1982) (Supreme Court of Ohio).
23. *American Bar Association Journal* June 1988, p. 118. See generally Nicholas von Hoffman, *Citizen Cohn* (1988).
24. *X v. Federal Republic of Germany* 39 CD 58, 62 (1971) (European Commission of Human Rights).
25. *Re Nicholson's Settlement* [1938] 1 All ER 109, 111.
26. *Reekie v. M'Kinven* (1921) SC 733, 735.
27. Above, n. 4 at p. 320.
28. *In Re Johnson* 20 QBD 68 (1887) (Court of Appeal).
29. See R. F. V. Heuston, *Lives of the Lord Chancellors 1885–1940* (1964), p. 333.
30. *Pie-Powder by A Circuit Tramp* (1911), p. 22.
31. *Beevis v. Dawson* [1957] 1 QB 195, 201 (Singleton LJ for the Court of Appeal).
32. *The Times* 17 Feb. 1968.
33. Ibid. 20 Feb. 1968. Shimon Shetreet, *Judges on Trial* (1976), p. 249, wrongly cites this episode as one where the judge had walked out of court as a rebuke to counsel for bickering.
34. *Independent* 18 Oct. 1988 and *The Times* 22 Oct. 1988.
35. *Parashuram Detaram Shamdasani v. King-Emperor* [1945] AC 264, 267, 269–70 (Lord Goddard for the Privy Council on appeal from the High Court at Bombay).
36. *Roberts v. Commission on Judicial Performance* 661 P 2d 1064, 1066 (1983) (Supreme Court of California).
37. *Cannon v. Commission on Judicial Qualifications* 537 P 2d 898, 913n–914n (1975) (Supreme Court of California).
38. *USA Today* 11 Aug. 1988 and *American Bar Association Journal*, Sept. 1988 at p. 25.
39. *Curran v. Superior Court in and for Fresno County* 236 P 975, 978 (1925) (District Court of Appeal, California).
40. *McMillan v. Superior Court of San Diego County* 158 Cal Rptr 17, 19 (1979) (Court of Appeal, California).
41. *Offutt v. US* 348 US 11, 16n (1954) (US Supreme Court).
42. *State of Wisconsin v. Walberg* 325 NW 2d 687, 690 (1982) (Supreme Court of Wisconsin).
43. *Observer* 6 Nov. 1988.
44. *Ryan v. Commission on Judicial Performance* 754 P 2d 724, 739–40 (1988) (Supreme Court of California).

45. Sir William Holdsworth, *A History of English Law* (4th edn., 1936), vol. 2, p. 313.
46. *Peck v. Stone* 304 NYS 2d 881, 883, 886 (1969) (Supreme Court of New York, Appellate Division).
47. *Jensen v. Superior Court of the County of San Diego* 201 Cal Rptr 275, 279, 281 (1984) (Court of Appeal of California).
48. *La Rocca v. Lane* 338 NE 2d 606, 613 (1975) (Court of Appeals of New York).
49. *Sandstrom v. State of Florida* 336 So 2d 572, 573 and 578 (1976) (Supreme Court of Florida).
50. *The People of the State of California v. Rainey* 36 Cal Rptr 291 (1964) (District Court of Appeal of California).
51. On wigs and gowns see David Pannick, *Judges* (1987), pp. 142–7.
52. John Mortimer, *The First Rumpole Omnibus* (1983), p. 191.
53. See, for example, *Jones v. National Coal Board* [1957] 2 QB 55 (Court of Appeal) and *R v. Renshaw*, *The Times* 23 June 1989 (Court of Appeal).
54. *R v. McFadden and others* 62 Cr App Rep 187 (1975), 119 *Sol J* 868 (1975) and 125 *NLJ* 298 (1975).
55. *Eizerman v. Behn* 132 NE 2d 788, 799 (1956) (Appellate Court of Illinois).
56. *State v. Crum* 74 NW 992 (1898) (Supreme Court of North Dakota).
57. *Holman v. State* 5 NE 556 (1886) (Supreme Court of Indiana).
58. *Bradley v. Fisher* 80 US 335, 337, 356 (1871) (US Supreme Court).
59. *State v. Driscoll* 555 P 2d 136, 137–8 (1976) (Supreme Court of New Mexico).
60. *Re Kumaraendran* (1975) 2 MLJ 45.
61. See generally 'Attorney's failure to attend court, or tardiness, as contempt' 97 ALR 2d 431 (1964) and John E. Theuman, 'Attorney's failure to attend court, or tardiness, as contempt' 13 ALR 4th 122 (1982). See also *Arthur v. Superior Court of Los Angeles County* 398 P 2d 777 (1965) (Supreme Court of California).
62. *R v. Jones* 42 CCC (2d) 192, 195 (1978) (Ontario Court of Appeal). See similarly *R v. Hill* 73 DLR (3d) 621, 630 (1976) (British Columbia Court of Appeal) and *R v. Anders* 136 DLR (3d) 316 (1982) (Ontario Court of Appeal).

63. *Muirhead v. Douglas* (1979) SLT (Notes of Recent Decisions) 17.
64. *Re Luben and another* (1987) *Pacific Law Digest* 32, noted in (1989) *Commonwealth Law Bulletin* 226.
65. See generally John J. Michalik, 'Attorney's Addressing Allegedly Insulting Remarks to Court During Course of Trial as Contempt' 68 ALR 3d 273 (1976).
66. *State ex rel Cheadle v. District Court of the Tenth Judicial District in and for Fergus County* 10 P 2d 586 (1932) (Supreme Court of Montana).
67. *MacInnis v. US* 191 F 2d 157, 160 (1951) (US Court of Appeals), cert. denied 342 US 953 (1952) (US Supreme Court).
68. *Re Lawrence Buckley* 514 P 2d 1201 (1973) (Supreme Court of California), cert. denied 418 US 910 (1974) (US Supreme Court).
69. *In the Matter of George D. Gates* 248 A 2d 671 (1968) (District of Columbia Court of Appeals).
70. *State of Washington v. Caffrey* 422 P 2d 307, 308 (1966) (Supreme Court of Washington).
71. *Re L. A. Paulsrude* 248 NW 2d 747, 748 (1976) (Supreme Court of Minnesota).
72. *US v. Schiffer* 351 F 2d 91, 98 (1965) (US Court of Appeals), cert. denied 384 US 1003 (1966) (US Supreme Court).
73. *In Re Dellinger* 370 F Supp 1304, 1319 (1973) (US District Court), appeal dismissed 502 F 2d 813, 815 (1974) (US Court of Appeals), cert. denied 420 US 990 (1975) (US Supreme Court).
74. *In Re Dellinger* 502 F 2d 813, 815 (1974) (US Court of Appeals), cert. denied 420 US 990 (1975) (US Supreme Court).
75. *R v. Rosenstein* (1943) TPD 65, 69.
76. *Public Prosecutor v. Seeralan* (1985) 2 MLJ 30, 32 (Supreme Court of Malaysia).
77. See *Hobbs v. Tinling (CT) and Company Ltd.* [1929] 2 KB 1. The cause of counsel's irritation was Lord Chief Justice Hewart. See A. M. Sullivan, *The Last Serjeant* (1952), pp. 307–8, and H. Montgomery Hyde, *Norman Birkett* (1964), pp. 264–6.
78. *R v. Swartz* (1977) 2 WWR 751 (Manitoba Court of Appeal).
79. *Brassington v. Brassington* [1962] P 276, 282 (Holroyd Pearce LJ for the Court of Appeal).
80. *Re Lechmere Charlton* (1837) 2 My & Cr 316.

81. *Izuora v. R* [1953] AC 327, 336 (Lord Tucker for the Privy Council on appeal from the West African Court of Appeal). See also *Weston v. Central Criminal Court Courts Administrator* [1977] QB 32 (Court of Appeal).
82. *Lord Eldon's Anecdote Book* (ed. Anthony Lincoln and Robert McEwen, 1960), pp. 42–3.
83. *R v. Jordan* (1888) 36 WR 797.
84. *Hilborne v. Law Society of Singapore* [1978] 1 WLR 841 (Judicial Committee of the Privy Council on appeal from the Court of Appeal of Singapore).
85. *Watt v. Ligertwood and Daniel* (1874) LR 2 Sc & Div 361.
86. Rudy Narayan, *Barrister for the Defence* (1985), p. 205.
87. *In Re a Barrister* 139 NLJ 327 (1989).
88. *Commonwealth of Pennsylvania v. Martorano* 563 A 2d 1193 (1989) (Superior Court of Pennsylvania).
89. *In the Matter of Lee A. Freeman* 292 F 2d 806 (1961) (US Court of Appeals).
90. *In the Matter of Macaulay* 1 Sierra Leone Law Reports 141, 145 (1960) (Court of Appeal of Sierra Leone).
91. *The Times* 16–17 Dec. 1981.
92. *Vernon v. Oliver* (1885) 11 SCR 156, 163 (Gwynne J for the Supreme Court of Canada).
93. *Lord Advocate v. Jamieson* (1822) 1 Shaw 285.
94. *Re Pryor* 18 Kan 72 (1877) (Supreme Court of Kansas).
95. *White v. State* 31 SE 2d 78, 79–80 (1944) (Court of Appeals of Georgia).
96. *In the Matter of Thomas James Wallace* (1866) LR 1 PC 283, 286, 294.
97. *In Re O. S. Miller* 54 Nova Scotia Reports 529 (1921) (Supreme Court of Nova Scotia).
98. *Attorney-General v. Kuang* (1987) 1 MLJ 206.
99. *Re Sarbadhicary* 23 TLR 180 (1906).
100. *Ex parte Pater* (1864) 5 B & S 299.
101. *Tanner v. US* 62 F 2d 601 (1933) (US Court of Appeals), cert. denied 289 US 746 (1933) (US Supreme Court).
102. *Johnson v. Trueblood* 476 F Supp 90, 96 (1979) (US District Court), vacated because of a denial of natural justice 629 F 2d 302 (1980) (US Court of Appeals), cert. denied 450 US 999 (1981) (US Supreme Court).
103. *Independent* 13 Sept. 1989.

104. 422 HL 251–2 (1 July 1981).
105. 416 HL 374 (20 Jan. 1981).
106. *Australian* 12 Oct. 1972, cited in Julian Disney, Paul Redmond, John Basten, and Stan Ross, *Lawyers* (1986), p. 860.
107. *Guardian* 20 May 1989.
108. *The Times* 1 Aug. 1989.
109. Ibid. 2 Aug. 1989.
110. *Albano v. Commonwealth* 53 NE 2d 690, 692 (1944) (Supreme Judicial Court of Massachusetts).
111. *State v. Johnson* 18 P 2d 35 (1933) (Supreme Court of Washington).
112. *R v. Benson* (1914) AD 357.
113. *Horn v. District Court, Ninth Judicial District* 647 P 2d 1368, 1372, 1375 (1982) (Supreme Court of Wyoming).
114. *Cohran v. Sosebee* 169 SE 2d 624 (1969) (Court of Appeals, Georgia).
115. See ch. 6, pp. 191–3 on the verbosity of litigants in person and judicial attempts at control.
116. See the *Independent* 24 Feb. 1988 and *The Times* 8 Mar. 1988.
117. *R v. Huntingdon Magistrates' Court ex parte Bugg* (Judgment of the Divisional Court, 17 Nov. 1988), per McCowan J (transcript at p. 33).
118. *Rondel v. Worsley* [1967] 1 QB 443, 492, 494.
119. *O'Laoire v. Jackel International Ltd* [1990] ICR 197, 207.
120. *Phillips v. Hedges* (1736) 125 ER 1004.
121. *Chandler, Assignee v. Page* Trin. 18 Geo. III. 1778, cited in 125 ER 1004 n.
122. *R v. Jermy* (1752) 96 ER 799.
123. *Anonymous* (1710) 1 Salk 84.
124. *Witham v. Witham* (1669) 21 ER 723. *Oswald's Contempt of Court* (3rd edn., 1910, by George Stuart Robertson), p. 94 n, says that 'the language used by the offenders in some of these cases was amusing, but not suitable for repetition, such is the prudery of a twentieth-century law book'.
125. *Nicholas Fuller's Case* (1607) 12 Co Rep 41, 43.
126. *Proceedings against James Whitelocke* (1613) 2 St Tr 765.
127. *Twyn's Case* (1663) 6 St Tr 513, 548.
128. *Anon.*, cited in *R v. Sumer and Hillard* (1677) 1 Sid 271n, cited in *Oswald's Contempt of Court* (3rd edn., 1910, by George Stuart Robertson), p. 54 n.

129. *The Times* 12 Jan. 1989.
130. *Lewis v. Ogden* 53 ALR 53, 57, 60 (1984).
131. *Steinmann v. De Courte* (1899) 17 NZLR 805, 813.
132. *Jellicoe v. Wellington District Law Society* (1900) NZPCC 310.
133. *R v. Silber* (1952) 2 SALR 475, 481, 484.
134. *Re Duncan* 11 DLR (2d) 616, 618 (1957).
135. *Re Wiseman* [1969] NZLR 55.
136. *Vidyasagara v. R* [1963] AC 589, 595–6 (Lord Guest for the Privy Council on appeal from the Supreme Court of Ceylon).
137. *In Re Lonrho PLC and others* [1990] 2 AC 154, 178.
138. *Maharaj v. Attorney-General for Trinidad and Tobago* [1977] 1 All ER 411, 415–16.
139. *Maharaj v. Attorney-General of Trinidad and Tobago (no. 2)* [1979] AC 385.
140. See (1979) *Commonwealth Law Bulletin* 190.
141. *Hobbs v. Tinling (CT) and Company Ltd.* [1929] 2 KB 1, 48. See n. 77 above for the context in which this comment was made.
142. *The Times* 6 Oct. 1989 and *Sunday Times* 8 Oct. 1989.
143. Patricia Campbell Hearst (with Alvin Moscow), *Patty Hearst* (1988 edn.), p. 406. See *US v. Hearst* 638 F 2d 1190 (1980) (US Court of Appeals).
144. *Garrison v. Louisiana* 379 US 64 (1964).
145. *In Re Snyder* 472 US 634, 646–7 (1985) (US Supreme Court). See also *In Re Sawyer* 360 US 622 (1959) (US Supreme Court) and Sandra M. Molley, 'Restrictions on Attorney Criticism of the Judiciary: A Denial of First Amendment Rights' 56 *Notre Dame Lawyer* 489 (1981).
146. *R v. Barker* (1980) 4 WWR 202, 221 (Alberta Court of Appeal).
147. *R v. Kiernan* (1855) 5 ICLR 171, 173–4 (Crampton J in the High Court in Ireland).
148. *Rockhold Ltd. v. Secretary of State for the Environment* (1986) JPL 130, 131 (Forbes J).
149. *R v. Secretary of State for the Home Department ex parte Brind* [1991] 1 AC 696, 717 (Lord Donaldson MR in the Court of Appeal).
150. Marcus Fabius Quintilianus, *Institutio Oratoria* (transl. H. E. Butler, Loeb edn., 1985), IV. i. 16, pp. 13–15.
151. E. S. Turner, *May it Please Your Lordship* (1971), p. 225.
152. *William Jones v. Rev. William Davies Shipley, Dean of St Asaph* (1784) 21 State Trials 847, 954.

153. *Pie-Powder by A Circuit Tramp* (1911), p. 50.
154. See *The Oxford Book of Legal Anecdotes* (ed. Michael Gilbert, 1986), p. 64.
155. See John Campbell, *F. E. Smith, First Earl of Birkenhead* (1983), p. 112.
156. Maurice Healy, *The Old Munster Circuit* (1939), p. 199.
157. Iain Adamson, *The Old Fox* (1963), p. 147.
158. *British Sugar Manufacturers Ltd v. Harris* [1938] 2 KB 220, 238 (intervention by Sir Donald Somervell A-G). The Court of Appeal decided not to deal with the second point. Cited in R. E. Megarry, *Miscellany-at-Law* (1955), pp. 5–6.
159. Above, n. 82 at p. 124.
160. *Forensic Fables by O* (Theo Mathew) (1961), pp. 267–8.

4. Duties and Powers

1. Rudy Narayan, *Barrister for the Defence* (1985), p. 205.
2. Jesse Berman, 'The Cuban Popular Tribunals' 69 *Columbia Law Review* 1317, 1341 (1969), cited by Charles Fried, *Right and Wrong* (1978), p. 178.
3. *Abse v. Smith* [1986] QB 536, 546.
4. *Orchard v. South Eastern Electricity Board* [1987] QB 565, 571 (Sir John Donaldson MR for the Court of Appeal).
5. *Kennedy v. Broun* (1863) 13 CBNS 677, 737 (Erle CJ).
6. *Rondel v. Worsley* [1967] 1 QB 443, 502 (Lord Denning MR). See ch. 5, p. 135.
7. *Tombling v. Universal Bulb Company Ltd.* [1951] 2 TLR 289, 297 (Denning LJ). See also *Rondel v. Worsley* [1969] 1 AC 191, 227 (Lord Reid), cited at ch. 3, n. 9.
8. *Code of Conduct of the Bar of England and Wales* (27 Jan. 1990), para. 207.
9. *R v. Thomas Williams* (1797) 26 St Tr 653, 687–8.
10. *Sacher v. US* 343 US 1, 13–14 (1952) (US Supreme Court).
11. *R v. Ensor* [1989] 1 WLR 497, 502 (Lord Lane CJ for the Court of Appeal). See n. 40 below. For an example, see ch. 7, n. 55.
12. *Strickland, Superintendent, Florida State Prison v. Washington* 466 US 668 (1984) (US Supreme Court).
13. *R v. Corporation of Helston in Cornwall* 88 ER 693, 694 (1713).

14. *The Works of Jeremy Bentham* (ed. John Bowring, 1843), vol. 2, p. 396.
15. Franz Kafka, *The Trial* (1925) (Penguin edn., 1953), p. 138.
16. See ch. 5, p. 133.
17. *In Re G. Mayor Cooke* (1889) 5 TLR 407, 408 (Court of Appeal).
18. *Johnson v. Emerson and Sparrow* [1871] LR 6 Ex 329, 367.
19. *Abraham v. Jutsun* [1963] 2 All ER 402. The third judge, Lord Justice Pearson, declined to consider 'whether there ever could, in some hypothetical circumstances, be a case in which it might constitute misconduct for a solicitor appearing as an advocate to take a bad point. It could obviously only be in an extreme case that such a conclusion could be reached, but I think that it is better not to consider in advance what the position might be in other hypothetical cases which are not before this court.'
20. *Gallagher v. Municipal Court of City of Los Angeles* 192 P 2d 905, 908–9 (1948) (Supreme Court of California).
21. *Earl Beauchamp v. The Overseers of Madresfield* LR 8 CP 245, 253 (1872).
22. *In the Matter of Samuel A. Bithoney* 486 F 2d 319, 322 (1973).
23. *Richardson v. R* 3 ALR 115, 121 (1974) (High Court of Australia).
24. C. P. Harvey QC, *The Advocate's Devil* (1958), p. 13.
25. Sir William Blackstone, *Commentaries on the Laws of England* (1776) (4th edn., 1876), vol. 3, p. 27.
26. *Flint v. Pike* (1825) 4 B & C 473, 478 (Bayley J).
27. *Munster v. Lamb* 11 QBD 588, 603–4 (1883) (Court of Appeal), approved in *Rondel v. Worsley* [1969] 1 AC 191, 229 (Lord Reid), 252 (Lord Morris), and 266–7 (Lord Pearce).
28. *Munster v. Lamb* 11 QBD 588, 603–4 (1883) (Court of Appeal).
29. *Needham v. Dowling* (1845) 15 LJCP 9.
30. *Mackay v. Ford* (1860) 5 H & N 792.
31. *Hodgson v. Scarlett* (1818) 1 B & Ald 232, 243.
32. *Butt QC v. Jackson* (1846) 10 ILR 120; *Lessee Sturgeon v. Douglass* (1846) 10 ILR 128n; *R v. Kiernan* (1855) 5 ICLR 171.
33. See, for example, *Lee v. Nash* 671 P 2d 703 (1983) (Court of Appeals of Oregon), petition for review denied 675 P 2d 491 (1984) (Supreme Court of Oregon); and *Anderson v. Rossman & Baumberger PA* 440 So 2d 591 (1983) (District Court of Appeal of Florida), petition for review dismissed 450 So 2d 485 (1984) (Supreme Court of Florida).

34. *Batchelor v. Pattison* 3 Cases in the Court of Session (4th Series) 914, 918 (1876) (Court of Session, Scotland), cited with approval in *Rondel v. Worsley* [1969] 1 AC 191, 241 (Lord Morris), 259–60 (Lord Pearce), and 282 (Lord Upjohn).
35. *Swinfen v. Lord Chelmsford* (1860) 5 H & N 890, 920–4. On the limits to counsel's implied powers in these and other respects see *Halsbury's Laws of England* (4th edn., reissue, 1989), vol. 3(1), paras. 518–21.
36. *Swinfen v. Lord Chelmsford* (1860) 5 H & N 890, 892–3.
37. See Lord Denning's account of the case in *Rondel v. Worsley* [1967] 1 QB 443, 498–9.
38. *R v. McLoughlin* [1985] 1 NZLR 106, 107.
39. *R v. Irwin* [1987] 1 WLR 902 (Court of Appeal).
40. *R v. Ensor* [1989] 1 WLR 497, 502 (Court of Appeal).
41. *Clark v. Couchman* (1885) 20 LJ 318 (Warwick County Court).
42. *Rondel v. Worsley* [1967] 1 QB 443, 448 (submission of Graham Swanwick QC).
43. *Saif Ali v. Sydney Mitchell & Co. (A Firm)* [1980] AC 198, 216 (Lord Diplock).
44. *Rondel v. Worsley* [1969] 1 AC 191, 232 (Lord Reid), 246–7 (Lord Morris), 261–3 (Lord Pearce), and 281 (Lord Upjohn).
45. *Saif Ali v. Sydney Mitchell & Co. (A Firm)* [1980] AC 198, 212 (Lord Wilberforce).
46. *Rondel v. Worsley* [1969] 1 AC 191. On the background to the decision, see two articles by Ronald F. Roxburgh: '*Rondel v. Worsley*: The Historical Background' 84 *LQR* 178 (1968) and '*Rondel v. Worsley*: Immunity of the Bar' 84 *LQR* 513 (1968).
47. *Giannarelli v. Wraith* (1988) 62 ALJR 611. This was a 4–3 decision of the High Court of Australia in which the majority concluded that advocates have an immunity from liability for negligence for the conduct of the case in court, the minority reached a contrary conclusion because of their interpretation of a statute, and one judge in the minority (Mr Justice Deane) expressed disagreement with the conclusions as to public policy adopted by the majority from the reasoning of the House of Lords.
48. See *Demarco v. Ungaro* (1979) 95 DLR (3d) 385 (Krever J in the Ontario High Court of Justice); *Karpenko v. Paroian, Courey, Cohen & Houston* (1980) 117 DLR (3d) 383 (Anderson J in the Ontario High Court of Justice); *Pelky v. Hudson Bay Insurance*

Co and others (1981) 35 OR (2d) 97 (Catzman J in the Ontario High Court of Justice).

49. See ch. 6, part V, p. 197.
50. *Rondel v. Worsley* [1969] 1 AC 191, 246 (Lord Morris).
51. Ibid. 287 (Lord Pearson).
52. *Saif Ali v. Sydney Mitchell & Co. (A Firm)* [1980] AC 198.
53. Ibid. 220 (Lord Diplock).
54. See ibid. 215 (Lord Wilberforce), 224 (Lord Diplock), and 232 (Lord Salmon). See also *Giannarelli v. Wraith* (1988) 62 ALJR 611 (High Court of Australia) approving the test stated by the New Zealand Court of Appeal.
55. *Rees v. Sinclair* [1974] 1 NZLR 180, 187 (McCarthy P).
56. *Somasundaram v. M. Julius Melchior & Co. (A Firm)* [1988] 1 WLR 1394, 1403 (Court of Appeal).
57. *Biggars v. McLeod* [1977] 1 NZLR 321 (Somers J in the Supreme Court of New Zealand).
58. *Orchard v. South Eastern Electricity Board* [1987] QB 565, 581 (Dillon LJ in the Court of Appeal).
59. *Rondel v. Worsley* [1969] 1 AC 191, 232 (Lord Reid), 243–4 (Lord Morris), 267 (Lord Pearce), and 284–5 (Lord Upjohn) (with Lord Pearson undecided at p. 294). See also *Saif Ali v. Sydney Mitchell & Co. (A Firm)* [1980] AC 198, 215 (Lord Wilberforce), 224 (Lord Diplock), and 227 (Lord Salmon). See also *Majid v. Muthuswamy* [1968] 2 MLJ 89 (Federal Court in Singapore).
60. Section 62(1) of the Courts and Legal Services Act 1990.
61. Article 2(1) of the Supply of Services (Exclusion of Implied Terms) Order 1982 SI No. 1771.
62. *Somasundaram v. M. Julius Melchior & Co. (A Firm)* [1988] 1 WLR 1394, 1397–1403.
63. *Turner v. Philipps* (1792) Peake 166.
64. *Mulligan v. M'Donagh QC* (1860) 2 LT 136.
65. *Rondel v. Worsley* [1969] 1 AC 191, 287 (Lord Pearson).
66. Ibid. 261 (Lord Pearce).
67. *Robertson v. Macdonogh* (1880) 6 LR Ir 433, 438 (Chief Justice May for the Queen's Bench Division of the High Court of Ireland).
68. *Re Le Brasseur and Oakley* [1896] 2 Ch 487, 493 (Lindley LJ). See similarly Lopes LJ at p. 495.
69. Sir William Blackstone, above, n. 25, loc. cit.

70. *Thornhill v. Evans* (1742) 26 ER 601, 602.
71. *Mostyn v. Mostyn* LR 5 Ch App 457, 459 (1870)
72. *Re Le Brasseur and Oakley* [1896] 2 Ch 487, 494 (Lindley LJ). See also *Wells v. Wells* [1914] P 157 (Court of Appeal).
73. See nn. 43–45 above.
74. *Kennedy v. Broun* (1863) 13 CBNS 677, 738 (Erle CJ).
75. *R v. Doutre* (1884) 9 App Cas 745, 751.
76. *Morris v. Hunt* (1819) 1 Chit 544, 555.
77. *Code of Conduct of the Bar of England and Wales* (27 Jan. 1990), para. 502(*d*).
78. *Re Le Brasseur and Oakley* [1896] 2 Ch 487, 493–4 (Lindley LJ). See similarly *Saif Ali v. Sydney Mitchell & Co. (A Firm)* [1980] AC 198, 230 (Lord Salmon).
79. *Code of Conduct of the Bar of England and Wales* (27 Jan. 1990), Annexe D.
80. *Saif Ali v. Sydney Mitchell & Co. (A Firm)* [1980] AC 198, 230 (Lord Salmon). See similarly *Rondel v. Worsley* [1967] 1 QB 443, 521 (Salmon LJ).
81. *Rondel v. Worsley* [1967] 1 QB 443, 460–1.
82. *Watt and Cohen v. Willis* [1910] NZLR 58 (Edwards J in the Supreme Court of New Zealand) and *Robinson and Morgan-Coakle v. Behan* [1964] NZLR 650 (Perry J in the Supreme Court of New Zealand).
83. *Rees v. Sinclair* [1974] 1 NZLR 180, 187 (McCarthy P) and 190 (Macarthur J).
84. Section 61 of the Courts and Legal Services Act 1990. The Bar maintains a rule that barristers do not enter into a contract by accepting professional instructions: *Code of Conduct of the Bar of England and Wales* (27 Jan. 1990), Annexe D, paras. 19–20 (as amended 22 Oct. 1990).
85. *Trial of Queen Caroline* (1821), vol. 2, p. 8, cited in David Mellinkoff, *The Conscience of a Lawyer* (1973), pp. 188–9.
86. 40 *Law Times* 16, 17 (1864).
87. *Re Griffiths* 413 US 717, 731 (1973) (US Supreme Court, Burger CJ dissenting).
88. *Strauss v. Francis* (1866) LR 1 QB 379, 381.
89. *Rondel v. Worsley* [1967] 1 QB 443, 502 (Lord Denning MR).
90. *Beevis v. Dawson* [1957] 1 QB 195, 201 (Singleton LJ for the Court of Appeal).
91. *Rondel v. Worsley* [1969] 1 AC 191, 274 (Lord Pearce).

92. *Hutchinson v. Stephens* (1837) 1 Keen 659, 668 (Lord Langdale MR).
93. *People ex rel. Karlin v. Culkin* 162 NE 487, 489 (1928) (Chief Justice Cardozo for the Court of Appeals of New York).
94. *Rondel v. Worsley* [1969] 1 AC 191, 282 (Lord Upjohn).
95. *Abse v. Smith* [1986] QB 536, 545 (Sir John Donaldson MR for the Court of Appeal).
96. *Rondel v. Worsley* [1969] 1 AC 191, 247 (Lord Morris). See also to similar effect *Re B* [1981] 2 NSWLR 372, 382 (Moffit P in the New South Wales Court of Appeal).
97. *Saif Ali v. Sydney Mitchell & Co. (A Firm)* [1978] QB 95, 103 (Lord Denning).
98. *Code of Conduct of the Bar of England and Wales* (27 Jan. 1990), para. 208.
99. *Tombling v. Universal Bulb Company Ltd.* [1951] 2 TLR 289, 297 (Denning LJ).
100. *Saif Ali v. Sydney Mitchell & Co. (A Firm)* [1980] AC 198, 220 (Lord Diplock).
101. *US v. Von der Heide* 169 F Supp 560, 567 (1959) (US District Court).
102. *Saif Ali v. Sydney Mitchell & Co. (A Firm)* [1978] QB 95, 103 (Lord Denning). See also *Code of Conduct of the Bar of England and Wales* (27 Jan. 1990), para. 606(*c*).
103. *Rondel v. Worsley* [1969] 1 AC 191, 282 (Lord Upjohn). See generally *Code of Conduct of the Bar of England and Wales* (27 Jan. 1990), para. 610(*c*) and *R v. Nunes, The Times* 31 July 1991.
104. See ibid., para. 610(*e*).
105. *Rondel v. Worsley* [1969] 1 AC 191, 227 (Lord Reid). See also *Oldfield v. Keogh* (1941) 41 SR (NSW) 206, 211 (Jordan CJ for the New South Wales Supreme Court approving some observations of Lord Macmillan in 'The Ethics of Advocacy' in *Law and Other Things* (1937), pp. 191–2).
106. *Saif Ali v. Sydney Mitchell & Co. (A Firm)* [1980] AC 198, 220 (Lord Diplock).
107. *Rondel v. Worsley* [1969] 1 AC 191, 227–8 (Lord Reid). See generally *Code of Conduct of the Bar of England and Wales* (27 Jan. 1990), para. 610(*c*).
108. *Rondel v. Worsley* [1967] 1 QB 443, 469 (Lawton J).
109. *Glebe Sugar Refining Company Ltd v. Trustees of the Port and Harbours of Greenock* (1921) WN 85, 86. See ch. 7, nn. 73–74.

110. See generally *Code of Conduct of the Bar of England and Wales* (27 Jan. 1990), para. 606.
111. *Emerson v. Dallison* (1660) 21 ER 547.
112. *Hill's Case* (1603) 21 ER 15.
113. *Bishop v. Willis* (1749) 5 Beav 83n.
114. *R v. Weisz ex parte Hector MacDonald Ltd.* [1951] 2 KB 611. See similarly *Re Elsam* (1824) 3 B & C 597. And see also *Coxe v. Phillips* 95 ER 152 (1737): an action brought not to determine a right or resolve a dispute but to deceive the court and to embarrass a third person was a contempt of court.
115. *R v. B* [1966] 1 WLR 1612. See similarly *Re Mithal* AIR 1924 Allahabad 253, 254 (Mears CJ for the High Court of Allahabad, India). And see *Code of Conduct of the Bar of England and Wales* (27 Jan. 1990), Annexe H, *Standards Applicable to Criminal Cases*, at para. 6.3.
116. *Mingay v. Hammond* (1618) 79 ER 411.
117. *R v. person unnamed* 87 ER 62 (1686).
118. *Clyne v. Bar Association of New South Wales* [1960] ALR 574 (High Court of Australia).
119. *US v. Thoreen* 653 F 2d 1332 (1981) (US Court of Appeals), cert. denied 455 US 938 (1982) (US Supreme Court).
120. *R v. Schumiatcher* 64 DLR (2d) 24, 31 (1967) (Saskatchewan Queen's Bench). On appeal, the fine was reduced from $2000 to $500: (1969) 1 CCC 272 (Saskatchewan Court of Appeal).
121. *Ex parte Bellanto* (1963) SR (NSW) 190, 191 (New South Wales Supreme Court).
122. *Re Swanwick* 1 Queensland Law Journal Reports 66 (1982).
123. *Linwood v. Andrews and Moore* (1888) 58 LT 612.
124. *Re Robert A. Branch* 449 P 2d 174, 181 (1969) (Supreme Court of California). See also *Thornton v. US* 357 A 2d 429 (1976) (District of Columbia Court of Appeals), cert. denied 429 US 1024 (1976) (US Supreme Court); *People v. Lowery* 366 NE 2d 155 (1977) (Appellate Court of Illinois); *Lowery v. Cardwell* 575 F 2d 727 (1978) (US Court of Appeals); *People v. Schultheis* 638 P 2d 8 (1981) (Supreme Court of Colorado); *In the Matter of Goodwin* 305 SE 2d 578 (1983) (Supreme Court of South Carolina).
125. See ch. 5, p. 160.
126. *Meek v. Fleming* [1961] 2 QB 366, 379–80.

127. *Tombling v. Universal Bulb Company Ltd* [1951] 2 TLR 289, 293, 297 (Court of Appeal).
128. *Abraham v. Abraham and Harding* (1919) 120 LT 672.
129. *Holowaty v. Holowaty and McDermid* [1949] 1 WWR 1064, 1068 (Brown CJKB in the Saskatchewan King's Bench).
130. *Swinburne v. David Syme & Co* [1909] VLR 550, 570–1.
131. *Sabella v. Southern Pacific Company* 449 P 2d 750, 756 (1969) (Supreme Court of California), cert. denied 395 US 960 (1969) (US Supreme Court).
132. *Poole v. Whitcomb* 12 CBNS 770 (1862). Cf. *Reekie v. M'Kinven* (1921) SC 733 (Court of Session, Scotland).
133. *Praed v. Graham* 24 QBD 53, 55 (1889) (Court of Appeal).
134. *Chattell v. Daily Mail Publishing Co. Ltd.* (1901) 18 TLR 165, 168.
135. Edward Marjoribanks, *The Life of Sir Edward Marshall Hall* (1929), pp. 183 and 190.
136. *Uren v. Australian Consolidated Press Ltd* (1965) NSWR 371, 375 (Supreme Court of New South Wales).
137. Roy Grutman and Bill Thomas, *Lawyers and Thieves* (1990), p. 131.
138. *Horn v. Atchison, Topeka and Santa Fe Railway Company* 394 P 2d 561, 565 (1964) (Supreme Court of California).
139. *Stewart v. Speer* [1953] 3 DLR 722, 725–7.
140. *Hoffman v. Brandt* 421 P 2d 425, 427–8 (1967) (Supreme Court of California).
141. *Wright v. Hearson* (1916) WN 216.
142. *Harman v. Crilly* [1943] KB 168 (Lord Greene MR for the Court of Appeal).
143. *Hoffman v. Brandt* 421 P 2d 425, 429n (1967) (Supreme Court of California).
144. *Graham v. Sutton, Carden & Co.* [1897] 1 Ch 761, 766 (Rigby LJ in the Court of Appeal). See also *Re Arthur and Town of Meaford* (1915) 34 OLR 231 (Middleton J in the Weekly Court at Toronto, Canada).
145. *Meadwell Enterprises Ltd v. Clay and Company* 44 BCLR 188, 200 (1983) (Locke J in the British Columbia Supreme Court).
146. *R v. Ruddick* (1865) 4 F & F 497, 499 (Crompton J). See also *R v. Thursfield* (1838) 8 C & P 269 (Gurney B), *R v. Holchester and others* (1865) 10 Cox CC 226, 227–8 (Blackburn J) and *R v. Webb* (1865) 4 F & F 862 (Mellor J). And see generally *Code of*

Conduct of the Bar of England and Wales (27 Jan. 1990), Annexe H, *Standards Applicable to Criminal Cases*, especially at paras. 1.1 and 1.2.

147. *Donnelly v. DeChristoforo* 416 US 637, 648–9 (1974) (Douglas J dissenting in the US Supreme Court).
148. *R v. Thomas (No. 2)* [1974] 1 NZLR 658, 659 (Wild CJ for the New Zealand Court of Appeal). See also *Berger v. US* 295 US 78, 88 (1935) (US Supreme Court).
149. See *Practice Note* [1982] 1 All ER 734 for the Guidelines issued by the Attorney-General on the duty to disclose to the defence information relevant to cases to be tried on indictment.
150. *R v. Thomas Williams* (1797) 26 St Tr 653, 711–20.
151. *Di Carlo v. US* 6 F 2d 364, 368 (1925) (US Circuit Court of Appeals).
152. *Remus v. US* 291 F 501, 511 (1923) (US Circuit Court of Appeals).
153. *R v. Banks* [1916] 2 KB 621 (Court of Criminal Appeal).
154. *Re Nathan House* (1921) 16 Cr App Rep 49, 52.
155. *People v. Caylor* 54 NE 2d 514, 516, 517 (1944) (Supreme Court of Illinois).
156. *Commonwealth v. Meyers* 139 A 374, 377 (1927) (Supreme Court of Pennsylvania).
157. *Boucher v. R* [1955] SCR 16, 19 (Kerwin CJ in the Supreme Court of Canada). See similarly *State v. Clark* 131 NW 369, 370 (1911) (Supreme Court of Minnesota).
158. *R v. Sir Walter Raleigh* (1603) 2 St Tr 1, 7, 26.
159. *State v. Gunderson* 144 NW 659, 660 (1913) (Supreme Court of North Dakota).
160. *Greenberg v. US* 280 F 2d 472, 475 (1960) (US Court of Appeals).
161. *Berger v. US* 295 US 78, 88 (1935) (US Supreme Court).
162. *Henderson v. US* 218 F 2d 14, 19, 21 (1955) (US Court of Appeals).
163. *Shank v. State* 72 SW 2d 519, 523 (1934) (Supreme Court of Arkansas); *People v. Pratchner* 50 P 2d 75 (1935) (District Court of Appeal, California); *People v. McElheny* 190 NW 713 (1922) (Supreme Court of Michigan); *State v. Hipplewith* 164 A 2d 481, 486–7 (1960) (Supreme Court of New Jersey).
164. *US v. Young* 470 US 1 (1985) (US Supreme Court).
165. *Gridley v. US* 44 F 2d 716, 739 (1930) (US Circuit Court of Appeals), cert. denied 283 US 827 (1931) (US Supreme Court).
166. On the duty of the advocate not to express his personal

opinions of the case see also ch. 5, p. 135.

167. Charles Dickens, *A Tale of Two Cities* (1859), Bk. 2, ch. 3.
168. Arthur Koestler, *Darkness at Noon* (1940) (Penguin edn., 1964), p. 199.
169. Tom Wolfe, *The Bonfire of the Vanities* (1988), p. 103.
170. Sir Harry Woolf, *Protection of the Public—A New Challenge* (1990), p. 6.
171. *Dictionary of National Biography 1951–1960* (ed. E. T. Williams and Helen M. Palmer, 1971), p. 495.
172. *Dictionary of National Biography 1971–1980* (ed. Lord Blake and C. S. Nicholls, 1986), p. 656.
173. *Saif Ali v. Sydney Mitchell & Co. (A Firm)* [1978] QB 95, 103 (Lord Denning). See also *Re Ontario Crime Commission* 37 DLR (2d) 382, 391 (1962) (Ontario Court of Appeal).
174. *Code of Conduct of the Bar of England and Wales* (27 Jan. 1990), para. 504(*e*). See also para. 209(*c*).
175. Ibid., para. 209 (*a*).
176. *Rondel v. Worsley* [1969] 1 AC 191, 272.
177. Ibid. 228.
178. *Abse v. Smith* [1986] QB 536, 546 (Sir John Donaldson MR for the Court of Appeal).
179. *Saif Ali v. Sydney Mitchell & Co. (A Firm)* [1980] AC 198, 220 (Lord Diplock).
180. *Kennedy v. Broun* (1863) 13 CBNS 677, 738.
181. *Rondel v. Worsley* [1969] 1 AC 191, 228.
182. *Kennedy v. Broun* (1863) 13 CBNS 677, 737.
183. Above, n. 25, loc. cit.
184. On contempt of court in this context, see generally *Borrie and Lowe's Law of Contempt* (2nd edn., 1983), pp. 27–36; Arlidge and Eady, *The Law of Contempt* (1982), pp. 182–91; and Peter Butt, 'Contempt of Court and the Legal Profession' (1978) *Criminal Law Review* 463.
185. *R v. General Council of the Bar ex parte Percival* [1991] 1 QB 212, 218 (Watkins LJ for the Divisional Court).
186. *In the Matter of Samuel A. Bithoney* 486 F 2d 319, 324 (1973) (US Court of Appeals).
187. *In Re Rouss* 116 NE 782, 783 (1917) (Cardozo J for the Court of Appeals of New York).
188. *Clyne v. Bar Association of New South Wales* [1960] ALR 574, 583 (High Court of Australia).

189. Geoffrey C. Hazard, Jr, *Ethics in the Practice of Law* (1978), p. 20.
190. See generally *Halsbury's Laws of England* (4th edn., reissue, 1989), vol. 3(1), para. 419, and *Re S (A Barrister)* [1970] 1 QB 160.
191. *In Re T (A Barrister)* [1982] QB 430 (Visitors to Lincoln's Inn).
192. See *Doe d. Bennett v. Hale and Davis* (1850) 15 QB 171.
193. *Re S (A Barrister), Guardian* 9 Oct. 1990.
194. *R v. General Council of the Bar ex parte Percival* [1991] 1 QB 212 (Divisional Court).
195. *Dictionary of National Biography 1961–1970* (ed. E. T. Williams and C. S. Nicholls, 1981), p. 523. The case was *R v. Governor of Brixton Prison ex parte Enahoro* [1963] 2 QB 455.
196. *Independent* 6 Jan. 1990 (obituary by Harold Lever of the complainant, Lord Paget of Northampton).
197. *Ex parte Clyne* [1962] SR (NSW) 436, 449–50 (per Manning J).
198. *In the Matter of Alger Hiss* 333 NE 2d 429, 436–7 (1975) (Supreme Judicial Court of Massachusetts).
199. *R v. Davison* (1821) 4 B & Ald 329, 335.

5. Morality

1. *Sandstrom v. State of Florida* 309 So 2d 17, 21 (1975) (District Court of Appeal of Florida).
2. On the advocate's duties to the court see ch. 4, p. 105.
3. *Smith v. Smith* (1882) 7 PD 84, 89.
4. John Mortimer, *Rumpole and the Age of Miracles* (1988), p. 6.
5. Jonathan Swift, 'A Voyage to the Houyhnhnms' in *Gulliver's Travels*. (1726), ch. 5.
6. William Hazlitt, *The Spirit of the Age* (1825) (OUP, 1970) p. 256.
7. See ch. 7, part V for analysis of an exception: Rumpole.
8. Charles W. Wolfram, *Modern Legal Ethics* (1986), p. 1.
9. Jeremy Bentham, *Works* (ed. John Bowring, 1843), vol. 6 p. 350.
10. Ibid., p. 100.
11. Ibid., vol. 7, p. 479, comments of John Stuart Mill, editor of Bentham's *Rationale of Judicial Evidence* (see John Stuart Mill,

Autobiography, ed. Jack Stillinger, OUP, 1971, pp. 69–71).

12. Lord Macaulay, *Essay on Bacon*, cited in Charles W. Wolfram, *Modern Legal Ethics* (1986), p. 581.
13. Anthony Trollope, *Phineas Redux* (1874), ch. 61.
14. Plato, *Gorgias* (transl. Walter Hamilton, Penguin Classics, 1960), p. 148.
15. Ibid., p. 139.
16. *US v. Wade* 388 US 218, 256–8 (1967) (US Supreme Court, White J dissenting in part, joined by Justices Harlan and Stewart).
17. Travers Humphreys, *Criminal Days* (1946), p. 105.
18. Lord Denning, *The Family Story* (1981), p. 99.
19. John Lord Campbell, *Lives of the Chief Justices of England* (3rd edn., 1874), vol. 2, pp. 165–6.
20. *R v. Baxter* (1685) 11 St Tr 493, 498–9.
21. *Lord Eldon's Anecdote Book* (ed. Anthony Lincoln and Robert McEwen, 1960), pp. 127–8.
22. John Lord Campbell, *Lives of the Lord Chancellors* (5th edn., 1868), vol. 6, pp. 121–2.
23. 514 HL 1192 (25 Jan. 1990) (debate on the Courts and Legal Services Bill).
24. Paul Hill with Ronan Bennett, *Stolen Years* (1990), p. 126.
25. Lord Macmillan, 'The Ethics of Advocacy' in *Law and Other Things* (1937), p. 181.
26. *The Times* 30 Jan. and 3 Feb. 1976, cited in Geoffrey Robertson, *Obscenity* (1979), p. 113.
27. *Code of Conduct of the Bar of England and Wales* (27 Jan. 1990), para. 610(*b*).
28. See ch. 4, p. 105 on counsel's duties to the court.
29. *R v. Palmer* (1856), cited in David Mellinkoff, *The Conscience of a Lawyer* (1973), pp. 235–6.
30. Lord Herschell, *The Rights and Duties of an Advocate* (1889), cited in David Mellinkoff, above, n. 29 at pp. 262–3. On the duties of prosecuting counsel not to tell the court that they personally think that the defendant is guilty of the offence with which he is charged, see ch. 4, pp. 117–20.
31. Charles Dickens, *The Pickwick Papers* (1836–7), ch. 34.
32. *US v. Butler* 297 US 1, 44 (1936) (the argument of counsel, George Wharton Pepper), cited in Charles P. Curtis, 'The Ethics of Advocacy' 4 *Stanford Law Review* 3, 15 (1951).

33. *Rondel v. Worsley* [1969] 1 AC 191, 227 (Lord Reid).
34. *Code of Conduct of the Bar of England and Wales* (27 Jan. 1990), para. 203.
35. 516 HL 194 (20 Feb. 1990) (debate on the Courts and Legal Services Bill).
36. *Code of Conduct of the Bar of England and Wales* (27 Jan. 1990), para. 203.
37. 516 HL 215 (20 Feb. 1990) (debate on the Courts and Legal Services Bill).
38. 516 HL 207 (20 Feb. 1990) (debate on the Courts and Legal Services Bill).
39. 516 HL 200 (20 Feb. 1990) (debate on the Courts and Legal Services Bill).
40. *Code of Conduct of the Bar of England and Wales* (27 Jan. 1990), paras. 501–3.
41. See Julian Disney, Paul Redmond, John Basten, and Stan Ross, *Lawyers* (1986), pp. 600–8. See also John Phillips, *Advocacy with Honour* (1985), p. 2.
42. William H. Harbaugh, *Lawyer's Lawyer: The Life of John W. Davis* (1978), p. 199.
43. Above, n. 8 at p. 571.
44. *American Bar Association Model Rules of Professional Conduct*, Comment to Rule 6.2: see Charles W. Wolfram, above, n. 8 at pp. 573 and 1145.
45. Charles Dickens, *The Old Curiosity Shop* (1841), ch. 63.
46. Above, n. 8 at p. 411. See also at p. 455.
47. *People v. Rhodes* 524 P 2d 363, 367 (1974) (Supreme Court of California). See similarly *People v. Fife* 392 NE 2d 1345 (1979) (Supreme Court of Illinois).
48. Alan M. Dershowitz, *Reversal of Fortune* (Penguin edn., 1991), p. 52.
49. Above, n. 4 at p. 18.
50. 56 *American Bar Association Journal* 552 (1970).
51. *Code of Conduct of the Bar of England and Wales* (27 Jan. 1990), para. 102.
52. Rule 1(2)(*b*) of the *American Bar Association Model Rules of Professional Conduct*, discussed and cited in Charles W. Wolfram, above, n. 8 at pp. 570 and 1101.
53. *Ex parte Lloyd* (1822) Montagu's Reports 70n, 72 (Lord Chancellor Eldon).

54. *Rondel v. Worsley* [1969] 1 AC 191, 227 (Lord Reid).
55. Ibid. 275 (Lord Pearce).
56. 55 *Parliamentary Debates, House of Lords* (5th series), 10 Aug. 1840, cols. 1401–2, cited in David Mellinkoff, above, n. 29 at pp. 143–4.
57. *Ex parte Lloyd* (1822) Montagu's Reports 70n, 71 (Lord Chancellor Eldon).
58. Wilfrid R. Prest, *The Rise of the Barristers: A Social History of the English Bar 1590–1640* (1986), p. 295.
59. Cited in *Cohen v. Hurley* 366 US 117, 139n (1961) (US Supreme Court, dissenting judgment of Black J).
60. David Lemmings, *Gentlemen and Barristers: The Inns of Court and the English Bar 1680–1730* (1990), p. 122, citing a letter from Talbot's wife.
61. *In Re Anastaplo* 366 US 82, 114–15 (1961) (US Supreme Court, dissenting judgment of Black J).
62. See Simon Schama, *Citizens: A Chronicle of the French Revolution* (1989), pp. 822–7.
63. H. Montgomery Hyde, *Carson* (1953) (paperback edn., 1987), pp. 329–30.
64. 514 HL 1197 (25 Jan. 1990) (debate on the Courts and Legal Services Bill).
65. 516 HL 203 (20 Feb. 1990) (debate on the Courts and Legal Services Bill).
66. Ibid.
67. See n. 36 above.
68. See n. 37 above.
69. *Code of Conduct of the Bar of England and Wales* (27 Jan. 1990), para. 203. Cf. the observations of Lord Salmon who distinguished advocacy from the other work of a barrister and said that he did not 'know of any firm rule which obliges counsel to accept instructions to advise or to draft pleadings': *Saif Ali v. Sydney Mitchell & Co. (A Firm)* [1980] AC 198, 230.
70. See Andrew Hall and Brian Raymond, *NLJ* 2 Mar. 1990, pp. 284–5; Brian Raymond, *Guardian* 7 Mar. 1990; and Geoffrey Bindman, *Independent* 9 Mar. 1990.
71. See the editorial in *NLJ*, 9 Feb. 1990, p. 157.
72. *The Harassment and Persecution of Judges and Lawyers: July 1989–June 1990* (ed. Reed Brody, International Commission of Jurists).

73. John Mortimer, *The First Rumpole Omnibus* (1983), p. 280.
74. 505 HL 1343 (7 Apr. 1989) (debate on proposals for reform of the legal profession).
75. *John v. Rees* [1970] Ch 345, 402 (Megarry J).
76. *Rondel v. Worsley* [1969] 1 AC 191, 275 (Lord Pearce).
77. Lloyd N. Cutler, 'Book Review' 83 *Harvard Law Review* 1746, 1750 (1970).
78. James Boswell, *The Journal of a Tour to the Hebrides with Samuel Johnson* (1786) (ed. R. W. Chapman, OUP, 1970), pp. 175–6.
79. *R v. Thomas Paine* (1792) 22 St Tr 357, 412.
80. *R v. Thomas Williams* (1797) 26 St Tr 653, 715n.
81. *R v. Hopkins, The Times* 18 Mar. 1989.
82. James Boswell, *Life of Johnson* (1791) (ed. R. W. Chapman, corrected by J. D. Fleeman, 1970), p. 388.
83. See also ch. 4, pp. 92–3 on the role of the advocate in this respect.
84. *Ex parte Lloyd* (1822) Montagu's Reports 70n, 72, cited with approval by Lord Justice Denning for the Court of Appeal in *Jones v. National Coal Board* [1957] 2 QB 55, 63.
85. Cited by Showell Rogers, 'The Ethics of Advocacy' 15 *LQR* 259, 262–3 (1899).
86. *Cordell v. Second Clanfield Properties Ltd* [1969] 2 Ch 9, 16–17.
87. Jerold S. Auerbach, *Unequal Justice: Lawyers and Social Change in Modern America* (1977), p. 307.
88. Rule 2.1 of the *American Bar Association Model Rules of Professional Conduct* discussed and cited in Charles W. Wolfram, above, n. 8 at pp. 157–9 and 1127.
89. *Of Law and Life and Other Things that Matter: Papers and Addresses of Felix Frankfurter 1956–1963* (ed. Philip B. Kurland, 1965), p. 151.
90. Marcus Fabius Quintilianus, *Institutio Oratoria* (transl. H. E. Butler, Loeb edn., 1985), v. xiii. 51, p. 343.
91. Lord Birkett, *Six Great Advocates* (1961), p. 30.
92. Edward Marjoribanks, *The Life of Sir Edward Marshall Hall* (1929), p. 58.
93. Above, n. 22, vol. 3, p. 12.
94. Marcel Proust, *Remembrance of Things Past* (transl. C. K. Scott Moncrieff and Terence Kilmartin), vol. 2 (1982), p. 834.
95. John Campbell, *F. E. Smith: First Earl of Birkenhead* (1983), p. 288.

96. *Code of Conduct of the Bar of England and Wales* (27 Jan. 1990), para. 604. See ch. 6, p. 185.
97. Charles Fried, *Right and Wrong* (1978), p. 188 n.
98. *Independent* 20 June 1989. The substantive judicial review application, alleging that the common law crime of blasphemy prohibited insults to Islam, was later dismissed: *R v. Chief Metropolitan Stipendiary Magistrate ex parte Choudhury* [1991] 1 QB 429 (Divisional Court).
99. Radio 4 *PM*, 26 Feb. 1990.
100. Above, n. 8 at p. 77.
101. Ibid., pp. 193–4.
102. *The King-Emperor v. Barendra Kumar Ghose* 28 *Calcutta Weekly Notes* 170, 184–5 (1923).
103. *US ex rel Wilcox v. Johnson* 555 F 2d 115, 122 (1977) (US Court of Appeals).
104. *Johns v. Smyth* 176 F Supp 949, 954 (1959) (US District Court).
105. Sir Malcolm Hilbery, *Duty and Art in Advocacy* (1959), p. 9. See similarly *Code of Conduct of the Bar of England and Wales* (27 Jan. 1990), Annexe H, *Standards Applicable to Criminal Cases*, para. 3, and Sir David Napley, *The Technique of Persuasion* (3rd edn., 1983), p. 65.
106. *R v. Courvoisier* 173 ER 869 (1840). The background, the proceedings, and the aftermath are analysed in David Mellinkoff, *The Conscience of a Lawyer* (1973).
107. David Mellinkoff, ibid., pp. 132–3.
108. J. B. Atlay, *The Victorian Chancellors* (1908), vol. 2, p. 163 n. See n. 31 above for an extract from the speech of Serjeant Buzfuz.
109. David Mellinkoff, above, n. 106 at pp. 134–40.
110. Richard du Cann, *The Art of the Advocate* (1980), p. 41.
111. David Mellinkoff, above, n. 106 at p. 222.
112. Ibid.
113. *Tuckiar v. R* 52 CLR 335, 341, 346 (1934) (High Court of Australia).
114. See Monroe H. Freedman, 'Professional Responsibility of the Criminal Defence Lawyer: The Three Hardest Questions' 64 *Michigan Law Review* 1469, 1474 (1966). See also the reply by Richard L. Braun, 'Ethics in Criminal Cases: A Response' 55 *Georgetown Law Journal* 1048 (1967).
115. See also ch. 4, p. 110 on presenting perjured evidence.

116. On client perjury, see Charles W. Wolfram, above, n. 8 at pp. 660–3 and cases there cited.
117. *US v. Curtis* 742 F 2d 1070 (1984) (US Court of Appeals).
118. *McKissick v. US* 379 F 2d 754, 761 (1967) (US Court of Appeals). See also at 398 F 2d 342 (1968) (US Court of Appeals).
119. Geoffrey C. Hazard, Jr, *Ethics in the Practice of Law* (1978), pp. 2–3.
120. *Code of Conduct for the Bar of England and Wales* (4th edn., 1989), para. 24.11. These statements do not appear in the 1990 version of the Code.
121. Ibid., para. 22.6. Again, this statement does not appear in the 1990 version of the Code. See ch. 4 at n. 103.
122. *State of Arizona v. Macumber* 544 P 2d 1084 (1976) (Supreme Court of Arizona). See similarly *State of New Mexico v. Valdez* 618 P 2d 1234 (1980) (Supreme Court of New Mexico).
123. New South Wales Bar Association *Annual Report* (1981), p. 12, cited in Julian Disney, Paul Redmond, John Basten, and Stan Ross, *Lawyers* (1986), p. 685.
124. See David Luban, *Lawyers and Justice: An Ethical Study* (1988), pp. 26–30.
125. *US v. Benjamin* 328 F 2d 854, 863 (1964) (US Court of Appeals).
126. L. N. Tolstoy, *Resurrection* (1899) (transl. Rosemary Edmonds, Penguin edn., 1966), pp. 41 and 44–5.
127. *D v. NSPCC* [1978] AC 171, 231 (Lord Simon).
128. See ch. 6, part III on legal aid.
129. See above, n. 8 at pp. 949–53 and 1144–5.

6. Reform

1. *In the Matter of the Serjeants at Law* (1840) 6 Bing (NC) 235, 239n.
2. Cm. 570 (Jan. 1989).
3. Virginia Woolf, *Three Guineas* (1938), ch. 2.
4. *The Times* 16 Feb. 1989.
5. 505 HL 1331 (7 Apr. 1989) (debate on the proposals for reform of the legal profession).
6. *The Times* 22 Feb. 1989.

7. 505 HL 1369 (7 Apr. 1989) (debate on the proposals for reform of the legal profession).
8. *The Times* 15 Apr. 1989.
9. Ibid. 31 Jan. 1989.
10. 505 HL 1454 (7 Apr. 1989) (debate on the proposals for reform of the legal profession).
11. Sir William Holdsworth, *A History of English Law* (1924), vol. 6, p. 432.
12. *Doe, on the demise of Bennett v. Hale and Davis* (1850) 117 ER 423, 429 (Lord Campbell CJ).
13. See 18 *Law Journal* 617 (1883) reporting a case before Smith J; *Doxford and Sons Ltd v. The Sea Shipping Company Ltd.* (1897) 14 TLR 111 (Bruce J); and *Butterworth v. Butterworth* 57 *Sol J* 266 (1913) (Evans P).
14. *Brownsea Haven Properties Ltd v. Poole Corporation* [1958] Ch 574, 591 (Lord Evershed MR in the Court of Appeal).
15. The first solicitor to serve in the post was Sir Thomas Barnes: see *Dictionary of National Biography 1961–1970* (ed. E. T. Williams and C. S. Nicholls, 1981), p. 74.
16. *London Engineering and Iron Shipbuilding Company (Limited) v. Cowan* 16 LT Reports 573 (1867).
17. 24 *Law Journal* 28 (1889).
18. *Collier v. Hicks* (1831) 2 B & Ad 663, 672.
19. *Rondel v. Worsley* [1967] 1 QB 443, 509.
20. *Clarke v. Couchman* 20 *Law Journal* 318 (1885). See ch. 4, n. 41 on this case.
21. New South Wales Law Reform Commission, *Discussion Paper* (1981), pp. 47–9, cited in Julian Disney, Paul Redmond, John Basten, and Stan Ross, *Lawyers* (1986), pp. 28–9.
22. *The Times* 31 Oct. 1985.
23. *Abse v. Smith* [1986] QB 536.
24. *Practice Direction (Solicitors: Rights of Audience)* [1986] 1 WLR 545.
25. *Abse v. Smith* [1986] QB 536, 546 and 556.
26. Above, n. 11, vol. 4, p. 264. See also *People ex rel Karlin v. Culkin* 162 NE 487, 490 (1928) (Cardozo CJ for the Court of Appeals of New York).
27. *Oswald's Contempt of Court* (3rd edn. 1910, ed. George Stuart Robertson), p. 57.
28. Eric Crowther, *Advocacy for the Advocate* (1984), p. 47.

29. *Code of Conduct for the Bar of England and Wales* (July 1980), Annex 11, p. 46.
30. Keith Evans, *Advocacy at the Bar: A Beginner's Guide* (1983), p. 8.
31. Sir Malcolm Hilbery, *Duty and Art in Advocacy* (1959), pp. 2–3.
32. Daniel Duman, *The English and Colonial Bars in the Nineteenth Century* (1983), p. 46.
33. Bar Council, *Relaxing of Rules between Solicitors and Barristers* (1968), quoted in Michael Zander, *Lawyers and the Public Interest* (1968), p. 218 n.
34. The Senate of the Inns of Court and the Bar, *Annual Statement 1984–85*, pp. 43 and 45.
35. *Code of Conduct for the Bar of England and Wales* (4th edn., 1989), Annex 8, paras. 4, 5, and 14–15.
36. *Virginia State Board of Pharmacy v. Virginia Citizens Consumer Council* 425 US 748, 763 (1976) (US Supreme Court). The European Court of Human Rights considered freedom of expression and commercial speech in *Markt Intern v. Germany* (1989) 12 EHRR 161.
37. *Bates v. State Bar of Arizona* 433 US 350, 364 (1977) (US Supreme Court). The US Supreme Court has further considered the limits of acceptable advertising by lawyers in *Re Primus* 436 US 412 (1978), *Ohralik v. Ohio State Bar Association* 436 US 447 (1978), *In Re RMJ* 455 US 191 (1982), and *Zauderer v. Office of Disciplinary Counsel of the Supreme Court of Ohio* 471 US 626 (1985). See generally Anthony Lester QC and David Pannick, *Advertising and Freedom of Expression in Europe* (1984) (International Chamber of Commerce).
38. Cmnd. 7648 (1979), vol 1, p. 375.
39. *Bates v. State Bar of Arizona* 433 US 350, 370–1 (1977) (US Supreme Court).
40. John Lord Campbell *Lives of the Lord Chancellors* (5th edn., 1868), vol. 6, p. 357.
41. *Bates v. State Bar of Arizona* 433 US 350, 371–2 (1977) (US Supreme Court).
42. See ch. 5, pp. 246–7 and ch. 8, pp. 148–9.
43. Oliver Wendell Holmes, 'Law in Science and Science in Law' (1899) in *Collected Legal Papers* (1920), p. 230.
44. See David Pannick, *Judges* (1987), pp. 173–4.

45. See now *Code of Conduct of the Bar of England and Wales* (27 Jan. 1990), para. 307.1.
46. *Code of Conduct for the Bar of England and Wales* (4th edn., 1989), para. 26.
47. *Code of Conduct of the Bar of England and Wales* (27 Jan. 1990), Annexe H, *General Standards*, para. 5.12.
48. See above, n. 44 at pp. 142–7.
49. *Code of Conduct of the Bar of England and Wales* (27 Jan. 1990), para. 604.
50. Richard L. Abel, *American Lawyers* (1989), pp. 232–3.
51. *The Times* 20 Sept. 1990.
52. 459 HC 1221 (15 Dec. 1948), cited in Brian Abel-Smith and Robert Stevens, *Lawyers and the Courts: A Sociological Study of the English Legal System 1750–1965* (1967), pp. 325–6.
53. Robert G. Storey, 'The Legal Profession Versus Regimentation: A Program to Counter Socialization' 37 *American Bar Association Journal* 100 (1951).
54. *Wallersteiner v. Moir (No. 2)* [1975] QB 373, 394 (Lord Denning MR in the Court of Appeal).
55. *Pittman v. Prudential Deposit Bank Ltd* (1896) 13 TLR 110, 111.
56. *Wallersteiner v. Moir (No. 2)* [1975] QB 373, 402 (Lord Justice Buckley in the Court of Appeal).
57. *Contingency Fees* (Cm 571, Jan. 1989), paras. 2.5–2.7 and 4.1–4.2.
58. *Legal Services: A Framework for the Future* (Cm 740, July 1989), para. 14.2.
59. Marcus Fabius Quintilianus, *Institutio Oratoria* (transl. H. E. Butler, Loeb edn., 1985), v. xii. 8, p. 303.
60. *Rondel v. Worsley* [1969] 1 AC 191, 228.
61. Ibid. 255–6.
62. *Bowler v. Warden, Maryland Penitentiary* 236 F Supp 400, 404 (1964) (US District Court).
63. *Ex parte Lewis* (1888) 21 QBD 191, 193 (Divisional Court).
64. *Ley v. Kennedy (Finance) Pty Ltd* (1975) (Supreme Court of New South Wales), cited in Julian Disney, Paul Redmond, John Basten, and Stan Ross, *Lawyers* (1986), pp. 544–5.
65. *R v. Morley* [1988] QB 601, 604–5 (Lord Justice Woolf for the Court of Appeal).
66. *R v. Webb and another ex parte Hawker*, *The Times* 24 Jan. 1899.
67. *Sheddon v. Patrick and the Attorney-General* LR 1 Sc & Div 470,

474–5 and 546 (1869) cited in *Oswald's Contempt of Court* (3rd edn., 1910, ed. George Stuart Robertson), p. 54n.

68. *Moorhouse v. Dooland* (1954) 36 TC 1, 7.
69. *R v. Ford (Royston)* [1989] QB 868, 877 (Court of Appeal).
70. *Practice Direction (Court of Appeal: Presentation of Argument)* [1989] 1 WLR 281. See also *Practice Direction (Court of Appeal: Skeleton Argument Time Limits)* [1990] 1 WLR 794.
71. *J. H. Rayner (Mincing Lane) Ltd v. Department of Trade and Industry* [1990] 2 AC 418, 483.
72. *Banque Financière de la Cité SA v. Westgate Insurance Co Ltd* [1990] 3 WLR 364, 380.
73. *Guardian* 22 Oct. 1990.
74. Robert J. Martineau, *Appellate Justice in England and the United States: A Comparative Analysis* (1990), p. 131.
75. *Rondel v. Worsley* [1969] 1 AC 191, 272–3 (Lord Pearce).
76. *R v. Southwark Crown Court ex parte Santana, The Times* 26 Apr. 1989.
77. *Rondel v. Worsley* [1969] 1 AC 191, 268 (Lord Pearce).
78. Ibid. 283 (Lord Upjohn).
79. Ibid. 227 (Lord Reid).
80. See ch. 4, pp. 98–101.
81. Cmnd. 7648 (1979), vol. 1, p. 333.
82. *Saif Ali v. Sydney Mitchell & Co. (A Firm)* [1980] AC 198, 228 (Lord Salmon).
83. *Code of Conduct of the Bar of England and Wales* (27 Jan. 1990), paras. 301(*e*) and 302.
84. *Saif Ali v. Sydney Mitchell & Co. (A Firm)* [1980] AC 198, 214 (Lord Wilberforce).
85. Ibid. 231 (Lord Salmon).
86. *Montriou v. Jeffreys* 172 ER 51, 53 (1825).
87. *Saif Ali v. Sydney Mitchell & Co. (A Firm)* [1980] AC 198, 220 (Lord Diplock). On mistakes by advocates, see ch. 7, pp. 212–13.
88. *Kirsch v. Duryea* 578 P 2d 935, 938 (1978) (Justice Clark for the Supreme Court of California).
89. *Saif Ali v. Sydney Mitchell & Co. (A Firm)* [1980] AC 198, 220 (Lord Diplock).
90. Ibid. 221 (Lord Diplock).
91. Ibid. 220–1 (Lord Diplock).
92. *Rondel v. Worsley* [1969] 1 AC 191, 228 (Lord Reid).

93. Ibid. 251 (Lord Morris).
94. *Kirsch v. Duryea* 578 P 2d 935, 939 (1978) (Justice Clark for the Supreme Court of California).
95. See ch. 4, p. 121.
96. *Demarco v. Ungaro* (1979) 95 DLR (3d) 385, 406 (Ontario High Court of Justice).
97. *Rondel v. Worsley* [1969] 1 AC 191, 228–9 (Lord Reid).
98. Ibid. 273 (Lord Pearce).
99. Ibid. 247–8 (Lord Morris).
100. Ibid. 283 (Lord Upjohn).
101. *Saif Ali v. Sydney Mitchell & Co. (A Firm)* [1980] AC 198, 222 (Lord Diplock).
102. See ch. 4, pp. 95–6.
103. See, for example, *Fray v. Blackburn* 3 B & S 576, 578 (1863) (Crompton J) and *Re McC (A Minor)* [1985] AC 528 (House of Lords).
104. *Saif Ali v. Sydney Mitchell & Co. (A Firm)* [1980] AC 198, 233 (Lord Russell).
105. *Rondel v. Worsley* [1969] 1 AC 191, 250–1 (Lord Morris).
106. *Saif Ali v. Sydney Mitchell & Co. (A Firm)* [1980] AC 198, 223 (Lord Diplock).
107. See *Somasundaram v. M. Julius Melchior & Co. (A Firm)* [1988] 1 WLR 1394, 1397 where the Court of Appeal struck out on this ground a claim by a man convicted of a criminal offence that his solicitors had given him negligent advice about the conduct of his defence.
108. See Charles W. Wolfram, *Modern Legal Ethics* (1986), pp. 218–21.
109. See ch. 4, p. 98 and ch. 7, n. 61.
110. *Rondel v. Worsley* [1969] 1 AC 191, 281 (Lord Upjohn).
111. *Rondel v. Worsley* [1967] 1 QB 443, 478 (in the course of argument). But see also p. 488 (argument of Graham Swanwick QC) on the differences between the barrister and others who have a duty to accept all clients.
112. *Saif Ali v. Sydney Mitchell & Co. (A Firm)* [1980] AC 198, 221 (Lord Diplock). See also Lord Keith at p. 236.
113. Above, n. 108 at p. 217.
114. *Rondel v. Worsley* [1969] 1 AC 191, 196.
115. *Giannarelli v. Wraith* (1988) 62 ALJR 611, 627.
116. *Rondel v. Worsley* [1969] 1 AC 191, 272 (Lord Pearce).

117. *Rondel v. Worsley* [1967] 1 QB 443, 519 (Lord Justice Salmon).
118. *Rondel v. Worsley* [1969] 1 AC 191, 225.
119. *Fell v. Brown* (1791) Peake 131, 132.

7. Success (and Failure)

1. John Lord Campbell, *Lives of the Lord Chancellors* (5th edn., 1868), vol. 8, p. 281 n.
2. Edward Foss, *Biographia Juridica: a Biographical Dictionary of the Judges of England 1066–1870* (1870), p. 591.
3. Bernard W. Kelly, *Famous Advocates and their Speeches* (1921), p. 60.
4. Travers Humphreys, *Criminal Days* (1946), p. 72.
5. *Rondel v. Worsley* [1967] 1 QB 443, 520 (Lord Justice Salmon).
6. Michael Hyam, *Advocacy Skills* (1990), preface.
7. H. Montgomery Hyde, *Norman Birkett* (1964), p. 506.
8. *Boswell: The English Experiment 1785–1789* (ed. Irma S. Lustig and Frederick A. Pottle, 1986), p. 8.
9. Cited in C. H. S. Fifoot, *Judge and Jurist in the Reign of Victoria* (1959), p. 22.
10. Cited ibid.
11. Richard du Cann, *The Art of the Advocate* (1980), p. 28.
12. Charles Dickens, *The Pickwick Papers* (1836–7), ch. 21.
13. James Boswell, *Life of Johnson* (1799) (ed. R. W. Chapman, corrected by J. D. Fleeman, 1970), p. 859.
14. Above, n. 8 at p. 40.
15. Anthony Trollope, *The Three Clerks* (1858), ch. 40.
16. Charles Dickens, *The Pickwick Papers* (1836–7), ch. 31.
17. Sir William Blackstone, *Commentaries on the Laws of England* (1765), vol. 1, p. 33.
18. Above, n. 1, vol. 6, p. 357.
19. Ibid., vol. 8, pp. 243–9.
20. J. B. Atlay, *The Victorian Chancellors* (1908), vol. 2, p. 20 n.
21. Edward Marjoribanks, *The Life of Sir Edward Marshall Hall* (1929), p. 41.
22. Eric Grimshaw and Glyn Jones, *Lord Goddard: His Career and Cases* (1958), pp. 31–2.
23. Above, n. 4 at p. 138.

24. Patrick Hastings KC, *Cases in Court* (1949), p. 109.
25. Cicero, *De Oratore* (transl. E. W. Sutton and H. Rackham, Loeb edn., 1942), II. xvii. 72–3, p. 253.
26. Lord Birkett, *Six Great Advocates* (1961), p. 78.
27. *Purves v. Landell* (1845) 12 Cl & Fin 91, 102–3.
28. *Rondel v. Worsley* [1967] 1 QB 443, 477 (during the course of argument).
29. Ibid. 519 (Lord Justice Salmon).
30. *People ex rel. Karlin v. Culkin* 162 NE 487, 492 (1928).
31. John Mortimer, *The Second Rumpole Omnibus* (1987), p. 455.
32. *Conway v. George Wimpey & Co. Ltd.* [1951] 2 KB 266, 276 (Asquith LJ).
33. Patricia Campbell Hearst (with Alvin Moscow), *Patty Hearst* (1988 edn.), p. 443.
34. *The Trial of Lady Chatterley: Regina v. Penguin Books Limited* (1961, ed. C. H. Rolph), p. 17.
35. Bernard Levin, *The Pendulum Years: Britain and the Sixties* (1977 edn.), pp. 282–3.
36. Above, n. 34, introduction by Geoffrey Robertson QC (1990 edn., p. xi). On the ethics of the prosecutor, see ch. 4 at p. 114.
37. Above, n. 25, I. iii. 12, p. 11.
38. Lord Macmillan, 50 *LQR* 275, 276 (1934), cited in R. E. Megarry, *Miscellany-at-Law* (1955), pp. 49–50.
39. *Famous Trials* (selected by John Mortimer QC, 1984), pp. 27–8.
40. Ann Dummett and Andrew Nicol, *Subjects, Citizens, Aliens and Others: Nationality and Immigration Law* (1990), p. 151.
41. Tom Wolfe, *The Bonfire of the Vanities* (1988), p. 169.
42. *Marbery v. Clarke* (1596) Hawarde's Reports 42, 43.
43. *Vestey v. IRC (No. 2)* [1979] Ch 198, 210, 215, and 216.
44. *Vestey v. IRC (Nos. 1 and 2)* [1980] AC 1148, 1172.
45. *Thorne RDC v. Bunting (No. 2)* [1972] 3 All ER 1084, 1088.
46. Sir James Fitzjames Stephen, *A History of the Criminal Law of England* (1883), vol. 2, p. 343.
47. *Smith v. Smith* [1923] P 191, 202, cited in R. E. Megarry, *Miscellany-at-Law* (1955), p. 48.
48. *Abse v. Smith* [1986] QB 536, 545.
49. *Yakub v. Chief Immigration Officer, Heathrow* [1988] Imm AR 177, 182 (Lord Justice Kerr for the Court of Appeal).

50. *R v. Immigration Appeal Tribunal ex parte Jones* [1988] 1 WLR 477, 482 (Lord Justice Kerr in the Court of Appeal).
51. *R v. Immigration Appeal Tribunal ex parte Kotecha* [1982] 1 WLR 487, 492 (Lord Chief Justice Lane for the Court of Appeal).
52. *R v. Immigration Appeal Tribunal ex parte Surinder Mohan* [1985] Imm AR 84, 94–5 (Lord Justice Kerr in the Court of Appeal).
53. *McDonagh v. Commissioner of Police of the Metropolis, The Times* 28 Dec. 1989 (Mr Justice Popplewell).
54. *Brisseau v. Martin & Robertson Ltd* [1978] 6 WWR 383.
55. *R v. Young and Robinson* (1978) *Criminal Law Review* 163, 164.
56. *R v. Davies* 39 OR (2d) 604, 607 (Ontario High Court).
57. *Re Knowles* [1984] VLR 751 (Supreme Court of Victoria, Australia).
58. *In Re A (A Minor), The Times* 25 Feb. 1988, *Law Magazine* 4 Mar. 1988, and (1988) *Family Law* 339. See also *Davy-Chiesman v. Davy-Chiesman* [1984] Fam 48, 66 (Lord Justice May for the Court of Appeal).
59. *Re Raymond A. Brownlow* 252 A 2d 903, 905 (1969) (District of Columbia Court of Appeals).
60. *In the Matter of Douglas D. Seely Jr* 427 NE 2d 879 (1981) (Supreme Court of Indiana).
61. *R v. Leith* (1984) *Commonwealth Law Bulletin* 315.
62. *Duffey v. Munnik* (1957) 4 SALR 390, 394.
63. *Tolley v. J. S. Fry and Sons Ltd* [1930] 1 KB 467, 473.
64. *Greenhalgh v. Mallard* [1947] 2 All ER 255, 259 (Lord Justice Evershed in the Court of Appeal).
65. *R v. Governor of Brixton Prison ex parte Enahoro* [1963] 2 QB 455, 464 (Lord Chief Justice Parker for the Divisional Court).
66. *R v. Horsham Justices ex parte Farquharson* [1982] QB 762, 796 (Lord Justice Shaw in the Court of Appeal).
67. *The Times* 27 June 1985 and (1985) *Commonwealth Law Bulletin* 989.
68. *R v. Immigration Appeal Tribunal ex parte Bahadur Singh* [1988] Imm AR 582 (Court of Appeal).
69. *Fay v. Prentice* (1985) 14 LJCP 298, 299, cited in R. E. Megarry, *Miscellany-at-Law* (1955), p. 250.
70. *The Times* 7 Oct. 1989.
71. *Evening Standard* 6 Nov. 1989.
72. *R v. Kynaston, The Times* 14 Dec. 1926, noted in 43 *LQR* 155 (1927).

73. *Glebe Sugar Refining Company Ltd v. Trustees of the Port and Harbours of Greenock* [1921] 2 AC 66, 71.
74. *Glebe Sugar Refining Company Ltd v. Trustees of the Port and Harbours of Greenock* (1921) WN 85.
75. *Penrikyber Navigation Colliery Company Limited v. Edwards* [1933] AC 28, 33.
76. *In Re H (Minors) (Local Authority: Parental Rights) (No. 2)* [1989] 1 WLR 1025.
77. *Bonalumi v. Secretary of State for the Home Department* [1985] QB 675, 682 (Lord Justice Stephenson for the Court of Appeal).
78. *Cassidy v. Ministry of Health* [1951] 2 KB 343, 363.
79. *Cardwell v. The Midland Railway Company* (1904) 21 TLR 22, 23 (Court of Appeal).
80. Marcel Berlins, 'Rights of Audience' 129 *NLJ* 1116, 1117 (1979).
81. Marcel Berlins, 'Counsels of Despair' *Spectator* 25 Nov, 1989.
82. Warren E. Burger, 'The Special Skills of Advocacy' 42 *Fordham Law Review* 227, 234 (1973).
83. Robert J. Martineau, *Appellate Justice in England and the United States: A Comparative Analysis* (1990), p. 88.
84. *Doe, on the demise of Bennett v. Hale and Davis* (1850) 117 ER 423, 429 (Lord Campbell CJ).
85. *Hawkins v. Harwood* (1849) 154 ER 1312, 1313.
86. John Lord Campbell, *Lives of the Chief Justices* (3rd edn., 1874), vol. 4, pp. 297–8 n.
87. *Saunders v. Richmond-upon-Thames LBC* [1978] ICR 75, 82 (Employment Appeal Tribunal).
88. *Skyrail Oceanic Ltd v. Coleman* [1981] ICR 864, 872 (Lord Justice Shaw dissenting in the Court of Appeal).
89. See generally David Pannick, *Judges* (1987), ch. 4.
90. *Congreve v. Home Office* [1976] QB 629, 652–3 (Lord Denning in the Court of Appeal).
91. Sir Harry Woolf, *Public Law—Private Law: Why the Divide? A Personal View* (1986) *Public Law* 220.
92. *Liversidge v. Anderson* [1942] AC 206, 244 (Lord Atkin).
93. *R v. Immigration Appeal Tribunal ex parte Coomasaru* [1983] 1 WLR 14, 19.
94. *Sudbrook Trading Estate Ltd. v. Eggleton* [1983] 1 AC 444, 487 (Lord Russell, dissenting).
95. *Gatehouse v. Vise (Inspector of Taxes)* [1956] 3 All ER 772, 776.

96. *Pratt v. South Eastern Railway Company* [1897] 1 QB 718, 721.
97. Peter V. MacDonald QC, *Court Jesters* (1987), p. 49.
98. Above, n. 86 at p. 339.
99. See ch. 5, pp. 158–9.
100. *Dictionary of National Biography* (ed. Sydney Lee, 1896), vol. 45, p. 196.
101. *Dictionary of National Biography* (ed. Sidney Lee, 1892), vol. 30, p. 411, and R. E. Megarry, 'Dispatented, Disbenched, Disbarred' 90 *LQR* 463 (1974).
102. Above, n. 7 at p. ix.
103. *Pie-Powder by A Circuit Tramp* (1911), p. 173.
104. Marcus Fabius Quintilianus, *Institutio Oratoria* (transl. H. E. Butler, Loeb edn., 1985), V. vii. 26, p. 183.
105. Above, n. 26 at p. 20.
106. Richard Ellman, *Oscar Wilde* (1987), pp. 424–5, and H. Montgomery Hyde, *Carson* (1953) (paperback edn. 1987), pp. 140 and 143.
107. See Richard du Cann, *The Art of the Advocate* (1980), p. 113.
108. Above, n. 7 at pp. 307–9.
109. Cited by Hodson LJ in *Hornal v. Neuberger Products Ltd* [1957] 1 QB 247, 263.
110. *Dictionary of National Biography* (ed. Sidney Lee, 1897), vol. 49, p. 190.
111. Roy Grutman and Bill Thomas, *Lawyers and Thieves* (1990), p. 56.
112. Above, n. 104, VI. ii. 6, pp. 419–20.
113. Marcel Proust, *Remembrance of Things Past* (transl. C. K. Scott Moncrieff and Terence Kilmartin), vol. 2 (1982), p. 394.
114. Ibid., vol. 3 (1982), p. 281.
115. Sir Malcolm Hilbery, *Duty and Art in Advocacy* (1946), p. 28.
116. Above, n. 21 at p. 254.
117. Ibid., pp. 89 and 95.
118. Above, n. 24 at pp. 275–6.
119. Ibid., p. 332.
120. Cited in C. P. Harvey QC, *The Advocate's Devil* (1958), p. 23, and Peter Carter-Ruck, *Memoirs of a Libel Lawyer* (1990), p. 94.
121. Judge Edward Abbott Parry, *The Seven Lamps of Advocacy* (1923), p. 11.
122. Above, n. 24 at pp. 330–1.
123. *Freeman v. Home Office (No. 2)* [1984] QB 524, 557.

124. John Mortimer, *The First Rumpole Omnibus* (1983), pp. 205–6.
125. John Mortimer, *The Second Rumpole Omnibus* (1987), p. 213.
126. Above, n. 124 at p. 87.
127. John Mortimer, *Rumpole à la Carte* (1990), p. 24.
128. Above, n. 125 at p. 456.
129. Ibid., p. 40.
130. Above, n. 127 at p. 122.
131. Ibid., p. 113.
132. Above, n. 125 at p. 499.
133. Ibid., p. 501.
134. Ibid., p. 584.
135. Ibid., p. 667.
136. Ibid., p. 495.
137. Ibid., p. 508.
138. Above, n. 127 at p. 8.
139. Ibid., p. 125.
140. Above, n. 125 at p. 665.
141. Ibid., p. 667.
142. Ibid., p. 489.
143. Ibid., p. 657.
144. Above, n. 124 at p. 167.
145. Above, n. 125 at p. 33.
146. Charles W. Wolfram, *Modern Legal Ethics* (1986), p. 585.
147. Above, n. 21, at p. 58.
148. Introduction by John Mortimer QC to Edward Marjoribanks, *Famous Trials of Marshall Hall* (1989) (condensed version of *The Life of Sir Edward Marshall Hall*), p. x.
149. Above, n. 113, vol. 1 (1981), p. 536.
150. Jonathan Swift, 'A Voyage to the Houyhnhnms' in *Gulliver's Travels* (1726), ch. V.
151. Above, n. 15.
152. R. F. V. Heuston, *Lives of the Lord Chancellors 1885–1940*, (1964), pp. 149–50.
153. John Mortimer, *Rumpole and the Age of Miracles* (1988), p. 109.
154. The opinion of Norman Birkett after his appointment to the High Court: see H. Montgomery Hyde *Norman Birkett* (1964), pp. 480 and 540.
155. Above, n. 86, vol. 2, pp. 401–2.
156. Felix Frankfurter, 'Mr Justice Jackson' 68 *Harvard Law Review* 937, 939 (1955).

157. Above, n. 26 at p. 41.
158. Lord Macmillan, 'The Ethics of Advocacy' in *Law and Other Things* (1937), p. 197.
159. Above, n. 24 at p. 334.

8. Conclusion

1. Sir William Holdsworth, *A History of English Law* (4th edn., 1936), vol. 2, p. 312.
2. Thomas More, *Utopia* (1516) (transl. Paul Turner, Penguin Classics, 1965), p. 106.
3. David Mellinkoff, *The Language of the Law* (1973), pp. 208–9.
4. *Cobbett's Parliamentary Debates* (1810), vol. 15, cols. 552–3.
5. *Bradwell v. The State of Illinois* 83 US 130, 141–2 (1872).
6. Albie Sachs and Joan Hoff Wilson, *Sexism and the Law* (1978), p. 28.
7. *In Re Summers* 325 US 561 (1945).
8. *Martin v. Law Society of British Columbia* [1950] 3 DLR 173 (British Columbia Court of Appeal).
9. *In the Matter of Richard M. Nixon, an Attorney* 385 NYS 2d 305 (1976) (Supreme Court of New York, Appellate Division).
10. *Florida Board of Bar Examiners: Re NRS* 403 So 2d 1315, 1317 (1981) (Supreme Court of Florida).
11. *R v. The Chancellor, Masters and Scholars of the University of Cambridge* (1723) 1 Str 557, 566.
12. *Powell v. Alabama* 287 US 45, 69 (1932) (US Supreme Court).
13. *Gideon v. Wainwright* 372 US 335, 344 (1963) (US Supreme Court).
14. *Galos Hired v. The King* [1944] AC 149, 155 (Judicial Committee of the Privy Council on appeal from the Protectorate Court of Appeal of the Somaliland Protectorate).
15. *The State v. Donoghue* [1976] IR 325 (Supreme Court of Ireland).
16. *McInnis v. The Queen* 143 CLR 575, 589 (1979) (High Court of Australia).
17. *Cobbett v. Hudson* (1850) 15 QB 988, 989.
18. *Gideon v. Wainwright* 372 US 335 (1963) (US Supreme Court). See Anthony Lewis, *Gideon's Trumpet* (1966).

19. *Argersinger v. Hamlin* 407 US 25, 37 (1972) (US Supreme Court). However, in the view of the US Supreme Court, an indigent defendant has no constitutional right to counsel where he is convicted of shoplifting and fined, even though the court had the power to send him to prison: *Scott v. Illinois* 440 US 367 (1979) (US Supreme Court). And the constitutional right to counsel does not necessarily extend to hearings, civil or criminal, where there is no threat of loss of liberty, although the consequences may be very detrimental to the fundamental interests of the litigant: see, for example, *Lassiter v. Department of Social Services of Durham County, North Carolina* 452 US 18 (1981) (US Supreme Court), concerning a finding that a woman was an unfit mother and so should lose the right to custody of her minor child.
20. *Herring v. New York* 422 US 853 (1975) (US Supreme Court).
21. *Monnell and Morris v. United Kingdom* (1988) 10 EHRR 205, 225 at para. 67 (European Court of Human Rights).
22. *Airey v. Ireland* (1979) 2 EHRR 305, 317 at para. 26 (European Court of Human Rights).
23. *Mason v. Mason* 11 *Family Law* 143 (1980) (Court of Appeal).
24. 416 HL 409 (20 Jan. 1981).
25. See *The Sunday Times v. The United Kingdom* (1979) 2 EHRR 245, 275 at para. 59 (European Court of Human Rights).
26. *Whitney v. California* 274 US 357, 377 (1927) (Mr Justice Brandeis J, with whom Mr Justice Holmes agreed).
27. For discussions of the justifications for freedom of expression see, generally, Kent Greenawalt, *Speech, Crime and the Uses of Language* (1989), pp. 9–39, and Eric Barendt, *Freedom of Speech* (1985), pp. 1–36.
28. *The Sunday Times v. The United Kingdom* (1979) 2 EHRR 245, 280 at para. 65 (European Court of Human Rights).
29. *Handyside v. The United Kingdom* (1976) 1 EHRR 737, 754 at para. 49 (European Court of Human Rights).
30. *Flint v. Pike* (1825) 4 B & C 473, 478. See similarly Mr Justice Holroyd at p. 480.
31. *The Talmud* (Steinsaltz edn., 1989), vol. 1, p. 238.
32. Edward Marjoribanks, *The Life of Sir Edward Marshall Hall* (1929), p. 13.
33. Marcus Fabius Quintilianus, *Institutio Oratoria* (transl. H. E. Butler, Loeb edn., 1980), II. xv. 11, p. 305.

34. Lord Birkett, *Six Great Advocates* (1961), p. 82.
35. Above, n. 32 at p. 13.
36. *Code of Conduct for the Bar of England and Wales* (4th edn., 1989), para. 1.1.
37. Peter Rawlinson, *A Price Too High* (1989), p. 58.
38. *Giannarelli v. Wraith* (1988) 62 ALJR 611, 624.

INDEX

Index